For

Jo Hunter: with very
best wishes.

Hubert Bonner
San Diego, May 28, 1968

THE

INTERNATIONAL SERIES

IN THE BEHAVIORAL SCIENCES

EDITED BY

John E. Horrocks

THE OHIO STATE UNIVERSITY

Houghton Mifflin books in Psychology
are under the general editorship of
LEONARD CARMICHAEL

Hubert Bonner

Professor of Psychology, Ohio Wesleyan University

On Being

Essay Toward

Mindful of Man

a Proactive Psychology

Houghton Mifflin Company · Boston

New York · Atlanta · Geneva, Ill. · Dallas · Palo Alto

FOR

DOROTHEA, RICHARD, AND HUGH,

whose lives validate my own

FOR

DOROTHEA, RICHARD, AND HUGH,

whose lives validate my own

Editor's Foreword

What is the nature of man? Where does he come from, what is his fate, and to what extent does he dare aspire to individuality and self-determination among his fellows? Are these matters of concern to the psychologist and his science? What problems should the psychologist be trying ultimately to solve? How and within what limits should he put his solutions into practice? Psychologists will offer widely differing answers to these questions. Dr. Bonner has taken a position which many academic psychologists in the United States will find untenable, while many European psychologists will heartily endorse it. In the marketplace of ideas, however, controversy is both expected and useful; and Dr. Bonner's proactive psychology and his concern for man more than deserve a hearing. In this book he proves himself a persuasive advocate.

Psychology has grown immensely in its relatively short history. It has brought more and more aspects of behavior under its purview and has attracted to its fold persons of many different persuasions. It has striven, often self-consciously, often defensively, to take its place as a "real" science in the ranks of the natural sciences and, in doing so, has often seemed to depart from its original preoccupation: the molar behavior of man. The appropriateness and ultimate significance of such departures, and the extent to which methods effective in other sciences may be applied with validity to psychology, are issues that lie beyond the scope of this book. The point here is that, for whatever reasons, man as a whole, man as a functioning, personal and social organism, has often disappeared from view. It is particularly appropriate at mid-twentieth century, when man stands so often with his back to the wall, when the civilization he has created seems at times to hang in the balance, that psychology should be "mindful of man."

Dr. Bonner has written an indictment of much contemporary psychology. He rejects, in both the psychoanalytic and behavioristic forms, the functionalist position that man is to be described almost exclusively as an adaptive organism whose behavior is stimulus-bound and habitual. He views man as an open system, not only adaptive but capable of unique expressive behavior, manifested in each individual's particular style of life. As Dr. Bonner sees it, the individual is not entirely bound by his past but is capable of transcending his environment to an appreciable extent. He cannot be wholly or meaningfully described by such disparate elements as drives, motives, memories, and cognitive structures. Dr. Bonner sees as particularly serious the banishment of human choice to the province of philosophy and theology, and he points to the need for a psychology that is truly therapeutic, that encourages self-affirmation and the courage to be an individual.

On Being Mindful of Man may be seen as a psychologist's affirmation of man's inextinguishable faith in perfectibility. Dr. Bonner presents a proactive psychology built upon the assumption that every man, however much like other men he may be, is yet unique and irreplaceable. Such a psychology rejects any attempt to separate the study of behavior from the process of living. Man is seen as a self-affirming being who strives, through his chosen goals, to realize his potentialities. Thus within the limits of his nature, man is his own master, responsible for his acts. He lives with his choices and his choices shape his conduct—one might almost say he becomes his choices. The hazard in living is that choice and responsibility go hand in hand, and so commitment, action, and guilt (or capacity for guilt) are inescapable.

Many of his colleagues will take issue with Dr. Bonner's faith in a man's ability to emerge "from the enculturation process as a relatively autonomous and liberated individual," and with the author's attack upon the positivist quest for simplicity and the positivist assumption that the methods of science can be transferred unchanged to the realm of human behavior. On the other hand, such American psychologists as Gordon Allport, Gardner Murphy, Carl Rogers, and Henry Murray share in a tradition that supports Dr. Bonner; and in Europe, Viktor Frankl and the logotherapists are of like mind.

It would be a grave mistake to conclude that Dr. Bonner rejects the utility of research or the promise of scientific method applied to the study of man. He states clearly that rigorous methodology is needed and that basic as well as applied research must go on. But he feels that psychology must evolve its own approaches, unintimidated by the pressures of the older sciences. He feels that method should be a means rather than an end; and that the end is the attainment of a view of man as "the self-actualizing organism" he is.

The view, then, is controversial, and Dr. Bonner's voice is in opposition to a trend. But the history of ideas teaches us that where there is no opposing voice, we approach sterility, though we may appear to flourish and progress. Dr. Bonner's interest in the presentation of man as a "unique, open, and creative individual" returns us to the problem with which psychology originally concerned itself, and to which its findings must eventually relate.

JOHN E. HORROCKS

Columbus, Ohio

Preface

This book presents no system and represents no school. Though it offers a more explicit elaboration of ideas more tentatively suggested in most of my earlier writings, it remains a provisional statement of a point of view, one which psychology has neglected but which cries out for its attention.

On Being Mindful of Man expounds my belief that man is a unique, open, and creative individual. The psychological processes of intentionality and proaction, and the uniqueness of individual human behavior, together compose the *Leitmotiv* of my thinking about psychological man. The sense of my whole discussion is that psychology must become more psychological and less preoccupied with statistical analyses of abstract, and for that reason, artificial and isolated processes. My long career of study has strengthened my conviction that psychology, though a representative among the sciences, can add little to the creation of a vital human culture if it is not fired with artistic imagination and insight. That study has also confirmed my beliefs that man is not merely a machine but an integral being, not merely a reality but a potentiality; not merely an ordinary creature, but a superior being.

The view of man that emerges here may be interpreted as a blend of two ancient conceptions, namely, the Hebraic idea of responsibility or duty, and the Hellenic model of excellence or the full actualization of human potentialities. The first stresses a life shared; the second, a life individually perfected. The first is a life of discipline and self-control; the second a life of aspiration and freedom.

Some readers will find in my exposition a disproportionate stress on physics. This is entirely the result of a practical decision stemming from physics' greater generality and simplicity and from considerations of economy of space. Another chapter would have been necessary to review the marvelous developments in the biological sciences, especially those in genetics and synthetic evolution. The work of geneticist Theodosius Dobzhansky and paleonthologist Gaylord Simpson gives us splendid confirmation of the unique, proactive, creative, and consciously self-directing character of man. If man has the ability to influence his own evolution, as these scientists have shown, what is there to prevent him from creating his own personality?

Although the ideas developed here are the products of a life-long study of man, they were markedly strengthened by several months of study in Vienna and the exchange of ideas with many scholars whom I met there and in Germany. For facilitating that study I am grateful to several persons for their special courtesies. I should like to express my thanks to Dr. Anton Porhansl, for making available to me the facilities of the Institute of European Studies, in the University of Vienna, and particularly to Dr. Viktor Frankl, for putting at my disposal the facilities of the Department of Neurology and Psychiatry of the Polyclinic of the City of Vienna, including its staff of psychiatrists and nurses, and many of its patients. From all of them I learned much.

I owe a special debt of gratitude to President Elden T. Smith, of Ohio Wesleyan University, the Personnel Committee, and the Committee on Grants-in-Aid, for an extended leave during the school year 1962–63, which provided me with leisure for study and reflection. To Mrs. Eileen Capehart I am grateful for her fine work in typing my manuscript, even while she was occupied with other responsibilities.

Finally, to Dr. John E. Horrocks, Editor of the International Series in the Behavioral Sciences, I am indebted for his early and astute perception of the possibilities inherent in the provisional formulation of the ideas which make up this book.

HUBERT BONNER

Delaware, Ohio

Contents

What is man that thou art mindful of him?

PSALM 8

Introduction

The guiding motto in the life of every natural philosopher should be, Seek simplicity and distrust it.

ALFRED NORTH WHITEHEAD

Psychology has failed to give us reasons for holding ourselves dear. Regrettably, it has assigned a reverence for man to philosophers, poets, and sentimental dreamers. The study of human behavior, it has warned us, is intricate enough without burdening it further by introducing elusive qualities to its difficult domain.

However, the price of simplification has been *over*simplification, and the excessive demands for operationism have impaired, if not destroyed, our smallish creativity. In its zeal for simplicity and measurement, psychology has divided man into mechanical part-functions, none of which is a meaningful description of the richness of the whole. Its well-aimed goals of quantification and objectivity have, in some quarters at least, eliminated human nature itself. The man whose behavior it measures so rigorously emerges from the psychological equations not as a joyous and suffering individual, but as a bloodless statistical unit.

As a scientific discipline, psychology can no longer afford to ignore the realities generated in human experience. It has disregarded those realities because it has been blinded by the positivist tradition of the nineteenth century. It has been oblivious to man's despair as he faces the terror of the contemporary situation. It has given us no intimation of the agonizing nature of the human condition. It has helped us not at all to face alone the possibility of our own annihilation. It has aided us even less in appreciating the idealism which has always kept man from taking refuge in savagery.

Why does psychology neglect so much? The answer is clearer than we think. Man as a unique person striving to actualize himself, challenges the simple mechanical structure of the human indi-

1

vidual which we have come to mistake for the viable human being.
The positivistic description of man denies the reality of his inner
life. It has so completely denatured him that he has no spirit left.
Instead of explaining man, it explains him away. In describing him
"correctly," psychology has ignored the poignant drama which animates his life. It gives us no hint of man's power to build his own
nature, his body and his mind. *Es ist der geist der sich den Körper
baut* ("It is the mind that builds itself a body").[1]

In its ambition to become a natural science, psychology has imposed a congruity and predictability upon human actions that are
belied by experience. In its zeal for creating a rational view of man,
psychology has overlooked the fact that rationality is also a form of
appreciation. Human nature refuses to be classified. It knows intuitively that in classification lies the stagnation and death of the
human spirit. Truly, at its best, science is also an art. As an art it
affirms that experience must be taken as it comes, at its face value,
and in its living fullness.

Nor can the psychologist account for human nature by comparing
it with the behavior of lower animals, or by tracing it to its infantile
origin. The human personality can be studied most fruitfully in its
florescence. Psychology should take man as he is, not as he was; as
he is coming to be, not as conditioning makes him.

The psychologist fears man's spontaneity, since it challenges his
demand for uniformity. He abhors man's unpredictability, since it
argues for behavioral novelty and freedom from a closed causality.
Creativeness generates insoluble problems and disturbs the psychologist's complacency. He is insensitive to the authentic forward
thrust of the healthy human organism. Like all of us, the psychologist finds it easier to ignore, or banish from view, those events which
do not fit his comfortable classifications, such as love, friendship,
courage, and self-sacrifice. Not being amenable to experimental
investigation, they are troublesome and to some, scientific absurdities. Knowledge of these phenomena, he feels, cannot but be vague
and ambiguous. Yet, as everyone knows, these are the qualities
that have made human history. And so, the science of psychology
looks backward, deriving its substance from accumulated experiments instead of the drama of living men.

This state of affairs is typical of the academic mind. This mind
tends to accept only the data which fit into the established cate-

[1] J. C. F. Schiller, *Wallensteins Tod*, in *Schillers Werke* (Leipzig u.
Wien: Bibliographisches Institut, n.d., vol. 4, line 1813).

gories. While the academic psychologist prides himself on his scientific methodology, he is better known for his fixed beliefs than for his techniques. Like many scientists, he feeds on outworn traditions. Defense of these traditions is a marked characteristic of contemporary psychology. Defense of the *status quo* generates stability but hardly novelty and clear directions. Sad to relate, psychology "has not one sure sense of direction but several quite unsure directions."[2]

In itself, this lack of a single direction is not a fatal defect, and may indeed reflect a desirable vitality. What is regrettable is that none of its directions points toward a serious concern with man as a unique individual. It is inspired by a mode of thinking that is almost exclusively mechanistic. In this mechanistic framework, personality, the self, and notably creative thinking, constitute a paradox if not an illusion. It is an illusion, on the contrary, to hold that because these human characteristics appear to be capricious and unique, which is to say discontinuous in the stream of psychological events, they lie outside the field of scientific psychology.

Psychology can no longer afford the luxury of universal parsimony. The day has come when, in the face of an urgent need for a psychology of the total person, we must place the "law" of plenitude on an equal footing with the demand for simplicity. Human nature in its fullness is not a "minimax" problem. The experiences of living beings in real life never exhibit the simplicity of an animal's behavior in a laboratory experiment. A law which holds under simple and controlled conditions does not necessarily obtain similarly under highly complex conditions of daily experience.

A similar *caveat* applies, as we shall show in more detail later, to the splendid virtue of objectivity. As an ideal it must be cherished and pursued, but in reality it is contradicted by human experience and scientific research. It is no longer necessary at this late date to invoke the astute observations of William James in order to establish the fact that the only direct encounter with reality that we can claim to be our own, is our own personal life. What we observe is frequently modified by the observation itself. Failure to take this fact into account invariably questions the reliability of our conclusions. Personality is a condition of the psychological events which we observe and measure. Accordingly, subjectivity and inwardness are significant conditions for psychological research.

[2] Dael Wolfle, in S. Koch (ed.), *Psychology: A Study of a Science* (New York: McGraw-Hill Book Company, Inc., 1959), vol. 2, p. 8.

Clearly, facts are not the scientist's only basis for choice of conclusions, for choices rest upon human nature, not only upon the mechanical model of behavior, or upon the deliverances of electronic computers, which themselves are products of human ingenuity. As Chauncey Leake has phrased it, "while our own anxieties may urge us to surrender this human ability [choice] to some future IBM machine, we must accept the strong probability that healthy human emotions are the indispensable basis for objective assessment of available facts and known uncertainties."[3] However, what Leake had in mind was not the "pale emotions so laboriously described in conventional psychological expositions," which are viscerally correct, "but which neither move men nor cause man to move mountains. Visceral movements require the passion of ideals . . . before they can be effective."[4]

Thus, it should by now be a commonplace that since all scientific operations are performed by individuals, the observer is always a part of what he observes. Despite all efforts to secure rigor and detachment, psychology, even more than other sciences, is deeply personal. The psychologist, like the poet and the novelist, is projecting his knowledge into the object he is describing. The rigor and objectivity which psychologists claim for their discipline are simply unobtainable, whatever the methodology they employ.

Although nomothetic laws are important ideals, the "ideal of coldly impersonal generality" is a part of our mythology. What we see in scientific investigation is invariably the finished product, never the fumbling processes which lead to its final formulation. Bridgman has called attention to this fact by showing that scientists "carefully erase all traces of the scaffolding by which they mounted to their final result, in the delusion that like God Almighty they have built for all ages."[5]

It is not an encouraging fact that up to now those psychological processes which have been rigorously investigated and measured have, with a few notable exceptions, bordered on the trivial. At the same time, the problems of great moment, the anguish of men, their alienation from themselves and the world, their concern with the meanings of life and death, their longings and disillusionments,

---

[3] C. D. Leake, "The Sciences and the Humanities" (Washington: *AAAS Bulletin*, 1961).

[4] H. Bonner, "Idealization and Mental Health," *J. Indiv. Psychol.*, 1962, *18*, 136–146.

[5] P. W. Bridgman, *The Way Things Are* (Cambridge: Harvard University Press, 1959), p. 5.

their loneliness and relatedness, their yearning for expression and self-actualization — these have fallen outside the sphere of scientific investigation. They can neither be defined operationally nor investigated experimentally.

In contemplating this disappointing situation, we are reminded again of the observation made a generation ago by Henry Murray. The human sciences, he commented ruefully, have the choice of two alternatives: to investigate unimportant problems by means of rigorous formal techniques, or important problems by means of inadequate methodologies.

Sad to relate, not only are the above-mentioned problems banished from psychology, but many that remain are relatively unimportant. Murray's plaint has been echoed by others, most recently by Brewster Smith. In his "Editorial" at the end of his service as Editor of the *Journal of Abnormal and Social Psychology*, Smith calls attention to this state of affairs. On the basis of his review of 2,825 manuscripts, he comments as follows:

> It seems that a remarkably high proportion of the research reported is clean, stringently conceived, and effectively executed, reflective of rigorous and painstaking thought and experimentation and remarkably trivial![6]

But the most lamentable of all the omissions is creative man, man the dreamer of dreams, the maker of himself, the being with the gift of creating his own heaven — and hell!

Alas! psychology has not been mindful of man. Our purpose in this volume, therefore, is to take man as a proactive being, seriously.

Proactive psychology is a synthesis and interpretation of the knowledge of man derived from empirical science, ontological analysis, and humanistic insight. Its methodology is pluralistic, relying on objective procedures, phenomenological description, and immediate cognition. The psychology which emerges from these integrated modes of investigation is a psychology of the total human being. It has a clear eye for the unpredictable contingencies in human behavior which sorely trouble the academic psychologist, since they disturb the comfortable order of his experimental procedures. Proactive psychology does not yield to the empiricist's fractionation of man into experimental or testable units, for man is not an object for simple partition. It bends method to substance,

[6] M. B. Smith, "Editorial," *J. abn. soc. Psychol.*, 1961, *63*, 461–465.

never human nature to technique. It stresses the subjective life of man, the inward nature of his decisions, his anxiety and guilt.

On the other hand, neither does proactive psychology temper its findings by religious orthodoxy, or by a genteel concern for the goodness of man. Its idealistic preferences are informed by the tragic sense of life. It opposes all facile and shallow appeals to adjustment and cultivation of a stiff upper lip. If by implication it should counsel man, it is the hard message that every individual must save himself. It demonstrates that adjustment may indeed be a form of neurosis. Adaptation to a destructive and inhibiting environment is not a sufficient criterion of mental health, but may be a sign of sickness and psychological death. It questions in the most radical way the belief that man is the helpless plaything of an all-controlling past. It affirms in the most forcible manner that the life of each individual, though embedded in society, is centered in himself rather than tossed about by blind external forces.

Proactive psychology is thus a human-centered discipline. It contrasts sharply with the two dominant approaches to human behavior: the poetic mythology of psychoanalysis and the mindless technology of behaviorism. Both present us with a very one-sided view of man. One describes man as a blind victim of his past, the other, as a driven creature of habits. In the first, man is, paradoxically, modified by a shaman who rids him of his anxieties by a complex ritual of self-revelation; in the second, he is reconditioned by a simple redirection of established habits. In one, man is an abreacted organism, in the other, a self-teaching mechanism. Although it is difficult to choose between them, psychoanalysis has the saving touch of dramatic tragedy — the tragedy of man condemned to helpless repetition of archaic impulses in a meaningless environment. The Pavlovian man, *à la* Skinner, in which the computer and the teaching machine, which is in principle the Skinner box, are substituted for the human consciousness, is a dangerous portent. In this view, man faces neither decision nor expiration, but like a machine merely wears out and is discarded. The view implies that the more we understand the human machine the less we need to admire man. And so at last, the more we understand man, the machine, the more replaceable becomes man, the creative being.

Proactive psychology rejects, as sufficient explanatory principles, universal determinism, reductionism, parsimony, operationism, and the all-embracing effectiveness of stimulus-response equivalence. In contrast to psychoanalysis and behaviorism, proactive psychology holds that we can understand another person's behavior, not only by knowing its antecedent conditions, but also, and more appreciatively, by knowing his intentions regarding his future. Indeed, the future dimension, in the form of forward-directedness, is more important than an individual's past. The being of a person consists in his becoming. In his becoming man is, to borrow Whitehead's phrase, perpetually perishing. His freedom is itself perpetually perishing. Since freedom means choice, and is a perpetual perishing, freedom is the generator of crises. Crises in turn give rise to alienation and estrangement from oneself and others. By the nature of his being as a unique individual, man is separated from other men. From our point of view, alienation is pathological only when it serves as a form of escape from, or rejection of, other beings; when it is the impairment of the uniqueness of others.

The concept of being-in-becoming lends to proactive psychology its dynamic character. In Freudian psychodynamics, man "grows" only in the very restricted sense that his present self is but a repetition of what he has been. Proactive psychology affirms that man changes as he moves in the direction of what he intends to become. It further holds that, although man is a part-product of his past, he is also an expanding self modified by his future. From this point of view, the true mark of the healthy man is a high degree of self-inductiveness. He does not linger in the past but dwells firmly in a foreworld. The ideals and values which have no acceptable place in conventional psychology, are the life and substance of the healthy individual. Through ideals and values we can observe the individual in the process of becoming a person. Without ideals man is not fully human, for the essence of humanness is the capacity to envision and actualize ideal ends. Proactive psychology asserts that each individual, in the light of his own experience and knowledge, chooses to create the life that he aspires to achieve. His personality is described in his self-affirmation: *"I am what I will do."*[7]

---

[7] H. Bonner, "The Proactivert: A Contribution to the Theory of Psychological Types," *J. Existential Psychiat.*, 1963, 3, 323–328.

PART
ONE

*The Supremacy
of Science*

1

The aim of science is . . . an incessant struggle toward a goal which can never be reached. Because the goal is of its very nature unobtainable. It is something that is essentially metaphysical and as such is always again and again beyond each achievement.

MAX PLANCK

Two Views of Science

In theory, every psychologist is ready to accept the proposition that there are different ways of interpreting the nature of science. He admits that science has never been a unified discipline, and that it is open to different though interrelated and consistent conceptualizations. Yet in practice many psychologists comprehend and use science as if it were a single and rigidly defined branch of learning. There are those, for instance, who hold that science proceeds by means of operational definitions of its concepts. Any term that cannot be operationally defined, they say, has no legitimate place in scientific psychology. Opposing these are the scholars who believe that, although operationism is a desirable ideal, terms which cannot be defined in this manner still have an acceptable place in psychology. They are useful terms which can lead to scientific truth by successive approximations.

The difference between equally competent and informed scientists is also, more frequently than is generally realized, a function of individual disposition and temperament. The controversy between Max Planck and Ernst Mach, as Einstein noted, was the result of a different feeling-tone with which each approached the problems of modern physics. Mach, the tough-minded positivist, did not take kindly to Planck's concern with the metaphysical bases and implications of physical events; and Planck in turn felt that Mach did not appreciate "the physicist's longing for perception of [the] pre-established harmony" in nature.[1] As Einstein remarks in describing Planck's attitude, the latter's state of mind resembles that of the "devotee" or the "lover."

SOME OBSERVATIONS ON SCIENCE

Before examining in detail the two views of science which make up the subject matter of the present chapter, it will be useful to examine briefly the broad characteristics of all science, whatever its specific subject matter may be.

The student of human behavior must first accustom his mind to the fact that almost nothing in science is certain. The naive notion that science deals with cold facts, must be abandoned. Almost every important axiom in science is challenged or denied by some investigator. Even physics, the most exact of the sciences, is riddled with contradictions and tormented by doubts. Some physicists are frankly skeptical about the mind's capacity to give us dependable knowledge of the external world. This fact alone impels the psychologist to temper his certainty regarding the behavior of the human animal; and of the internal reality, he can speak only falteringly and humbly. The principle of causality, the bedrock of scientific certainty, has itself been seriously challenged.

It is cause for surprise that psychologists should not perceive, or perceiving, grudgingly acknowledge, the subjective nature of their scientific research. Not only has causality been challenged but the perspective from which physical events are viewed has radically shifted. It is no longer possible, if it ever was, to view the universe objectively. It is an illusion to believe that we can banish the human equation from our scientific description of the world. This conclusion is not merely an expression of the skeptical spirit of our times, but the reasoned judgment of those who have guided the course of recent scientific developments. In psychology, the belief in scientific detachment is not even sound as an ideal, as it conceivably could be in physics. On the contrary, the net effect of this ideal has been destructive. In formulating human behavior objectively, psychology has given us largely its outward features. It has made of man a thing, the object of a subject. In this way psychology has been extending and prolonging the ancient split

---

[1] A. Einstein, "Preface," in M. Planck, *The New Science* (New York: Meridian Books, Inc., 1959), p. xi.

between subject and object, between inner and outer, between the basic and the derived.

In this bifurcation by the older science, and the leading psychologies based upon it, psychology impaired its claim to objectivity and impartiality. Insofar as "scientific" psychology has failed in establishing contact with man's inner reality, it has lacked the comprehensive validity for which it has been striving. Insofar as it has disavowed the personal nature of its own knowledge, it has been incomplete and therefore, unlike science at its best, not universally valid.

Again, the history of science bears witness to the view that scientific ideas are judged not only by their claim to truth but also by their value to human beings. Even if the value of physics, say, is wholly independent of the world to which it points, it gets its meaning largely from its human relevance. The questions regarding causality and the existence of the physical world are as much questions of value as of truth.

It is now an established fact in physics that the events which it investigates are affected by the measuring instruments with which the scientist examines them. The physicist delights in telling us that scientific measurement of physical events interferes with or modifies the events themselves. A favorite illustration of this paradox is the measurement of the position and velocity of an electron. In order to measure an electron in motion it is necessary to illuminate it with a powerful light ray, which in this case is the instrument, or the means, for its investigation. However, the light-ray interferes with the path of the electron, and the more intense the illumination the greater is the interference with the electron's path of motion. This means, as some writers have indeed affirmed, that science must deal with its own interferences with nature. Many measurements of physical phenomena, in short, are causal interventions in the stream of physical events.

Considerations like the foregoing are demonstrations of the tentative and uncertain character of modern science. They show, too, that science is open to different interpretations, and at its very best, is self-corrective and self-enhancing.

For the science of psychology this is an encouraging situation. It is an unmistakable warning to all who investigate behavior, that when they fractionate the human person by the measurement of part-functions, they destroy the unity of the whole. They have interfered with the person's behavior just as surely as the physicist has with the motion of the electron. Like the physicist, the psychologist must incorporate this knowledge in his generalizations of human behavior. In physics this is no longer an alarming situation, but the beginning of a revitalized search into the mystery of the universe. In psychology it can be equally salutary and open the way to a better understanding of the depth of human nature.

POSITIVISM, OLD AND NEW

Positivism, as a philosophy oriented around the natural sciences, is an old tendency in human thought. Its earliest, consciously articulated form can be traced to Francis Bacon, in the seventeenth century. It was reformulated in the empirical philosophy of Locke and Hume, in the eighteenth century. It was made explicit and formal about the third decade of the nineteenth century, by Auguste Comte.

The most important fact about this positivism was its untiring effort to banish metaphysical ideas from investigations into human nature. In effect, this meant that psychology and other social sciences should not transcend the empirical world in search of ultimate causes and hidden essences behind phenomenal appearances. Positive science dealt only with the facts of immediate perception, with what could be observed in the objective world, both physical and human.

Positivism thus argued for the application of the scientific procedures of the natural sciences, which had demonstrated their efficacy in the study of inanimate nature, to the realm of psychological and moral situations. It traced the bewildering complexities of the human mind down to its simplest operations in the nervous system. It turned psychological investigations away from thoughts to things, from mind to matter, from introspection to observation of external events. Objectivity thus came to be dogmatically identified with overt behavior.

Classical Positivism

It should be noted that the creators of positivism in the nineteenth century were mostly philosophers. Already in the time of Comte and Spencer, the most articulate exponents of positivism, the status and reputation of the natural sciences were extraordinary. It was therefore doubly valuable to the growing positivism that Ernst Mach, the Austrian physicist, added his weight and prestige to its influence on nineteenth-century thought, an influence which was felt in the early years of the present century.

Mach's empirical-critical position was no longer directed solely against the metaphysical excesses which the earlier positivists deplored, but against the condition of science as it was formulated in his own time, beginning with the developments in the 1880's and 1890's. He was markedly critical of the proclaimed rationality of science, holding instead that scientific areas are as mystical as those of metaphysics. His principle of "mental economy" proclaimed that scientific theories are but convenient shorthand statements or summaries of the known facts. Their value and truth consist in their economy of thought. This principle is but a more radical formulation of the principle of parsimony, or the demand for simplicity. It foreshadows the ideas of logical positivism, especially the radical physicalism of Wittgenstein, who proclaimed that any idea that cannot be rigidly formulated is meaningless, and has no acceptable place in science. "Whereof one cannot speak," he wrote, "thereof one must be silent."[2]

From Mach's point of view, then, the importance of a theory lies less in what we like to call its truth, than in the fact that it gives us a simple and economical account of observed phenomena. Indeed, truth and simplicity were in Mach's mind, as in the minds of many latter-day positivists, virtually synonymous. And since the concept of truth has never been satisfactorily defined, the concept of simplicity thus bears the same ambiguity and uncertainty as the meaning of truth itself.

Already in the positivism of Comte, mind had no meaningful place in science. Mind was conceived as a metaphysical entity which had no ontological status. Since introspection was repudiated, and mental phenomena could not be observed subjectively, they could not serve as objects of scientific investigation. We can, however, said the positivist in Comte's time, study them objectively as organic phenomena, as nervous processes. Comte's aversion to a mentalistic psychology thus led him to regard psychological processes as functions of the brain.

This view was reinforced by the many studies of brain functions initiated largely by Pierre Flourens, whose method of extirpating parts of the brain enabled him to study the functions of its various parts. Psychology thus tended to become increasingly "materialistic," a fact which was followed by an idealistic reaction to the excesses of the positivist emphasis.

<hr>

[2] L. Wittgenstein, *Tractatus Logico-Philosophicus* (London: Kegan Paul, Trench, Trubner and Co., Ltd., 1922), p. 188.

One need not be anti-positivist to recognize the severe limitations which positivism imposed upon science, especially on the evolving psychology in the nineteenth century. In the field of psychology, positivism was based on a very sweeping assumption. It believed that the method of positive science could be transferred unchanged to the realm of human behavior. The positivists were oblivious to the indubitable fact that psychological events are incomparably complex.

Scientific facts are not established by citing the authority of their discoverers. Nevertheless, it is fair to point out that the positivists in their arrogance banished many profound observations on the nature of man from the realm of human thought. In this way they improverished and mutilated our image of man. They displayed a lack of understanding and appreciation of what others had achieved; and in reducing psychological facts to physical structures they committed the fallacy of gross reductionism.

Logical Positivism

The anti-metaphysical bias of scientific thought reached its maximum zeal in the logical positivism of the twentieth century. This bias is not merely the expression of a long historical trend; it is an axiom. The battle-cry is, "Logic without ontology." In the radical thinking of Bertrand Russell, the leading spirit behind this movement, the validity of logical relations is no longer dependent on objective fact, and need not be descriptions of the external world. The sole criterion is validity, and the sole task of the logic of science is the analysis of the formal structure of logical relations. There is neither substance nor process to talk about and our scientific discourse concerns nothing more than the rules of procedure. The problems of human commitment and human destiny turn out to be, like all human problems, "either technical or ridiculous."[3]

The above conclusion by Ramsay is but the ineluctable consequence of a line of reasoning that was made explicit in the logic of the so-called "Vienna Circle," whose members, especially Wittgenstein, were influenced by the logical and mathematical ideas of Bertrand Russell. Since the end of the First World War this line of reasoning has had an influence on philosophic and scientific thought that cannot be over-estimated, even though it is now declining.

[3] F. P. Ramsay, *The Foundations of Mathematics and Other Logical Essays* (New York: Humanities Press, 1950), p. 290.

Operationism

For the purpose of this chapter it is not necessary for us to examine the technical symbolic logic of the positivist's position. We need to look only at that feature which has had the greatest impact on the scientific pretensions of contemporary psychology. Although operationism is neither historically nor logically an integral part of logical positivism, we discuss it here because of its close association with the latter.

Neo-positivist physicalism, as the positivist's position is also called, asserts that philosophy of science must eschew all metaphysical problems for, having no satisfactory answers, they are meaningless. The task of the logic of science is the rigorous analysis of the concepts and propositions of the special sciences. It holds, further, that although science starts with empirical descriptions of experience in the language of common sense (*Protokolsprache*), its real task is to "translate" these descriptions into the language of theory, or constructs (*Physikalischesprache*).

The method by which science proceeds in translating the empirical descriptions into the language of constructs is called the hypothetico-deductive method. From the empirical data, science constructs a theory, follows the implications of the theory, and tests it on the basis of still more data. Those theories are most scientific that have the widest acceptance.[4]

The question now concerns the manner in which universal assent is achieved in science. This brings us to a point of view which has been dogmatically advocated and spiritedly debated for no less than thirty years. Understanding its meaning and perceiving its ultimate sterility will help the reader to grasp the irrelevance and futility of radical behaviorism in contemporary psychology.

The road to both simplicity and universality in science is found in the operational definition of its concepts. This overworked idea means quite simply that an idea is scientifically meaningful only when it is defined through the mensurative process by which it was achieved. Thus, the meaning of length is obtained by means of measurements with a meter-stick, and of intelligence, by the ratio of mental-age score to the chronological age of the subject.

Clearly operationism, when stripped of the non-essentials that were added to it by its extreme devotees, is but a more rigorous

---

[4] For one of the earliest and most lucid statements of this point of view, see R. Carnap, "On the Character of Philosophic Problems," *Phil. of Science*, 1934, *1*, 5–19.

form of the principle of parsimony. It demands empirical referents for the terms employed. It banishes from science the use of fictitious entities or hidden agents which cannot be empirically verified. This more reasonable view of the operational nature of scientific ideas has not, however, been the position of most logical positivists. From Wittgenstein, Schlick, and Carnap to Bridgman, Reichenbach, and the psychologist Hull, operationism has been intolerant of non-empirical constructs.[5] There has been a widespread tendency among operationists to exclude from scientific consideration all concepts that are not subject to operational definition, on the ground that they are meaningless. The logic of science is thus scarcely more than a formal syntax, empty of all ontological referents. Logically, this would exclude the physical nature which it purports to investigate, thus coming perilously close to denying science altogether.

We have pointed out that the extreme demand for operationism is declining. Nevertheless, its negative and damaging effect on the philosophy of science and on psychology will take a long time to efface. A whole generation of psychologists was moved by its beguiling influence. In this way it has robbed psychology of its potential creativity and removed man's most vital qualities from the realm of scientific investigation. For a whole generation positivism in psychology has replaced the humanistic concern for what makes man truly human. Obsession with method has blinded many psychologists to what has been the perennial goal of psychology, namely, a rigorous yet humane interpretation of the nature of human nature. In its zeal for quantification and measurement and in its search for nomothetic generalizations, psychology has forgotten its chief objective: the identification of the individual. Many contemporary students of personality show little grasp and even less appreciation of the fact that, as will be argued fully later, the complexity of the individual can be better understood in the study of the single case. Psychology will become even more scientific when it is able to study the particular as well as the general trend in human behavior. What it will lose by a questionable operational rigor, psychology can compensate for by a deeper sensitivity to

[5] Toward the end of his life Bridgman expressed impatience and disillusionment with radical operationism, declaring that "we are pretty much driven to accept our primitive operations on the basis of feelings in our bones that we know what we are doing." See P. Bridgman, *The Way Things Are* (Cambridge: Harvard University Press, 1959), where this generally skeptical tone is expressed.

man's creative potentiality. In his eager haste to encapsulate man's behavior in statistical equations, to describe only his adaptive and coping behavior, the psychologist has merely succeeded in emptying man of his essential humanity.

The extreme concern for methodological rigor has by no means been confined to the operational approach to human behavior. The "euphoria of gadgets," as it has been described, has compounded the results of radical simplification. It has created the impression that formal technique is the touchstone of psychological research. It has caused some men to believe that the simplification of behavior in laboratory research with animals gives us its most important description. Since the variables are drastically reduced, it beguiles man into believing that *human* behavior is equally simple. The youthful student of psychology, particularly, is led early in his career, long before he has any basis for valid judgment, to commit himself to the most fashionable point of view in psychology.

Professional psychologists need hardly be reminded that the great psychologist, William James, was not preoccupied with formal method. Yet, his apprehension of the vital human person was so "true" and so subtly creative that few have equaled him in his provocative insights. His *Principles of Psychology* is a work of descriptive science and of personal art. It is for these reasons, as well as others, that his work is still both important and true.

Concluding Remarks

A glance at the history of science since the time of Bacon reveals an alternation of anti-metaphysical emphasis with inevitable reactions to its excesses. Positivism, representing the urge to transform the philosophy of nature into a rigorous physical system, has banished from psychology all mentalistic and empirically unverifiable concepts. That science in general and psychology in particular have profited from the demand for increasing rigor in both logic and experiment is an undoubted fact. Dependable knowledge, be it in science or philosophy, is essential to making the world intelligible.

However, virtues have a way of becoming vices, and strengths, weaknesses. Enhancement, when fanatically pursued, can end in sterility. The pursuit of positivism has impaired psychology's effectiveness in dealing with the most urgent problems of human nature. Positivism has concerned itself too much with necessity and not enough with contingency, too much with the general at the

expense of the particular. Its goal of precision and rigor has closed the door to human ambiguities.

To surmount the difficulties of positivism and make room for the uniquely human qualities of man, a different conceptualization of science is necessary. This conceptualization is not a new creation, but the adoption of a point of view already explicitly stated in the "new science." To this newer philosophical position we now turn.

SCIENTIFIC HUMANISM

Human nature defies and ridicules narrow scientism. It refuses to be classified. It is transformed by the very act of discovery. Man helps to make the very facts which he tirelessly investigates. He selects and interprets them in the light of his own motives and purposes. It is sheer conceit in the scientist to believe that there is only one way of interpreting natural events. It is artless simplicity on his part to imagine that a fullness of facts alone is sufficient to account for the richness of the human being. We now possess an abundance of facts regarding minute segments of behavior. On the basis of these facts psychologists have aimed to make predictions, but with indifferent success. However, it is of no small moment to point out that the untutored individual can be more successful in predicting an individual's behavior than the psychologist with his conceptual and experimental paraphernalia.

Why is this so? Simply because an individual *knowing* another can grasp the *being* of the other. He is involved in that other and yet remains unbiased about him. Rather than interfering with our understanding of another person our involvement in his existence enables us to grasp him more clearly. We can predict because we know what to expect, and we know what to expect because we are human beings like the other one. It is this simple fact that enables a mother to anticipate her child's behavior and the lover his beloved's, without benefit of scientific abstractions. It is all the more remarkable that scientific psychology, with all its facts and measurements, has generated few if any general laws of human nature and conduct. The scientist's understanding is based on "knowledge about," whereas one individual's understanding of another is the result of "acquaintance with," to borrow William James's happy phrasing.

The sense of the foregoing observation is that it points once more to a familiar fact: the progress of science is stifled by the power of an influential dogma. Positivism, old and new, has been an obstacle

to man's search behind the abstractions of science to the living human being. In order to perceive man as a living whole, psychology must admit to its calculations an alternative and enlarged criterion of truth, namely, that an event is true because it has been subjectively lived. This subjective criterion of truth depends not on empirical or logical proof but on immediate experience. Its general form is designated as scientific humanism.

A Working Definition

There is a growing agreement among psychologists as well as natural scientists that there is no real opposition between the scientific and the humanistic study of human behavior; that they are, indeed, mutually supportive. From this integrated point of view, the psychologist as a scientist investigates man's purposive behavior, his capacity to envision and strive for goals which he has generated himself, and his unceasing struggle to choose intelligently between competing and antithetical moral alternatives. Man is not exclusively guided by the need to relieve his visceral tensions but even more powerfully by his need to love, know, and revere. He is not solely a homeostatic organism but a moral and percipient being, as well.

Scientific humanism is scientific in an accommodated sense. It interprets scientific phenomena "experimentally;" for choice, aspiration, and other forms of proactive behavior are "provisional tries." Thinking, as John Dewey informed us many years ago, is a form of experimentation. When a man strives in his imagination for a goal which he has himself previsioned, his behavior is a natural process. His intention is not something which he merely injects into the world; it is, rather, a part of nature. The positivist's split of man from nature, subject from object, is contradicted by the natural history of the human mind. The view that mind is separable from nature and that human knowledge is composed of sensory data or abstract concepts is a quaint mythology. Experientially and experimentally, the conscious or percipient being always begins his thinking with a meaning or a belief, a condition of animal faith, some private or personal conviction. When he thus adds his own perception to the world, it is he who performs the act of attribution, thereby complicating nature itself — the same nature in the creation of which he has participated. When Einstein and Planck interpreted the experimental work of their fellow scientists, when they subjected physical events to *conceptual experimentation,* rearranging those events in their own imaginations, they gave mankind two most revolutionary ideas: relativity theory and quantum mechanics. These challenges to the Newtonian framework were derived not from their own laboratory experiments, but from inner rearrangements of the meanings of the "objective" data. Theirs was a form of inner experimentation which formal experiments later confirmed.

Descriptive Phenomenology

The old problem of the relation between subject and object, the inner and the outer, has never been solved to everybody's satisfaction. The positivists rejected the subjective altogether, defining it as a mentalistic condition lying outside the sphere of scientific investigation. In the early history of psychology, roughly from the period of Wundt to the advent of Watsonian behaviorism, the problem was disposed of by a verbal legerdemain. Knowledge was neatly divided into the "mediate" experience of physics and the "immediate" experience of psychology. Physics was described as dealing with mediate experience, experience *independent* of the experiencing person; whereas psychology was conceived as dealing with immediate experience, experience *dependent upon* the experiencing person, experience that goes on only when there is an experiencer.

Behaviorism, on the other hand, took the extreme position of eliminating the experiencer altogether. Psychology, it asserted, deals only with objective facts. Whatever is not objectively demonstrable is not a datum of scientific psychology. As a consequence of this position, which has been firmly established in American psychology for the last forty years, the science of behavior has renounced all interest in consciousness and the whole range of inner experiences that could not be investigated from an external point of view. By this single stroke, psychology consigned itself to sterility.

There are important signs of a reaction against the sovereignty of objectivism. The most inconspicuous of these indications is the diminishing timidity in the use of the term "subjective." Developments in the natural sciences have shorn it of its "unscientific" character, and today it is less often used as an epithet to discredit it. The rise of phenomenology, first as a form of philosophical analysis, and later as a psychological method, has aided its growing acceptance. It is becoming increasingly clear to all those who have divested themselves of the positivistic bias, that the separation of the organism from its surroundings is not only artificial but empirically impossible.

What is phenomenology? To avoid unnecessary complication we shall omit discussion of phenomenology as metaphysics and the varieties of phenomenological method. In its more restricted descriptive sense, phenomenology begins with the simple proposition that all human knowledge is based on experience. This experience is not only of empirically-centered objects, but the psychologically more relevant *lived* experience. This experience has both a structure and a property. The structure can be communicated in "technical" language with no special difficulty, for it resembles similar experiences in others. The properties, the unique qualities, can be most satisfactorily conveyed only by means of immediate intuition. Although it may be "formalized" with more or less success, its "feeling-tone" can best be apprehended by the "entering" of one person into the life of another. It is the process of "feeling with," not "feeling toward."[6]

Again, phenomenology deals not only with objective facts, like other sciences, but unlike them, it has a special interest in objects as possibilities, objects in the process of becoming. Accordingly, it is not only a study of empirical facts, but a science of the possible, of the emerging, of the coming-into-being. Unlike behaviorism and the whole positivistic movement, which have explicitly denied the validity of the phenomenological view, descriptive phenomenology affirms the world of subjective experience. In its radical sense, phenomenology proclaims that truth for each of us has meaning, that is, is relevant to us, when it has been lived by ourselves. It holds for us a certainty which is characteristic of many creative ideas. One is at once reminded of the immediate, subjective certainty that Poincaré, the mathematician, experienced at the moment of acute inspiration.[7]

By means of the phenomenological strategy the "objectively" true, the truth of natural science, is integrated with the "subjectively" true, the truth of human experience. The truth of experience is the kind that facts may challenge, but cannot destroy, for it is the truth of poetry and feeling. One suspects that in this way of viewing human life one can account, though feebly, for the vitality of psychoanalysis. Even if Freud's dramatic portrayal of

---

[6] To the "closed-circuit" thinker, this way of phrasing the lived experience is both mystical and repugnant. He should be reminded that it is mystical only because its aim is unclear; because it is full of anticipation rather than actualization, potentiality rather than completeness.

[7] See H. Poincaré, *Science et Méthode* (Paris: Flammarion, 1908), p. 52.

man should one day turn out to be largely mistaken, it will remain to remind us that, although man is driven by the dark forces of his inner nature, he is still capable of heroism and grandeur, Freud's pessimism to the contrary notwithstanding.

In this mode of conceptualizing the human enterprise, or the life of reason and science, the certainties of logic and mathematics are not abridged or nullified. Having lived with mathematics, no matter how tenuously, man knows from his encounter with it that its truths are, for the present moment, indisputable. Yet, having lived with love and beauty, art and poetry, he is no less certain of *their* revelations. If in the course of events, of experience and knowledge, one mode should oppose the other, it will but serve as an occasion for further creative effort: for the problem a solution must be found.

Although descriptive phenomenology stems from Husserl, its modern creator, it is much less a theory than a point of view, much less a philosophical method than a mode of improvisation. This must be so since proactive psychology meets life on the wing, before it has become history. For the proactive man, history is indeed, as it is for Stephen in Joyce's *Ulysses,* a nightmare from which he is trying to awake. Phenomenology aims to bring into the light of reason and the heart the phenomena of life as they are experienced, in their primary sources. It goes a long way in acknowledging the truth of Proust's observation that "the subjective impression, however inferior the material may seem to be and however improbable the outline, is a criterion of truth."[8] Since the awesome complexity and variability of the human person are never caught by the abstractions of positivistic psychology, the phenomenological description of man cannot be justly criticized. This description is in intimate touch with the being who sees and feels, who is conscious of being conscious, the being who is not identical with other beings, but who is unique and irreplaceable.

SOME PRINCIPLES OF SCIENTIFIC HUMANISM

Like every philosophy of science, scientific humanism is recognized by its assumptions, concepts, and general principles. Also like every philosophy of science, scientific humanism bases its ideas on the interpretation of the important hypotheses and generaliza-

---

[8] M. Proust, *The Past Recaptured.* Trans. Frederick A. Blossom (New York: A. & C. Boni, 1932).

tions of current scientific investigations and practices. If the controversy in science is over the nature of matter, or of causal relationship, then the current philosophy of science will engage in discussions of the logical, epistemological, or methodological questions regarding those scientific questions. Since controversy by its nature is divisive, it generates differences of opinion among the disputants. At the present time the disputants over matters of great importance fall roughly into two camps — the *empiricists* and the *idealists*. On most controversial issues — certainly on the question of determinism–indeterminism — the idealists constitute the majority.

Briefly, the empiricist stays as close as possible to the experimental data, claiming that on disputed issues we must assume that *if* we had sufficient data to solve the problems, our solutions would be consistent with the established principles of science. The idealist, on the other hand, holds that in the face of insufficiency of data, the scientist is free to take the opposite position, even if that position challenges and contradicts widely accepted opinions.

Because the course of psychological development is eventually affected by the controversies in the natural sciences, and because the proactive psychology expounded in this book is firmly based upon the idealist's answers to the physicist's questions, we shall briefly discuss the more important ones. They are causality, determinism, reductionism, and self-anchored methodology.

Causality

This is the oldest, and until recently has been the most firmly established, law in science. The daily thinking of every individual in Western society is deeply conditioned by this law and his actions are firmly based on its functioning. It is not only a law regulating the behavior of events but the basis of scientific prediction. The ability to foretell the future of an event by knowing its past has been until recently not merely an article of faith but a principle of certainty.

But in this area of scientific endeavor, as in Western civilization itself, we have reached a critical moment. The axiom of causality, like other axioms of science, is challenged and denied by one or another worker in the field. It is no longer accepted as a universal postulate, and some scientists have suggested its exclusion from natural science. It has become difficult to establish the fact that every elementary event in nature is completely determined by laws without reference to other events. Thus whether causal events are determined in the classical sense depends upon the scientist's choice of alternatives. While he may prefer a strict causal explanation of all events, simply because a well-defined answer to a question is preferable to a one that is poorly defined, many a physicist has adopted the non-causal alternative, nevertheless. He does not deny that one event which regularly follows another event is causally related to it. What he denies is the proposition that regular succession is identical with causal relationship. He denies, too, the predictive certainty of the causal relationship, but holds, on the contrary, that it is at best only statistical. There is thus no strict mechanical causality in nature. What appears to be an invariable causal connection between events is in fact an illusion — an illusion stemming from the fact that the connection is almost, but not absolutely, true. Every physical law is in effect a law of probability, a law having only an approximate validity, a law expressing contingency, not certainty. In short, statistical laws do not depend on causality.

This state of affairs has been created by the researches of quantum mechanics, the physical theory of Max Planck. Quantum theory does not give the physicist a completely objective description of the physical world. The reasons for this situation are many and complicated, but for our purpose it is sufficient to point out that the data of physics are never known by means of direct observation and experimentation but by means of theoretical constructions. The external world is not directly knowable. The law of causation, from this perspective, is an excellent guiding rule, but not the statement of an established fact. It does not have universal validity, for in the world of atoms, as shown by the principle of indeterminacy, it has been a failure, as we have already seen. In the realm of statistical laws, irregularity, no less than regularity, characterizes natural events. Complete regularity or causal determination obtains only in what Planck calls the fictitious "world image," not in the immediate world of the senses.[9] In the real world of the senses, quantum theory challenges Einstein's conviction that God does not play dice with the universe.

The lesson conveyed by the foregoing developments in modern physics for the behavioral sciences is the important role of speculation in science. Indeed, many of the great physicists of the twentieth century, such as Einstein, Planck, and Heisenberg, have empha-

---

[9] M. Planck, *op. cit.*, p. 283.

sized the view that the scientist arrives at his theory of the physical world only by means of speculative thinking. Complete empirical proof is neither possible nor necessary in science. Proof is the "idol before whom the pure mathematician tortures himself."[10] The best we can hope for regarding causation in the "real" world is plausibility. As we shall see, this is infinitely more true of the world of man. The fictitious world image can be constructed out of mathematical symbols, but the world of man — of inner man particularly — can be built only on the insights of the human personality. If causality does not strictly obtain in the world of the atoms, it holds to an even lesser degree in the world of the human self.

Determinism

Causality and determinism are different and at the same time intimately related. Depending on the definition given of causality, the two words may or may not be identical. The physicist who holds that causality operates even in the field of quantum mechanics, will also affirm that determinism is universal. On the other hand, the physicist who claims that causality does not operate in quantum phenomena will assert that, although determinism is a causal system, not every causal system is completely determined. Since between these two modes of thinking the scientist is free to exercise a choice, the proactive psychologist prefers the indeterministic position. The uniquely human traits of reflection, conscious aspiration, creativity, and so forth, presuppose for their existence and understanding a human nature with the property of freedom of choice.

Unlike the speculative conclusions of the physicist, the evidence for indeterminism in the human realm lies in man's own consciousness. Man needs no awesome mathematical equations to establish his freedom. His own experience is the evidence of his freedom of choice. The starting point of every act of knowing, including the most rigorous scientific explanation, is the knower's own experience — the immediate data of his consciousness.

Max Planck, the renowned physicist, has stated the whole matter of determinism and causality in the realm of human conduct eloquently. He writes,

[10] A. S. Eddington, *The Nature of the Physical World* (New York: T. e Macmillan Co., 1929), p. 337.

In principle every man can apply the law of causality to the happenings of the world around him, in the spiritual as well as the physical order, according to the measure of his own intellectual powers; but he can do this only when he is sure that the act of applying the law of causality does not influence the happening itself. And therefore he cannot apply the law of causality to his own future thoughts or to the acts of his own will. These are the only objects which for the individual himself do not come within the force of the law of causality in such a way that he can understand its play upon them. . . .

It is a dangerous act of self-delusion if one attempts to get rid of an unpleasant moral obligation by claiming that human action is the inevitable result of an inexorable law of nature. The human being who looks upon his own future as already determined by fate, or the nation that believes in a prophecy which states that its decline is inexorably decreed by a law of nature, only acknowledges a lack of will power to struggle and win through.[11]

And so man, the only being who is conscious of himself, who can meditate upon the nature and meaning of his own life, is inevitably brought around to reflect upon the most practical question of his life, the freedom to choose. In denying this capacity in man, positivistic psychology has blinded itself for the sake of a foolish consistency and an illusory scientific prestige.[12]

It is possible, then, to assert that one of the oldest riddles of life, the question of independent behavior in a world of causal laws, is solved by the very human capacity of choice which the determinist denies.

Reductionism

The doctrine of reductionism is a corollary of the Comtean, or positivistic, arrangement of the sciences into a hierarchy, beginning with the simplest, which is physics, and ending with the most

[11] M. Planck, *op. cit.*, pp. 62–63.

[12] To the purist we can say that freedom means unpredictability, so that from an operational standpoint all human behavior that cannot be predicted is free. To the scrupulous physiologist, who would trace all behavior to an antecedent physiological source, we can reply that it is impossible to make predictions in certain microphysiological processes, and on the basis of any foreseeable future developments, we probably will not be able to predict every possible act of choice.

complex, which is sociology. Comte and his followers, down to the contemporary scene in science, have held that the concepts and processes of one science may be reduced to those of another, from the most complex to the simplest. The reduction of a complex form of behavior, such as cognition, some say, can and should be reduced to its simplest process, which is neurophysiological.

Rather than simplifying the scientific study of man, the principle of reductionism complicates it instead. In the present state of scientific knowledge it is impossible to determine with confidence when a phenomenon is, say, physiological or non-physiological. In this situation reductionism is meaningless.

Reductionist methodology is in a position of uncertainty, similar to the doctrines of strict causality and rigid determinism, with whose spirit it is closely allied. Neither of the doctrines is widely accepted, because there is insufficient tangible evidence to support it. In like manner, there is no empirical evidence and no valid logical argument to demonstrate that merely because one event precedes another one in time, the two are therefore causally connected. A prior event cannot be said to be more authentic than one that comes late in the series, and there is thus no necessary reason why the later should be reduced to the earlier. Reductionism stands or falls with the validity of the doctrine of causal determinism. Since choice between this doctrine and its alternative is not only permissible but widely practiced, there is no reason in fact or logic that should prevent us from accepting or rejecting determinism, in degree or in its entirety. And since we proceed in this book on the premise that complex psychological forms like consciousness, selfhood, and personality cannot be explained reductively without explaining them away, we deny the necessity of reducing the complex to the simple. For the principle of reduction we substitute the principle of expansion. What we possibly lose in methodological elegance we gain in a humanistic appreciation of the wholeness of man.[13]

Self-Anchored Methodology

The positivistic tradition in psychology, especially its behavioristic form, has been, with such notable exceptions as the behaviorism of B. F. Skinner, almost entirely statistical in its meth-

[13] A rule of thumb would be: reduce when you must, when it makes a segment of behavior more intelligible, but without distorting it; expand when, in order to forestall partition, you must preserve the integrity of the whole.

odology. Most scientific psychologists, those who are scientific in the narrow sense, not only bend behavior to statistical technique, but are convinced that statistical reduction is the only road to the science of man.[14] In America statistical method in psychology is not only widely used, but has achieved an honorific status as well.

It would be foolish to discredit the reasonable use of statistical technique in psychology. At the same time, it is foolish and narrow for the statistician to hold in disrepute all psychological results that have not been derived from a plenitude of subjects. Like Skinner and others, we should have greater confidence in the "intensive concentration on the single case."[15] There is nothing in the whole complex of psychological methodologies that can refute the belief that the scientific nature of psychology can be enhanced when it studies the single subject in its full complexity. A sound psychology of personality can be built on the study of a single case. We believe that a detailed knowledge of the traits of single individuals can increase psychology's predictive power.

This self-anchored methodology is wholly consistent with the scientific study of human behavior; indeed, it is the only method which enables us to study the whole person, instead of merely his part-functions. All psychologies that ignore the anchorage of experience within the human self are incomplete. They catch the peripheral elements in their measures of behavior, never its living center. They correlate and partition, they sample and test significance, but somehow the living human being always escapes them.

The self-anchoring technique creates nothing but consternation in the psychologist's mind. The heavy hand of tradition blinds him to the simple truth that there is no other way to knowledge, as we have shown, than through the person's own experience. There is not a phenomenon in psychology, from mass communication to the self-image, which is not deeply anchored in the self who investigates them. But just as it is difficult for many persons to accept the fact that a straight line is also bent—so difficult is it to think in relativistic concepts—so is it equally hard for the academic psychologist, nurtured by the bias for statistical analysis, to believe in the credibility of single-person observations. Once the old bias has been removed from our thinking, the self-rootedness of

[14] See, for example, F. V. Smith, *Explanation of Human Behavior,* 2nd ed. (London: Constable and Co., 1960).
[15] B. F. Skinner, "A Case History in Scientific Method," in S. Koch (ed.), *Psychology: A Study of a Science.* (New York: McGraw-Hill Book Co., Inc.), vol. 2, p. 370.

human knowledge becomes commonplace. The reason for this condition is not difficult to find: since human beings, despite their uniqueness, are also very much alike, it is safe to assume that what is true as an explanatory principle of me, is similarly true of others. It is now firmly established that Freud's massive description and analysis of man, though confirmed by many cases in his practice of psychotherapy, was based almost entirely upon exceptionally keen observations of his own personality.[16]

For a whole generation William Stephenson, the factor analyst, has been propounding in a rigorous way what the early existentialists, especially Kierkegaard in his *Concluding Unscientific Postscript*, had advocated at the end of the last century. Stephenson calls this non-sampling approach to human behavior the *centrality-of-self methodology*. Its similarity and relevance to the present discussion of self-anchored psychology is obvious.[17]

Self-anchored analysis in psychology and causal description in physics are very much alike. Both are explanations of "facts" by means of self-descriptions. They are "operations" performed by an individual, and the consequences of the operations result in personal knowledge. There is here an unexpected similarity between the operations performed by Skinner's animals and by the human individual. Self-anchored knowledge is knowledge from the point of view of the experiencing person: there is no other kind. It is knowledge in which man is asking questions about himself and giving his own answers. Thus, as Stephenson remarks, "one no longer works on a hundred men to prove a point, but basically on only one."[18]

Why do psychologists not accept the simple and obvious fact that self-anchored descriptions are the data of all sciences, including psychology? We have already suggested a partial answer. Outside of Skinner and his devoted followers, psychologists have

---

[16] This information, though startling to the narrow methodologist, is consistent with Freud's daring probing into the human psyche, and is very natural to the phenomenologist, existentialist, and proactive psychologist.

[17] These similar approaches were developed independently. Stephenson was influenced by the specialist's knowledge of statistics and factor analysis; the writer's own is largely a reaction to the inhibiting effect of logical positivism and operationism in his early training. For a lucid and comprehensive introductory discussion of the centrality-of-self methodology see W. Stephenson, "Scientific Creed — 1961; The Centrality of Self," *Psychological Record*, 1961, *11*, 18–25.

[18] W. Stephenson, *op. cit.*, p. 22.

been beguiled by the importance of sheer numbers. In this respect they differ little or not at all from the "man on the street." Tell the latter that *thousands* of individuals have found *Dentine* tooth-paste best for preventing cavities, and he is ready to use it himself. Another reason for this state of affairs is the prestige of statistical methodology. Since psychologists are sensitive to the opinions of their colleagues, they are not ready to discard their hard-won status in the scientific bureaucracy. A final reason lies in the psychologist's inability to admit that "objective" knowledge can be obtained by "subjective" means. He can point to Freud's self-anchored psy-chology as proof of the invalidity of the single-case technique. He cannot be so cavalier, however, in dismissing the scientific work of Skinner, who is not impressed by sampling procedures and the power of numbers, yet who is one of his contemporary heroes. As for earlier exemplars of the self-anchored technique, such as Ebbinghaus, for example, whose authority in the field of memory and learning has lost none of its original luster, the psychologist either does not know or has forgotten. As Stephenson gently re-minds us, Ebbinghaus, already fifty years ago, investigated memory entirely upon himself, and yet "his work has long been regarded as a landmark in the application of the theory of errors of observation to the examination of higher mental processes."[19]

Since the objective of this chapter is to prepare the conceptual and philosophical foundations of proactive psychology, not to indoctrinate the reader with the shortcomings of current behavior theory, it is enough to point out that, if psychology is going to deal with the human person instead of his part-reactions, it must engage in a radical change in its view of scientific method, away from statistical analysis, especially the theory of sampling, to the accept-ance of self-anchored methodology, self-observation, introspection, and personal experience.

CONCLUSION

The great physicist, Niels Bohr, was fond of making the point that physical science always presupposes man, and that man is not a mere spectator of physical events, but an active participant in their occurrence. There is no human world without percipient man. Reality is not exclusively "external." Man creates his world. This is no poetic fancy. As a knowing and reflecting subject, man

[19] *Ibid.*, p. 19.

is the key to the science of both nature and man. Only bias and dogmatic positivism have kept man from perceiving clearly that the only reality anyone can truly know is the reality of his own subjective experience. Logically and scientifically man can only *deduce* the nature of the objective world and the subjective experiences of his fellow man.

It is a grave error to define science in its current positivistic sense, especially its form in American behaviorism. The current definition would have us believe that science is largely a process of data collection, and the manipulation of these data by means of statistics and operationism. However, it should be clear by now that this mode of scientific manipulation has resulted in squeezing the life out of the living human being.

The definition of science as *scientia,* as *Wissenschaft,* is as valid today as it was before the advent of the positivistic philosophy. In Europe, where basic science had its birth and where it is still most highly valued, this has been its meaning. Thus the science of Max Planck, for instance, is largely the integrated generalizations resulting from hard thinking about experimental research. This meaning of science helps us to penetrate deeper into the "dark" currents inside man. It enables us to see that the psychologist does to man what the physicist does to matter: he changes him. As the physicist modifies the object that he investigates, so the psychologist, in using human consciousness and reflection, modifies the behavior of man. Finally, this view permits us to describe man not only quantitatively but by artistic modes of expression as well, thus helping to bring art and science together again.[20]

[20] Several months after this chapter was completed, Sigmund Koch published an important critique of behaviorism and phenomenology, which supports many of the ideas which we have expounded in this chapter. See T. W. Wann (ed.), *Behaviorism and Phenomenology* (Chicago: University of Chicago Press, 1964).

PART
TWO

Reactive Man

2

People, it seems, are busy leading their lives into the future, whereas psychology, for the most part, is busy tracing them into the past.

GORDON W. ALLPORT

The Tyranny of the Past

The concept of time has been largely the concern of the physicist and the philosopher. The psychologist has made very little explicit use of it, even though it is an underlying premise of every system of psychology. When Freud decribes an individual's present behavior as the recapitulation of archaic responses; or when the behaviorist attributes a man's contemporary act to the process of conditioning in the individual's past; each is placing the behavior within a temporal framework. Every habit presupposes a past. Even psychologists—perhaps because they *are* psychologists—are baffled by a form of present behavior which seems to have no functional connection with an individual's past. Life is replete with instances of criminal acts committed by a person in whose life there is not a remote suggestion of future violence; or examples of gentle persons whose past should have foredoomed them to criminal behavior; or of criminals who have successfully reformed. Nevertheless, the past tyrannizes the psychologist when he analyzes and explains human motivation or describes the process of human socialization.

It has been known for a long time that people in different cultures conceptualize and orient themselves differently on the temporal continuum. More recently the hypothesis has been advanced and generally confirmed, that temporal goal orientations are related to levels of social class. Thus, children of the lower class do not generally deny themselves present pleasures for future gains. The future is a vague region of time, and serves as a weak

37

motivating force in their lives. Rewards and punishments in the future are largely inoperative and function efficiently only in the present. They confirm the reinforcement theory that rewards and punishments should be meted out at once if they are to be effective. In the upper-lower, middle, and lower-upper classes, the orientation is much more toward the future. An adult may plan for his retirement when he is very young. Inhibition and deferment of action is characteristic of his goal orientation. In the upper class, the individual perceives himself in the temporal orientation of several generations, thus looking backward and guiding his behavior by tradition.[1]

For our purpose the foregoing observations are interesting, but they do not form the immediate content of this chapter. We are interested in examining the extent to which much contemporary psychology explains human behavior as a product of antecedent conditions.

MAN, THE CONCUPISCENT ANIMAL

It has become something of a pastime among unknowing psychologists to ridicule psychoanalysis for its lack of scientific rigor. They unwittingly equate Freud's penchant for literary metaphor with fuzzy thinking. Whatever the final verdict of history may be regarding Freud's psychoanalytic view of man, Freud was uncompromising in his refusal to rely on any method but that of empirical science. He was a positivist who often spoke the humanist's language. He never wavered or equivocated in his preference for determinism and rigid causal connectedness of psychological events. The unsurpassing character of his scientific work has the fascination of Greek tragedy. If in the unlikely event that psychoanalysis should turn out to be nothing but mythology, it will nonetheless remain as great literature. Freud never flinched in his remorseless portrayal of man as a concupiscent animal, driven by an innate biological energy, called *libido*. Although he eventually saw the error of describing man exclusively in libidinal terms, by going beyond the pleasure principle, Freud never de-emphasized the appetitive nature of man. This and other principles of psychoanalysis as a form of reaction psychology, and the heavy burden

---

[1] See L. L. LeShan, "Time Orientation and Social Class," *J. abn. soc. Psychol.*, 1952, 57, 389–392.

of the past in the life of every individual which it stresses, we shall discuss in the present section.

The Pleasure Principle

Every organism is activated by the possession of a primary energy, by inborn automatic reflex actions. The function of these primary processes is to reduce the tensions of the organism. Tensions are experienced as discomfort, displeasure, or pain. The reservoir of these tensions is the *id*, the source of most psychobiological energy, the center of all the purely hedonistic drives. The id has no conscience and knows no logic. Contradictory and conflicting impulses exist in it side by side. It has no foresight and is blind to the consequences of its own satisfactions. Thus, although Freud was an unyielding empiricist who could not logically admit teleological elements into his psychology, he suffered no embarrassment in declaring that the entire psychobiological apparatus of the organism is bent on realizing but one purpose: the attainment of pleasure and the avoidance of pain.

Freud justified this seeming purposivism by giving it a biological basis. Pleasure when discharged diminishes or exhausts the accumulated tensions of the id. Conversely, since pain increases stimulation and tension, it must be extinguished. It makes no difference to the organism whether pleasure is gained or pain is lost; the end-product is always the same, namely, the reduction or elimination of unbearable tensions. Thus, although the life-urge, expressing itself in the form of libidinal energy, works in the service of individual and phylogenetic propagation and survival, as a psychological model for the study of the personality, Freud's concept is a thoroughly tension-reductive formulation. In this formulation, the individual acts wholly in response to irritants, to the reduction of the tensions and discomforts generated by the libido. Of these irritants sexual tension, aroused in different bodily regions, or erogenous zones, is the most important. The bodily needs create erotic wishes in the individual. Even when the erogenous zones are not stimulated, the individual engages in fantasy behavior in the form of images of past pleasure-fulfilling experiences, called wish-fulfillments. These images or wishes constitute the reality of the id. It must be emphasized that the libido consists not only of sexual or procreative energy, but even more of the mental energy of the total human psyche. Indeed, the libido *is* the mental side of the total energy. It must be stressed at the same time, that the libido is only an hypothesis. Freud never claimed any ontological status for it. It is a heuristic construct, a useful postulate, like the concept of energy in physics.

The Unconscious

Freud's most radical departure from the psychology of his time and of the present, is his concern with the unconscious dimension of the mental life. Preoccupation with the unconscious aspects is due to the belief of all psychoanalysts that most of man's mental life goes on without his awareness. The unconscious occupies an important place in psychoanalysis also because it is the locus of all impulses and desires which are repressed by virtue of social and moral demands placed upon the individual by society and his own conscious mind. It is important too because most infantile patterns of behavior, which in the Freudian system are exceedingly important, take place in the unconscious. According to Freud, the early patterns of reaction occurring in the unconscious are largely responsible for the reactions and adjustments of the adult. Accordingly, any failure or deformation in the solutions of life's problems in childhood is carried into maturity, where it results in maladjustments.

A person's early modes of dealing with life thus become established habits. Frequently, an adult will regress to one of these earlier behavior patterns, the stage of regression being determined largely by a previous regression. The first few years of a person's life are the most crucial in the establishment of all later forms of behavior.

The pleasure principle governs the course of the development at every step, and determines the three stages of the libidinal history. The first of these, known as the *oral* stage, and lasting for about a year, is the period when the child's libido finds its fullest expression in activities associated with the mouth. The *anal* stage is the period during which the child's activities center around the anal zone, expressing themselves in anal and urethral eliminations. The third stage, called variously the *phallic* or the *genital* stage, is characterized by sexual and aggressive pleasures, particularly masturbation and erotic fantasy activities, which Freud called narcissism. This period is psychologically important because it ushers in the Oedipus complex, which all psychoanalysts agree is the origin of most of the conflicts of adult life. Normally, this stage emerges during the third year in a child's development and lasts until the fifth year. It marks an important stage in the development of the libido. During this time, the egoistic, self-seeking child seeks to possess his mother as a love object. But in this erotic attraction to his mother, the child finds himself his father's rival. Out of this erotic triangular drama arises fear of punishment and a sense of guilt on the child's part.

This is the normal course of development of a child in Western society, according to all Freudians. However, it is subject to fixations, distortions, and perversions. The child who grows up into a normal adult has successfully resolved the conflicts in the Oedipus situation by surrendering the parents as erotic objects and constructing new ideals out of the image of each of them. Both now serve the child as guiding principles in the growth toward maturity. That child, on the other hand, who has failed to resolve the Oedipus conflict, who has not envisioned ideals in his parents, may remain at or return to a former erotic level, a libidinal fixation, neurosis, or other compromise or abnormal resolution of his erotic conflicts.

The foregoing is only the barest sketch of what is by all odds the most complex and intricate theory of human nature in the history of modern psychology. It testifies to the fact that a theory of personality may break the rule of parsimony and yet be conceived in the spirit of science.

It is an egregious mistake to consign psychoanalysis to the outer darkness of a higher metapsychology. This is the more true in view of the fact that in his last major revision of his ideas before his death, Freud explicitly described some of the important, empirically unverified concepts, in the language of constructs. Thus, the most controversial of his ideas, the concept of a basic drive or "instinct" (*Trieb*), was named a "mythical being" (*mythische Wesen*).[2] Likewise, no one was more conscious of the limitations of psychoanalysis as a form of psychotherapy than Freud himself. Contrary to his critics, Freud was always ready to revise his ideas in the light of contradictory evidence. Although he obstinately held to the belief in the validity of the fundamental idea of psychoanalysis, Freud was never doctrinaire. In his exposure of the subterranean forces of the human psyche to the searching light of his own intellect, Freud made a signal contribution to the understanding of man.

[2] S. Freud, *New Introductory Lecture on Psychoanalysis* (New York: Carlton House, 1933), p. 131.

What one misses in Freud's penetrating analyses is not the way of science, but the way of the self-developing man. What one deplores in his writings is not his placing of man in the animal kingdom, since this is an incontrovertible fact, but his vision of the dwarfish nature of man. On the magnitude of man in his uniqueness and wholeness, Freud is quaintly silent.[3]

Since our task in this chapter is to show the reactive, or more precisely the retroactive, nature of the individual in Freud's psychology, we turn our attention to this phase of our discussion.

SOME LIMITATIONS OF FREUDIAN PSYCHOLOGY

In view of what we have said here and elsewhere, it is clear that we hold Freudian psychology in high esteem.[4] Its penetration into the deeply embedded and indirectly accessible motives of human conduct, is in our humble judgment as yet unequalled. Freud's grasp and delineation of the dramatic conflict within every individual has been exceeded only by a few great dramatists and poets.[5] What gives them the power and authenticity is Freud's observation of them in living and suffering individuals, with an unsurpassing clinical mind.

We begin our verdict with the strong conviction that, first, although psychoanalysis goes far indeed in describing man's personality, it does not go far enough; and second, that, although the human being it portrays is indeed an animal driven by blind forces to which he responds mechanically, it completely neglects those qualities of man which enable him to transcend his crippling past to create a healthy future.

[3] It is only fair to Freud to note here that, although he considered man as a total individual who, for scientific reasons, had to be partitioned and then put together again, he never conveyed a picture of man in a holistic, or organismic, sense. His approach to scientific problems was completely mechanistic, a position in the history of science which always placed the parts before the whole, and conceived totalities as additive relationships.

[4] See H. Bonner, *Psychology of Personality* (New York: The Ronald Press Co., 1961), Ch. 2.

[5] *Zwei Seelen wohnen, Ach! in meiner Brust*–Goethe; *Je sens deux hommes en moi.* – Hugo. Human conflict, both internal and external, is the subject matter of the plays of Euripides, Sophocles, and Shakespeare, as is well known.

Mechanistic Bias

For all his search for psychodynamic interpretations of human behavior, Freud's description of man is thoroughly mechanistic. What does this mean?

Mechanism is a philosophical position in science which implies a conception of nature in which entities and events are related to one another externally, rather than organically. In psychology, Freudian or behavioristic, this view makes of personality, the self, consciousness, etc., epiphenomena, or by-products, of something fundamental, such as libido, or the pleasure principle. Historically, mechanism has from its inception in ancient philosophy, denied an organizing principle in physical, biological, and psychological events. Processes are seen, instead, as purposeless and yet determined by law. If today the paradox of this position is called to the mechanist's attention he usually falls back on the Humean explanation that a law is but an observed regularity in nature, or if he is more positivistically sophisticated, that a law is a statistical formulation of a uniformity in the behavior of phenomena. That these formulations are human thoughts without proof of objective reference, does not seem to bother the mechanist; and Freud would have dismissed it, as he dismissed similar and related problems, as lying in the field of philosophy, of which he had a low esteem.

The psychoanalytical thesis that an adult's present behavior is the recapitulation of earlier modes of adjustment, is thoroughly mechanistic. It is based on the so-called laws of association. It explains the behavior of the whole, or of the person, in terms of its parts. No attempt is made to explain how the separate parts come together to make a whole. Logically and ontologically, each part must exist by itself, without definable relation to any other. How the laws of causation, which are universally affirmed by mechanists, operate to make it possible for one part to affect another part, remains one of those mysteries which Freud, in company with other mechanists, indignantly scorned.

On the mechanistic view the parts are therefore *sui generis,* or independent elements. The elements or parts are antecedent to the whole, and the whole is a derived product. Logically and in essence, this means that the modalities of personality—its libido, motives, attitudes, its pleasure-seeking, its tension-reduction—are primary, whereas the personality which "has" them is a derivative, an epiphenomenon.

Thus, although by intent Freud was aiming at a description of the total individual, in practice he was dissecting personality into part-reactions. Although Freud's purpose was to account for the human person as an organization or structure of libidinal strivings, he could not go beyond the atomistic principles inherent in the mechanistic assumption. Even if one were to grant, as we do not, that man is only a machine, it would be impossible on that ground to derive a unified reaction by means of a piecemeal synthesis. Such a synthesis is possible only on the basis of another assumption, whose validity has been established in philosophical and biological research, namely, that parts are not antecedent to structures, not primary in their relation to organized wholes.

This obliviousness to the primacy of wholes over parts, of persons over part-reactions, has been a fatal defect of psychoanalysis. In its preoccupation with libido, the pleasure principle, and the id— with sex in its broadest meaning as a generalized pleasurable feeling —psychoanalysis subordinated personality to part-functions. Personality is, in fact, the mere balancing of libidinal strivings, of pains and pleasures. Tension-reduction is, in its very nature, a homeostasis, never a productive behavior; and all behavior is indeed, as we have shown, a recapitulation of archaic and mechanically-related wish-fulfillments.[6]

Deterministic Dogma

Viewed historically, all mechanistic philosophies of science have been deterministic. This is a logically consistent and necessary position. In mechanistic relations the parts, we have seen, are mutually independent. Causation proceeds in a lineal fashion from part to part and culminates in a whole. The relations are determined at every position in the process. Man is never free to act on his own initiative. Every act is determined by an antecedent act dating back to the very origin of man's being in the intrauterine environment. Man is not free to act, and he cannot choose his behavior.

---

[6] This dependence of the contemporary act upon infantile sexual strivings is maximized in the psychoanalytic theory of neurosis. So important is this notion that Freud was sure that psychoanalysis as a theory of both normal and abnormal personality fails or succeeds in accordance with its establishment of the primacy of the sexual function. However, since neurosis and pathological behavior are not our concern in this book, we shall say no more.

In this bias for determinism Freud was a child of nineteenth-century positivism, which even he could not—or would not—transcend. The bedrock of nineteenth-century science was causal determinism, a concept which was erroneously assumed to be necessary in order to make prediction possible. So natural was this mode of thinking in Freud's time that the great psychoanalyst was never able to face, let alone resolve, the dilemma of trying to cure patients of illnesses which were themselves completely determined.

Psychotherapy is not alone in being impossible, if the deterministic dogma is correct. The whole process of human socialization, including education and moral improvement, is made inexplicable in the face of it. Psychoanalysis has not progressed beyond the Fall of Man—a fall which was itself, ironically, a consequence of Adam's freedom of choice. Nor need we stop with a Biblical metaphor: human behavior is not genetically predetermined. Modern genetics has given us extensive proof of man's behavioral plasticity within the framework of enculturation, education, and interpersonal relations. Cultural evolution goes hand in hand with biological evolution. The determinism of nineteenth-century evolutionary doctrine was basically amoral; the evolutionary view of today "involves knowledge, including the knowledge of good and evil."[7]

Freud's negative view of man was not the mere expression of a deep-rooted pessimism. It was based on the premise of rigid necessity in the course of events. Freedom in his view was as much an illusion without a future as the religion which he so deftly annihilated.[8]

There is merit in the argument that Freud, both in his work and in his person, is the strongest refutation of his deterministic assumption. Without freedom to choose, Freud could neither have cured his patients nor created the marvel that is psychoanalysis. Thus the values which he denied in theory, he affirmed in practice. This is a paradox, for Freud himself strove for, and apparently believed in, the perfectibility of man.

Although Freud's life is a refutation of the deterministic principle, this philosophical canon has rendered psychoanalysis danger-

[7] G. G. Simpson, *The Meaning of Evolution* (New Haven: Yale University Press, 1949).

[8] See S. Freud, *The Future of an Illusion* (New York: Liveright Publishing Corp., 1953).

ous and unacceptable. One is inclined to agree with Frankl's judgment, that more perilous than Freud's pansexualism in human conduct, is the psychoanalytic assumption of "pan-determinism."[9]

Hedonistic Fallacy

Nowhere in psychoanalysis is man's servitude to the id more evident than in its pleasure principle. Nowhere is the tyranny of the past more crippling of the personality than in its all-encompassing influence. The infantile strivings of the pleasure-seeking id chain the adult to his narcissistic origin.

Few things in psychoanalysis—and in psychology generally—are more astonishing than its inability to see what is obvious to those who have no doctrine to defend, namely, that men often follow a course of action that leads only to pain and suffering. Throughout their history, men have suffered and sacrificed for others, or for a goal wholly devoid of pleasure in the psychoanalytical meaning. Even physical survival is not a universal goal. In the concentration camps of the Second World War, some men preferred starvation and death to the surrender of their deepest values and commitments. Many men have engaged in activities whose fulfillment was even at best highly problematic. Idealism may be out of fashion in psychology, but it is alive in the hearts of men.

The defender of the psychoanalytic faith always counters with the familiar reply. The man who gives his life for a cause, he says, is motivated by the pleasure he experiences in the act of pursuing it. This is a specious argument invented to hold intact an indefensible position. It denies the face value of human experience in favor of the rigid doctrine of unconscious motivation. It flies in the face of current evolutionary evidence that man can determine his own destiny.[10]

The hedonic dogma is the contemporary manifestation of the ancient predilection for depicting Satan more attractively than the

[9] V. E. Frankl, *Man's Search for Meaning: An Introduction to Logotherapy* (Boston: Beacon Press, 1962), p. 132.

[10] This view of the nature of man is held by an increasing number of evolutionists. See T. Dobzhansky, *Mankind Evolving: The Evolution of the Human Species* (New Haven: Yale University Press, 1962); J. Huxley (ed.), *The Humanist Frame* (New York: Harper and Bros., 1961); and G. G. Simpson, *op. cit.*

Deity. In psychoanalysis man is full of flaws but empty of nobility. Early fixations account for everything, later idealizations, for nothing. From the psychoanalytical point of view we are all, in Hermann Muller's arresting phrase, "hastily made-over apes." In this view, foresight and the envisioning of ideals are purely adaptive mechanisms, incapable in themselves of generating novel behavior. Man is not a self-actualizing being, but a recapitulating animal.

Concluding Remarks on Psychoanalysis

The complaint has been voiced by defenders of the positivistic doctrine, that objections to its picture of man are motivated by religious, moral, and even aesthetic sensibilities. That this is true of some critics cannot be denied. Our own reaction is based on more persuasive considerations, even though we find the others compatible with our own.

Man is not wholly a concupiscent animal, chained to his infantile past. The weight of biological and psychological evidence contradicts the psychoanalyst's mechanistic oversimplification. Man's ethical conduct is an option among alternatives. Neither education, nor ethics, nor psychological healing is possible in a predetermined universe. The moral choices which men everywhere make in their daily lives presuppose their freedom. If man is able to master his environment, as history has proved that he can, something more than blind instincts must operate to make his mastery possible. Rome was built not only by means of pleasurable reward but also by painful sacrifice.

Man's renunciation of his infantile pleasures—a renunciation denied by orthodox psychoanalysts—is a prerequisite of mature conduct. The latter is not deducible from the pleasure principle, and most adult behavior contradicts it. The free choice among alternative values is not a mere wish, but a biological fact. Dobzhansky has stated the matter clearly. He writes:

> The ability of man to choose freely between ideas and acts is one of the fundamental characteristics of human evolution. Perhaps freedom is even the most important of all the specifically human attributes. Human freedom is wider than "necessity apprehended," which is the only kind of freedom recognized by Marxists [and one might add, psychoanalysts]. Man has freedom to defy necessity, at least in his imagination.

Ethics emanate from freedom and are unthinkable without freedom.[11]

MAN, THE LEARNING MACHINE

Most behavioristic psychologists disclaim the kinship of their science with psychoanalysis. They criticize or reject it on the ground that it is unscientific, even mystical. It affirms the existence, they say, of agents or forces that have no empirical status, such as libido, id, and superego. These cannot be defined operationally, nor are they legitimate hypothetical constructs or intervening variables.

Thanks to the judicious and impartial comparison of psychoanalysis with current learning theory, Hilgard has established some important links between them.[12] Some of the similarities will become obvious in our exposition of the fundamental ideas of what may be labeled "behaviorism." This term must be understood as a purely descriptive one, for unlike psychoanalysis, behaviorism is not a rigid doctrine, nor a school of psychology. What identifies the different theories as a distinct psychological point of view is their central and over-riding interest in the learning process.

Finally, psychoanalysis and behaviorism share in common an emphasis on the hedonistic character of all behavior and the conceptualization of man as a reactive animal. Thus, both are fundamentally reaction psychologies—psychologies which define behavior in terms of a stimulus and response framework. In psychoanalysis the stimulus-situation is for the most part internal, consisting of the libidinal irritants that clamor for reduction or elimination. In behaviorism, the stimulus-situation consists mostly of external irritants, such as food, which set the organism into action for removing them.[13] The common denominator of both psychoanalysis and the several forms of behaviorism is the stimulus-response linkage. In the rigorous and highly sophisticated behaviorisms of Miller, Dol-

---

[11] T. Dobzhansky, *The Biological Basis of Human Freedom* (New York: Columbia University Press, 1956), p. 134.

[12] E. R. Hilgard, *Theories of Learning*, 2nd ed. (New York: Appleton-Century-Crofts, Inc., 1956), Ch. 9.

[13] It would be a mistake to assume that behaviorism ignores internal stimuli, such as hunger and sexual tension. But what interests the behaviorists is the acts which the animal performs in trying to eliminate the tensions. This point will become clear in the full exposition of the behavioristic point of view.

lard, and Mowrer, especially with the two-factor, learning theory of the latter, there is much borrowing of psychoanalytical ideas, even though none of them can be described as a psychoanalytical psychologist.

The Stimulus-Response Framework

Every science operates by means of a fundamental or irreducible unit of a larger process. In behaviorism, the fundamental unit is the stimulus-response (S-R) bond. Although each of the sub-units of this connection is sometimes investigated separately, the two compose a single and total unit.[14]

The terms, stimulus and response, although among the most commonplace words in psychology, are far from clear. The word "stimulus" has by no means a single, unequivocal meaning. At least four definitions of the word can be found in the literature of psychology. The most frequent definition is in terms of energy, so that it may be defined as any degree of energy sufficient to elicit a response in an organism. It may also be defined as any event, or class of events, in the environment which controls a specific activity in an organism according to a specific law. A third definition conceives it as a change in a part of the environment. And finally, a stimulus is an *inferred* or *hypothetical* energy or event which elicits a response in an organism.[15]

The difficulty is compounded by the fact that not all stimuli lead to responses and because there are responses with no discoverable stimuli. Instances of the first are found in distraction, as when reading a page my attention is drawn to something else; and in so-called subliminal advertising, where no clear stimulus can be identified. Examples of the second — responses without stimuli — are found in the large variety of expressive behavior, such as manner of speaking, walking, writing, dancing, etc.

Every stimulus-response psychologist explains the behavior of the learner by reference to the latter's past history. The psychologist's knowledge of the learner's behavior, despite his demand for objective evidence, is always an *inference* from observed behavior, never

[14] Hull, one of the leading American behaviorists, even used the term "configuration," of *Gestalt* psychology, in referring to "stimulus-configuration," thus showing that even the separate unit of the couplet is conceived holistically.

[15] For a detailed discussion of these definitions, see W. S. Verplanck, in W. K. Estes *et al.*, *Modern Learning Theory* (New York: Appleton-Century-Crofts, 1954).

a direct verification of the inference itself. Accordingly, the stimulus-response theorist's demand for precision lacks the precision which he demands of all psychological theory, including his own. Decisive proof of what a subject learns is impossible. Stimulus-response psychology has thus survived to our day, not because it is "true," but because it has successfully explained its own illustrations of learned behavior. The particular theory of learning that the stimulus-response psychologist chooses to accept depends, therefore, not on objective evidence, but on general systematic considerations.

The non-objective, inferential nature of what is learned, and the determination of choice of theory by systematic preferences, is further illustrated by the contrasting *cognitive* approach to learning. This approach, sometimes called *centralist*, infers the presence of central brain processes, such as expectancies or memories, as explanations of behavior. Since both theories rest upon inferences from observed behavior and not upon objective facts, which one a psychologist chooses will depend on how consistent it is with his basic theoretical assumptions.

The stimulus-response fallacy. Most behavioristic psychology is embedded in the nineteenth-century theory of mechanical, causal determinism. In the view of causal determinism there is complete regularity of events, every cause resulting in an effect, and every effect presupposing a cause. The process of cause-effect is a completely mechanical one. A fixed dogma in this conceptualization of cause-effect relationship was that the effect is equivalent to its antecedent cause, and could contain neither more nor less than the cause.

Early critics of the dogma, notably Jan Smuts, called attention to its sterility.[16] Creativeness, progress, adventure are impossible in the older view. As in psychoanalysis, so in behaviorism, this doctrine has never been seriously questioned. Novel behavior is thus impossible, and in both systems present behavior is largely the repetition or recapitulation of past behavior.

The narrow view of causality has had still another negative effect upon reaction psychologies, whether psychoanalytical or behavioristic. Causality is defined in terms of single factors or isolated lineal events. Wholes are foreign to this mode of explanation. Thus there

16 See J. C. Smuts, *Holism and Evolution* (New York: The Viking Press, 1926; Compass Books Edition, 1961), Ch. 1. In complete fairness it should be noted that some recent behaviorists have argued against the breaking of complex behavior into S-R components. But the S-R mode of analysis is still a strong tendency in American psychology.

exists the belief that if one could isolate the one variable in a chain of events and hold it constant, one could explain the entire chain. In behaviorism one could account for learning by a rigorous identification of the separate variables; and in psychotherapy one could effect a cure if the traumatic experience of childhood were known and its effects gradually eliminated. In each case an antecedent event is the efficient cause of a subsequent effect.

This kind of isolation of single events is the very substance of the mechanistic view of science. Parts produce their effects individually, and these effects are predictable. Mechanical relations among events predominate. In this system novel changes are impossible, and genuine creativity is but a vitalistic concept.

To regard behavior — even animal behavior — as a chain of responses to stimuli, is to ignore its extraordinary complexity. To contend that every response invariably and inevitably follows upon a particular stimulus is to assert a proposition that cannot be supported by tangible evidence.

Many years ago Woodworth amended this purely mechanistic doctrine by interposing the organism between the stimulus and response, thereby converting the formula into S-O-R.[17] Although this was an improvement over both the structuralism of Titchener and the anti-introspectionism of Watson, both of which Woodworth combatted, it lacked the holistic attribute of organization or regulation. The specific human response to a stimulus is affected by the inner state of the individual. Stimulus-response equivalence, although it is the bedrock of behavioristic psychology, is not only an assumption but a fallacious one besides. It is based on an exaggeration of the importance of the principle of homeostasis, the principle that every organism strives to retain its equilibrium. The principle is true, but it has been overworked. Homeostasis, constancy, and equilibrium, like all forms of conservatism and survival, make for lifelessness. Human behavior is characterized by purpose, by changes in goals, by proaction. Stimulus-response equivalence leaves no room for novelty and creativity. Yet, the human person leaves both tranquility and the dead past behind as he advances into the future.

Even if for the sake of argument one should admit that the individual units, the stimulus and the response, are bound to each other in a one-to-one mechanical relationship, and hence rigidly

[17] R. S. Woodworth, *Dynamic Psychology* (New York: Columbia University Press, 1918).

determined, the whole of which they are parts is not subject to their influence. In contrast to the parts which are determined, the whole, in the form of the human personality, is free, for beyond the psychic whole there is nothing external to it that will control it.

However, in the light of modern physics our hypothetical argument is unnecessary. Two contemporary events are said to happen in causal independence of each other. Accordingly, as Whitehead has shown, two contemporary events are such that neither can belong to the past of the other.[18] Each is free to "advance into novelty."

Finally, it is no small thing to observe that response, like stimulus, is what Tolman called a "slippery and unanalyzed" concept. It includes so much that its value as a scientific term is greatly diminished. The term may mean anything from "a secretion of 10 drops of saliva . . . [or] the slope of a Skinner box curve, to achieving a Ph.D., or to a symbolic act of hostility against one's father by attacking some authority figure."[19]

This exaggerated emphasis on what after all these years are still poorly defined terms, and the related preoccupation with the past have been responsible for a view of man without an inner life. Man is *reduced* to a series of carefully measured external responses to outer events, or a structure of elementary reactions. In reality all men are reduced to a condition in which no one can any longer be distinguished from anyone else. They cannot act as free individuals, but only as reacting victims of their past.

The reactive fixation on the past fits well the life of a white rat, that gentle rodent who has no symbolic system, and the young child who cannot talk. It is now pretty well established that early influences are strongest in the preverbal stage of human development, when a child's behavior is not yet under symbolic control. The adult, on the other hand, having acquired an extensive verbal control over himself and his environment, can transcend his preverbal experiences by means of verbal manipulation. Experiments have shown that non-verbal learning is very resistant to extinction. An adult can talk himself out of the control of his past experiences.[20]

[18] A. N. Whitehead, *Adventures of Ideas* (New York: The Macmillan Co., 1933), p. 146.

[19] E. C. Tolman, "Principles of Purposive Behavior," in S. Koch (ed.), *Psychology: A Study of a Science* (New York: McGraw-Hill Book Co., Inc., 1959), vol. 2, p. 95.

[20] For experimental research bearing on this problem, see E. R. Hilgard and D. G. Marquis, *Conditioning and Learning* (New York: Appleton-Century-Crofts, 1940).

Freud's dictum that man cannot forego any pleasure he has once experienced, may be true of the child, the immature human being, and the rat; but it is contradicted by the lives of grown-up men.

Drive-reductive Learning

The central concern of current behaviorism, we said, is the learning process. All but one or two contemporary learning theories, of which there are at least a dozen, are firmly based on the stimulus-response, drive-reduction, framework. It is safe to say that the learning theories which are getting the most serious attention today are drive-reductive, in different ways. All assert that when there is no drive, there is no learning.

A drive is the energizing function in the learning process, a stimulus to action, and so the first step in learning. Primary drives consist of physiological needs, such as hunger, thirst, and sex. Secondary drives are social in character, and include such needs as belongingness, friendship, and the kind of food prevailing in a social group.

Although both reward and punishment have played important roles in learning theory, the current emphasis is on reward, technically called *reinforcement*. While a drive will impel an organism to action, it is insufficient in accounting for continuous learning. A mode of behavior is repeated for any length of time only when it is reinforced. In the absence of reward the stimulus-response is weakened, or extinguished altogether. A reinforcement thus strengthens the stimulus, or drive, while it at the same time reduces it. While the reinforcement continues, the organism learns; and when it ceases, learning diminishes and eventually stops. Reinforcement is thus the most effective variable in the learning process.

Reinforcement strengthens the already established stimulus-response connections, and makes it difficult for new responses to occur. In order to eliminate this barrier to new learning the learner must be placed in learning situations, called learning dilemmas, where old responses will not be reinforced. In these situations the learner can establish new associations because the old ones are either absent or inappropriate. We cite here a case described by the author in another connection.[21] The child is a five-year-old boy who, though well past the age when speech normally appears in children, spoke hardly at all, or so poorly that his speech was unintelligible. His parents almost invariably anticipated the child's

---

21 H. Bonner, *op. cit.*, pp. 234–235.

wants without his needing to communicate them verbally. The child quickly learned that his wishes would be satisfied by his parents without any verbal efforts on his part. He was thus deprived of every opportunity to learn to speak. However, a speech therapist who was employed to encourage verbal communication did not reinforce the latter's silence and defective verbalization. The child was thus thrown upon his own resources. The dilemma soon forced him to verbalize, and his acquisition of verbal habits was accelerated. The problem-situation served as a strong drive-stimulus which impelled the boy to seek and find a way for reducing the tension which the learning situation had generated.

It would take us far beyond the boundaries of the present discussion to go into a detailed criticism of the drive-reduction theory of learning. It has advanced learning theory far beyond its crude forms in early behaviorism, and for that we owe a great debt to Hull, Dollard, Miller, and B. F. Skinner. There is, nevertheless, one serious flaw, and this can be stated simply.

It will be recalled that an important feature of the theory is that drive-reduction is reinforcing, and is therefore the main impetus to learning. Yet, tension-reduction cannot strengthen the cue which directs the drive into channels that will reduce the tension, nor strengthen the bond between the cue and the response-induced tension. If it did, drive-reduction would reinforce the tension-reducing response. Paradoxically, tension-reduction would increase tension.

Miller tried to meet this objection, but his explanation, though ingenious and complex, is too extensive to recount here.[22]

Concluding Remarks on Behaviorism

Contemporary behaviorism has given the objective study of behavior a marked advantage over other psychologies. It has given us rigorous experimental procedures and opened the way, as no other psychology has, to the prediction and control of behavior. The behaviorist has devised methods which must be used by every psychologist searching for irreducible data.

But the strengths of behaviorist's position are its weakness too. By his uncompromising stress on objective data and quantitative measurement, the behaviorist has placed himself in an anomalous position. He now finds himself holding a point of view that the

[22] N. E. Miller, "Learnable Drives and Rewards," in S. S. Stevens (ed.), *Handbook of Experimental Psychology* (New York: John Wiley & Sons, Inc.), Ch. 13.

physical scientists of a generation ago have since abandoned. Natural scientists now maintain that only conscious experience exists, whereas the behaviorist, whose psychological forebears argued for consciousness, are now engaged in denying it. The physicist "locates" the world in his consciousness; the psychologist banishes consciousness, now renamed behavior, and places it in the world external to himself.

By his narrowing of the scope of psychological investigations to external events, to what is measurable and operationally definable, the behaviorist has closed his mind to the wealth of human conduct which defies physicalistic explanations. Intention, proactive behavior, and all subjective processes which are sources of overt action, which cannot be appraised or measured by the behaviorist's methodology, are consciously ignored.

It is not irrelevant to point out that this preference for the study of psychological phenomena in terms of their objective consequences, is an integral part of the American pragmatic tradition. Behaviorism, like pragmatism, has steadfastly preferred fact to theory, action to contemplation, overt performance to self-reflection.

This is not to imply that behaviorism, either in its classical or its current form, based itself on, or was even conscious of, its philosophical presuppositions. We simply mean that behaviorism, like all sciences, was partly shaped by the spirit of the time which gave it birth. Despite its rejection of philosophical elements, behaviorism has a clear-cut philosophical point of reference. Behaviorism, like pragmatism, was established before the radical developments of current physical theory, with its recognition of consciousness and subjective experience as the filters through which physical phenomena are now perceived. Its philosophical basis is, accordingly, anachronistic and irrelevant.

Finally, behaviorism, like psychoanalysis, is a form of reductionism, although the phenomenon to which each reduces the human person is different. While some contemporary learning theorists reduce behavior to the actions of the nervous system, others to biological development, and others to molar stimulus-response configurations, most of them ultimately reduce man to a learning machine.[23] Man is the animal who, when stimulated by

---

[23] As happens often in such generalizations, Skinner is an exception to the rule. Although his view of man is "mechanistic" in a loosely defined sense, Skinner does not reduce one thing to something else. To him the problem is artificial, and can make no difference to the experimental results.

inner or outer tensions, by drives, needs, or hungers, engages in activities which are designed to reduce or eliminate them. Having been rewarded in pleasure by this reduction or elimination, he will repeat the activities on future occasions. What he learns, what habits become established in his behavioral repertoire, will be determined by what has been reinforced. Man does not consciously choose his behavior, but being the learning machine that he is, acts in the light of the established changes produced by prior reinforcements. Thus, although learning is invariably defined as changes in behavior, the changes are never truly novel or creative. They are wholly products of repetition and reinforcement. Thus, just as there can be nothing in the response that was not already present in the stimulus (for to claim more is to be vitalistic), so there can be nothing in my present behavior that was not already established by antecedent reinforcement. *Man is what he has learned.*

CONCLUSION

Psychoanalysis and behaviorism, although radically different in their method and approach, are in limited ways very similar. The past dimension of time is fundamental in both. Both are rigid reaction psychologies: one in depth, the other in a single dimension. Both are deterministic and reductionistic in their philosophical assumptions. In both views, the maximization of pleasure and the reduction of pain are the basic motivational forces driving man, with the pursuit of pleasure fundamental in each. Repetition compulsion, so characteristic of fixation and neurosis, are seen by the learning theorist as resistance to extinction.

Other similarities exist as well; but it would not be profitable to pursue them here. For the reader who may have forgotten, it is only fair to Freud to point out that the latter did not see — or seeing, did not care — about these similarities. They have been stressed and explored by those academic psychologists who believe that all behavior, even the most complex, autonomous, and creative, can be — and should be — reduced to the learning process.

The drive-reduction formula has proved itself to be a good paradigm for animal learning, especially as it is observed and precisely measured in controlled experiments. It is fair, however, to note that even at best it only scratches the surface of the breadth, the depth, and the proactive reach of the human person.

It is safe to believe that every psychologist is fully aware of the bewildering complexity of life; yet in his endeavor to ape an obsolescent science, he denies the legitimacy of his own experience. Even learning has been emptied of its significant contents, leaving us only a disembodied process. This condition follows in any form of research where the animal subject is limited in his responses by the nature of the experimental design. The animal can make only those responses that are permitted by the purpose of the experiment and by the form of the apparatus employed. Individual differences in the experimental subjects are eliminated by the simple device of reducing all stimulations to hunger tensions. It requires no special ability on the experimenter's part to predict that the animal will engage in such activities, and repeat them in similar future circumstances, as will reduce or eliminate the unpleasant tensions.

But, alas! even if human learning were as simple as the behaviorist would have us believe, it would tell us nothing whatsoever of those tensions which are uniquely human: the aspirations for an ideal, the transforming experience of love, guilt, suffering, tragedy, and man's creative advance into the future.

Both psychoanalysis and behaviorism, both the concupiscent animal and the learning machine, are outmoded ways of dealing with the psychological nature of man. Although psychoanalysis probes much deeper than behaviorism, both present us with a view of the human being that is a grotesque trivialization of the potential greatness of man.

PART
THREE

Proactive Man

3

And in this staggering disproportion between man and no-man, there is no place for purely human boasts of grandeur, or for forgetting that men build their cultures by huddling together, nervously loquacious at the edge of an abyss.

KENNETH BURKE

The Human Predicament

To a superficial observer of the human scene it may seem merely fashionable for writers to burden their readers with the tragic predicaments of man and society. However, ours is no longer a world of warring ideologies merely, though they frighten and annoy us every day; it is, rather, a world in which value-systems are disintegrating and collapsing. The "world in crisis" is no mere literary conceit, but a cruel reality.

There is growing evidence that man's fears and sufferings and the sources of his neurotic ailments, are not always those which psychoanalysis has done so much to discover and cure. To be sure, libidinal or "instinctual" conflicts are still the stuff of psychological suffering, and will continue to be; but the ills of modern man and the reasons for his despair, lie in a neglected dimension of psychological inquiry: the realm of the human spirit, the dimension of consciousness in which values and meanings are warring with one another. Man's troubles spring not only from his sexual, marital, and vocational difficulties and failures, but equally if not more, from his spiritual frustrations. These frustrations arise in the *noosphere,* as de Chardin calls it, the sphere of consciousness and self-reflection, in which man struggles with the meaning and destiny of his own life.[1]

[1] For an absorbing discussion of the noosphere, see F. Teilhard de Chardin, *The Phenomenon of Man* (New York and Evanston: Harper & Row, 1961), Torchbook Edition, Book Three.

Contemporary man is disrupted as he never was before. Inner and outer forces are at work to challenge or destroy the values by which man guided his life in the past. He is confronted as never before with agonizing decisions and choices among warring and life-destroying values. In this disturbing state men no longer entrust their conduct to religion or to a stable tradition. Few men appeal to God or a stabilizing frame of religious values. These are the luxuries of zealots and unquestioning believers, both sacred and secular. The thoughtful individual has only abstractions and theories to rely upon, and these are ineffectual and useless. He has only science left for his guidance, and in psychology this is encapsulated in a rigid determinism, which compounds and aggravates his feeling of helplessness and despair. To this condition we must now turn.

THE SOCIAL SITUATION

The two dominant systems of psychology, psychoanalysis and behaviorism, throw very little light on man's social dilemma. Freud's metapsychological analysis of the social situation and its effect on the human personality is incisive, but descriptive only of the middle-class Viennese society of his day. The psychic disturbances which engaged his attention throughout his long professional career were largely the ailments of middle-class neurotics. The pessimism with which he viewed society and the individual had too narrow a base. It was the price he paid for the one-sided view that civilization is bought at the cost of repression of libidinal urges. He was sociologically naive in describing society in terms of a simple class struggle. Did we not know that he was uncontaminated by Marxist doctrine, we would believe that he was one of its inept disciples. His analysis of contemporary civilization was the expression of a view that is very old: "the neglected classes will grudge the favored ones their privileges and . . . they will do everything in their power to rid themselves of their own surplus of privation."[2] From this state of affairs, which is too lifeless to generate the psychological conditions that trouble contemporary man, Freud derived his view of the social origins of the neuroses of

2 S. Freud, *The Future of an Illusion* (Garden City, N.Y.: Doubleday and Company, Inc., n.d.), p. 15. First English translation, 1928.

his day.[3] His analyses and conclusions are, therefore, largely irrelevant for a diagnosis of the current situation.

Some General Observations

It is an historical fact that societies, like individuals, show vitality, creativeness, and growth or their opposites. Societies grow or decline roughly in proportion to the vitality and authenticity of their value-systems, or their creative forces. In societies that long endured, in which their members could actualize their potentialities, the value-systems were essentially creative. They were based on self-transforming and self-renewing energies. They were societies which were marked by enduring values and creative genius.[4] Every society contains within itself the fructifying seeds of its regeneration and the morbid cause of its decline. Whether one views the rhythmic succession of growth and decline as historical recurrences, or as the progressive actualization of a world community, is not a question we have to answer. In the perspective of epochal time, one is not altogether amiss in believing that, despite the horrendous crises that have afflicted civilization, humanity is fundamentally proactive and self-renewing.

The shocks and stresses which are inherent in the drama of human history, on both the individual and collective levels, are not the concern solely of the philosophers of history. On the contrary, they are the stuff of which human psychologies are made. As both observer of and actor in the tragicomedy of human history, the psychologist is in the unique position of viewing man as both producer and product of the human situation; as a creative agent in the vast individual and social transformations of his time.

In this double role of seeing and doing, the proactive psychologist places man squarely between a higher integration and an apocalyptic disaster. He sees man in the awesome predicament

---

[3] Nevertheless, Freud possessed the insight to examine the social conditions of man, as a means to a deeper understanding of human nature. Behaviorists, by contrast, neglect society almost entirely. A few who give it attention focus exclusively on social learning. See N. E. Miller and J. Dollard, *Social Learning and Imitation* (New Haven: Yale University Press, 1941).

[4] Documentation of these observations is unusually extensive. We mention only two well-known references: P. A. Sorokin, *Social and Cultural Dynamics*, 4 vols. (New York: American Book Co., 1937–41); A. Toynbee, *The Study of History*, 10 vols. (New York: Oxford University Press, 1934–43).

of dissociation from nature, from himself, and from other men. He describes human nature on the background of a disrupted society and a broken self. The tragic sense of alienation, so eloquently detailed by existentialist thinkers, he perceives as a reality, not as the adventious idea of moody intellectuals. In short, he views man as engaged in his most human vocation: a soul-searching analysis of the foundations of his being.[5]

The Great Transformation

It is a commonplace and a unanimous verdict of students of contemporary civilization, that our social order is in a process of revolutionary change. The changes of the past 175 years almost defy the human imagination. The changes, carefully detailed in hundreds of publications, are the sources of the pathologies of our time. Man has been exposed to the unsettling views of modern science and the disrupting effects of an unprecedented mechanization of life. The older orientations provided by a static theology and a monistic ethic, have for all but a very few, been virtually destroyed. There is no "medieval" synthesis of life and thought; and this state of affairs, rather than serving as a source of healthy diversity, has been the cause of widespread anxiety.

Sociologists and other students of the social scene have made an academic livelihood from correlating the enormous changes and their consequent dislocations, with the individual and social ills of the day. They never grow weary (and for their labor we owe them a signal debt) of cataloging the alarming increase of crime, delinquency, marital discord, mental disorders, etc., "since the Industrial Revolution." Even the noises, traffic hazards, and forms of recreation, we are told, share in this responsibility, for they all create stresses to which the human organism had never before been exposed.

It would be obtuse to deny the general validity of the social scientist's observations; and it would be a mistake to minimize the role of the profound social changes in the causation of men's attitudes, personalities, and mental disorders.

But these changes in the social order, and their effects upon the human spirit, fade almost into insignificance when pitted against the

[5] This implies total rejection of the Freudian dogma that self-questioning and a concern for human destiny are symptoms of immaturity and neurosis.

convulsive and cataclysmic events of our own generation. Ours is no mere social crisis, but a massive spiritual chaos. The dislocations initiated by the great changes of the Industrial Revolution were also compensated for by great material benefits, and eventually by a more humane life for increasing numbers of people. However, the catastrophic changes since the First World War, but especially those since the beginning of the Second World War, have been value-negating and life-destroying on a scale not recorded in the annals of man's melancholy history.

It would be surprising, indeed, if the predicament of our time could be adequately contained in the framework of the leading reaction psychologies of our day. The ills from which contemporary man suffers so acutely are sicknesses of the spirit, failure of nerve, and loss of hope. These are not conventional neuroses, but profound distresses of the human soul.

The paradox of our time. The essence of modern man's predicament is a profoundly moral one: the forces that can foster the dignity of man tend to destroy it. Perhaps never before in human history has man possessed the means to enhance human life while being at the same time capable of unleashing forces that will annihilate it. The paradox is the more stupefying in view of the fact that the forces of elemental evil were let loose upon the world by a people historically credited with moral idealism and scientific genius. The Germans, who for centuries have been indoctrinated with scientific thoughtways and the humanistic spirit, with the religion of Luther and the poetry of Goethe, are also the people who committed the monstrous crime of exterminating millions of people. Theirs has not only been a crime that baffles beyond the powers of imagination; it was a debauch and degradation unparalleled in human history. The infamy is so profound that the final *Götterdämmerung*, which under different circumstances might have served as dramatic relief, by its very ghoulishness only magnifies our disbelief. It would seem that the more civilized a people becomes, the more driven it is to destroy civilization. Somehow, suffering can always be mitigated when it has meaning. But the suffering imposed upon those in the extermination camps of Europe is, in the context of any conceivable moral scheme, utterly meaningless and wholly irredeemable. It is pure, primordial evil.

There is an aspect of this disturbing paradox that is easily overlooked. In their self-deluding moral superiority, some people have a simple explanation. They see the horrendous evil as an expression of the unique character of the German people. This is a dangerous delusion. One does not absolve the German people of their shame and guilt by affirming that their madness can be duplicated by other people as well. A single example will have to suffice. It is well known that in World War II the Rumanians murdered almost a quarter million Jews and several hundred thousand Russian peasants. When the war was over many thousands of ethnic Germans had disappeared, and we can only assume that they were either killed or were allowed to perish in the horrible conditions of the times. Nevertheless, in the context of an ethics that transcends the narrow limits of ethnic and political boundaries, we are all more or less guilty. We went to war against Hitler, not to save innocent people from the gas chambers, but to destroy a political and military enemy. It is a well-documented fact that the world's leaders during the Nazi holocaust, men like Roosevelt and Churchill — in petrified disbelief, perhaps — did not cry out against the ghastly crimes. Even the Vicar of Christ, Pope Pius XI, declared a Concordat with Hitler, and his successor remained incredibly silent.

The mass society. We began the description of the social situation with the nightmare of the twentieth century. We must not, however, overlook the lesser terror; for time may indeed prove that the greater crime is the vicious child of the minor event, since the effect can be greater than the cause that produced it.

It is all too simple to ascribe the ills of modern life to industrialization and its attendant evils. Industrialization has had powerful allies in the form of science and technology. The triad of industry, science, and engineering together have been largely responsible for the collectivization that is now destroying the individual. We do not join the calamity-howlers who impute our ills to the "materialistic" forces of our economic life. Nevertheless, we should be greatly remiss if we failed to recognize the destructive force of the collectivization to which technology and industry have given rise.

A fatal defect of many rationalizations of the contemporary social scene is to allocate responsibility to specific ideologies. The popular scape-goat is the doctrine of communism. This explanation cannot be rationally defended. Collectivization is as virulent in capitalistic societies as it is in the Soviet Union and her satellites. It results, rather, from the widespread application of scientific knowledge and technological skill to the mode of making a living. The incisive analyses of Max Weber and Thorstein Veblen in this connection, as well as those of many others, are as relevant today as they were when these social economists first advanced them.[6] Rationalization, as it is called, is a mark of all large-scale organization of industry, be it capitalistic or communistic. It entails the rational direction and disciplined control of the productive forces of a society. Although this rational control consists in the organization of "free" labor in capitalist society and of "planned" labor in communist countries, in both cases it is all-pervasive and highly impersonal, a minutely specialized, hierarchical bureaucracy, in which "discipline" is very pronounced. This means that every worker performs the right act in the right place at a determinate time. In this bureaucratic arrangement maximum efficiency is the highest desideratum. Even the differentiating mark of earlier bureaucracy, namely, its relative independence of the political state, no longer obtains. All technological societies are characterized by extreme organization, ruthless efficiency, and unfeeling collectivization. The destructive consequence of this frightful *totalization* of human life is the deformation of personality and the annihilation of individuality. In Germany it was responsible for the national schizophrenia that came to a climax in the Nazi era.

But let us return to Weber's analysis of bureaucratic efficiency and the collectivization to which it has led. It is now quite clear that Weber's analysis of the role of religion, particularly Protestantism, had the scholar's defect of timidity and attenuation, neatly rationalized as scientific impartiality. The relation between Protestantism and modern capitalism was indeed that described by the great German sociologist. However, the "spirit" which he found in both was largely a virtuous one, and it in no way made it possible to prevision the coming brutal events. Protestantism has been too fully conceived in an honorific sense. But Martin Luther was not altogether a religious hero but a sadistic tyrant as well. His theology was a doctrine of abject submission, first to God, later to the secular Prince. A man was judged, not by his performance — his "works" — but by his faith: faith in God and faith in the ruler. *Submission* to authority, it did not matter which, became the cardinal moral virtue. In supremely Machiavellian fashion, in order to vouchsafe the power of the Evangelical church, Luther magnified the incipient Teutonic split, by absolving the ruler from ruling as a Christian. Thus, the ruling Prince, though a Christian, is not

[6] See M. Weber, *Gesammelte Aufsätze zur Religionssoziologie* (Tübingen: J. C. B. Mohr, 1924), vol. 1; T. Veblen, *The Instinct of Workmanship* (New York: The Macmillan Co., 1914).

obliged by that fact to rule in man's favor if that rule was contrary to the Prince's personal interest. And since the Devil has been adept at quoting Scripture, Luther, too, could find Biblical support for his beliefs. He had no qualms of conscience, therefore, in approving in the name of Christianity the terrible inequality of men so common in his time. He did not find it repugnant to describe men as cattle possessed by their master, like any other goods.[7] The dual character of "the German" — his automatic submission to hierarchical power and his tendency to tyrannize over his subordinates — is thus seen in the early history of the German people, especially as it was justified by the Protestant religion. The step from doctrinaire philosophy and authoritarian religion to the organized terror of the Nazi era is thus rendered a little more understandable.[8]

Collective Suicide

Moral idiocy, it should now be clear, is a defect, not of a single population, but of the human race. This becomes daily more vivid when we examine honestly the astounding dilemma of the nuclear age. The tragic facts of Hiroshima and Nagasaki scarcely cause a wince in people accustomed to the terrors of collective violence. And to those Satanic persons who measure destruction in megatons and casualty lists, those hapless communities, especially since they revived so quickly, were merely sacrificed for the "greater" cause of forestalling even greater butchery.

[7] See F. Troeltsch, *The Social Teaching of the Christian Churches,* Eng. trans. (Glencoe: The Free Press, 1949), vol. 2. If space permitted it would be instructive, even though speculative, to examine the aggressive and sadistic elements of Luther's character, as they are expressed in his anal preoccupations. See H. Grisar, *Luther,* E. M. Lamond, Eng. trans, 6 vols. (London: Kegan Paul, Trench, Trubner, 1913–17), vol. 6.

[8] We have already said that these qualities are not peculiarly German. There is a wholly unwarranted tendency, since World War I, to describe all Germans as demons and all others, especially if they fought for "righteousness" on our side, as paragons of civilized virtue. The passions become idiocies when, sometimes slyly, sometimes directly, the madness since 1914 is associated with the evil of Nietzsche and Wagner. Literary and historical criticism are in this manner made a mockery. It makes us forget that the men and women who were exterminated at Belsen, Auschwitz, and Buchenwald were not Jews, or Christians, or believers of various kinds, but *human beings* facing the terrifying fact of their own destruction. As we stand on "the edge of an abyss' it is unbecoming of us all to boast of our own grandeur. Self-righteousness is a symptom of the human predicament of our time.

Although mankind will never fully expiate for the massive genocide of the recent past, it is in danger of forgetting it, for our memories are poor and our characters are weak. The dilemma of today, however, does not issue from the *historical* past but from the frightening present as it is projected into the future. Our choice today is quite literally between an agonizing peace and mutual extermination. Never before in human history has the choice been so excruciatingly clear and yet so fraught with the possibility of unimaginable and convulsive violence.[9]

The collective suicide which we envision is not a hysterical belief but a nerve-racking possibility. Unlike the damage caused by conventional war, even one of such great magnitude as that of the 1940's, from which the participants nevertheless recovered, the damage from a nuclear holocaust precludes recovery. It has been estimated that a nuclear war would kill a hundred million persons, destroy the large cities, contaminate the earth, water, and atmosphere. The damage would be mutual, as Lippmann recently remarked, and there would be no victory. The United States, he added, possesses the nuclear might to reduce Russia to a smoldering ruin, and she in turn might kill as many as seventy million Americans.[10]

Numbers one can always somehow grasp, however dimly, and the horror of massive misery one can by a radical process of empathy, somehow vaguely and remotely feel. But that human beings can not only contemplate but plan to execute such diabolic acts, is beyond human comprehension. Perhaps in this stupefying incomprehension lies the hope of averting what many men feel to be a real possibility: the destruction of civilization.

This is admittedly a sanguine hope. Meanwhile, man in the twentieth century, remembering the macabre insanity of the 1940's, is grimly aware that collective lunacy is always possible in the face of unbearable strains, frustrations, and unrelenting provocation which the great adversaries feel.

This terrible dilemma will not be solved by men who are driven by hungers and fear, who are tossed about by every wind of doctrine. It will be solved, if it can be solved, by men who can choose intelligently from alternative courses of conduct, by men who try,

---

[9] The despairing idiocy to which we have referred has been recently manifested in the remarks of a minor statesman, when he proposed that "we drop the bomb first," before the Soviet Union drops one on ourselves!

[10] See W. Lippmann, "The Nuclear Age," *The Atlantic Monthly*, May 1962, p. 46.

because they know that they can within the limits of their own
finitude, to direct their own destiny. Only a psychology that endows
man with the capacity of self-transformation, is a psychology that
is fit for the needs of man in the mid-twentieth century.

Sad to relate, the dominant psychologies of the day are not
pointers to a saner future, but sufferers of the very defects which
have created the madness of the world. The man whom the
psychologist has created in the image of the rodent or the pigeon
lacks the spirit, the wisdom, and the good-will that are the necessary
and sufficient cause of creating a world fit for the potential grandeur
that is man. We can experiment, we can describe and measure the
behavior of man, but like the casualty lists of Hiroshima and
Nagasaki, or the ghoulish numbers games of the extermination
camps of Europe, we omit the creative potentialities of man. Outside the existentialists, whom most psychologists reject, contemporary students of behavior have nothing to say about, and even
less to prescribe for, the dread and anguish of contemporary man.

It is disheartening to read the psychologist's account of human
aggression, that destructive force in human history, so costly in
human misery. Neither Freud nor Skinner gives us a hint that man
may indeed possess, like some animal species, a deeply embedded
inhibition from destroying others. Few psychologists, *qua* psychologists, are receptive to the possibility that man and society may
survive by creating a "long-term ethics," as Arnold Gehlen has
called it. Yet, despite our neglect of it, moral behavior is a truly
human vocation. This ethics is as old as civilized man, for it is the
overt manifestation of man's capacity to envision other persons,
wherever they may be, as beings like himself. This is no mere
role-playing capacity, valuable as that is, but a profoundly affective
condition which psychologists are too timid to call by its name: love
as compassion.

In the unstable equilibrium in which we are living; in the agonizing stalemate which alone for the moment seems to save nations
from mutual extermination; this human compassion, this long-term
bond between human beings, is the last hope for conserving our
civilization. This, rather than the impulse for self-preservation, or
the instinct of species perpetuation, is the emotion that can make
universal peace in the nuclear age possible. If there is no alternative to peace — and we believe there is none — then civilization
must rely wholly on the long-term ethics which is functionally and
ontologically bound up with man's capacity to love. Compassion,
like the long-term ethics, is a proactive, life-affirming condition of

human existence. It alone can rescue man from the paralyzing state of mind in which he finds himself, as he stands on the edge of an abyss. It alone can in the long haul help man to choose between principle and expedient, between self-seeking national policy and individual conscience. Without it our current posture is ridiculous and hypocritical, a perfect instance of what some existentialists have described as inauthenticity or bad faith. Although politicians may ignore it, and scientific psychologists reject it, the men and women who are uncontaminated by social doctrine and unmoved by an arid scientism, understand its constructive potency.

The great creative moments in history show that this way of conceiving man's role in the crises of existence is a valid one. All the barbarities of a Stalin or a Hitler cannot destroy this memorable fact. Man's constructive efforts, guided by the vision of a long-term ethics, have been without exception magnificent forward leaps. Exhausted by his savageries, man has nevertheless comprehended his own condition and, through compassion and other-mindedness, built himself a new life. This is the creative function of personality, of which we shall say more in a later chapter. In the immediate world situation this ethical and creative capacity makes possible the vision of a new social order. Indeed, in the face of an unimaginable catastrophe, reliance on man's creative and moral character is the only practical alternative. All other means — political action, statesmanship, economic amelioration — can be achieved only on the premise that the basic human motive is neither conservation nor destruction, but a creative advance into the future.

THE HUMAN CONDITION

The profoundest truths about the nature of man have been disclosed by humanists and existentialists, not by academic psychologists. Together and separately they have clearly perceived the human being in his triumphs and in his spiritual agonies. They, not the Freudians, have revealed the dark depths of human nature — but also its grandeur and its self-renewing possibilities. They, not the professional psychologists, have given us dramatic glimpses of man facing, alone, the tragedy of human existence. This existence, this human condition, merits our most thoughtful examination.

Man's Finitude

We have shown that, although the principle of determinism operates widely, it is not a universal force in the affairs of men. A limited indeterminism is a fact of physical nature and of human life. Although life is governed by innumerable contingencies, it has a wide area of free choice. Although every individual is molded by the situations of his life, there are conditions which impel him to act and choose within the limits of his vitality and his personal endowments.

However, modern man is moved far less by his capacity to choose than by his awareness of his own finitude. Why is this so? The answer to this, as to all questions concerning human affairs, is complex, yet has been cast in oversimplifications. Nevertheless, we can answer it by pointing to two vital conditions.

First is the overwhelming, immediate fact of ruthless and life-destroying power. Since those fatal days of August, 1914, when the military juggernaut rumbled over the fields of Europe, Western man has suffered from an anguished feeling of hopelessness and helplessness. The values by which he had lived heretofore, though containing the seeds of coming events, gave man a sense of confidence and purpose nonetheless. Decadence there was, to be sure, before that event, but man could exult in the crowning achievements which somehow held the world together. The fractionation of man and his values had not yet reached the limits of its possibilities. A callous disregard for human sensibilities, though never absent in human history, had not yet become a destructive force in the lives of men.

Since 1914, all this has radically changed. Values that once were binding have been destroyed. Man's faith in reason and religion, although seldom strong enough to save him from taking refuge in savagery, was nevertheless a stabilizing and directive agent in the relations between men. Today, man has no sure anchorage, no personal basis of values. His work is meaningless, he is disoriented, he has no sense of direction within it. This condition, not the inherent degeneracy of a people, is the source of the diabolic behavior of men.

In the face of these and far more dangerous coming events, man is overcome and paralyzed by a profound feeling of futility and helplessness. While outwardly he gives no sign of his inner anguish — indeed he succeeds in concealing and denying it by a pseudo-imperturbability — the fact is that he is weighted down with incapacitating defenses and dispiriting anxieties. Accordingly, although he has the capacity and opportunity to choose freely, his effective conduct is grievously impaired. For the man who doubts his own humanity, of which the freedom of choice is a fundamental ingredient, confident self-direction soon becomes an impossibility.

The second reason for man's loss of nerve in the face of his finitude, is the overwhelming impact of science and technology on his image of himself. Science is *not* inherently incompatible with human values and man's freedom of choice. Nevertheless, the influence of *scientism*, of the doctrine that only empirical science can give us a dependable view of man's nature, has led modern man to devaluate himself and to lose confidence in his capacity to direct his own destiny.

Although the great makers of modern science are deeply concerned with human values and have spoken eloquently for the dignity of man, men and women still think about nature and man in the framework of nineteenth-century positivism and materialism. The *Weltanschauung* of contemporary man is embedded in the scientism of the last century. In this view man is the helpless victim of blind forces over which he has no effective control. The fact that this is an anachronistic view of science makes no difference to those who believe it. History is a sorry record of the destructive power of fallacious ideas.

Until human beings everywhere become conscious of the fact that empirical science presents but a partial view of man's nature, and that even this picture makes room for freedom of action, they will continue to impair their lives with needless fears and crippling anxieties. Constructive behavior is based on the self-confidence born of the awareness of one's finitude *and* one's potentiality for transforming intentions into actions. Helplessness, or the feeling of compulsion in one's actions, is a product, not of determinism in psychological events, but of the failure to actualize one's potentialities. Success in controlling or directing the contingencies of life, in full awareness of his finitude, is a measure of man's freedom and his humanity.

Anguish and Despair

The step from a feeling of helplessness, of a disconsolate finitude, to anguish and despair, is but a small one. We are speaking here of the anguish and despair of the "normal" individual, not of the mentally disturbed or of the person plunging into suicide. Anguish has been described by many writers, but by none so profoundly as the existential psychologists. Although it is quite similar to anxiety, the latter lacks the powerful affect, the feeling of hopelessness and despair, that characterize the condition of anguish. Its clearest and sharpest manifestation is found when man is confronted by his own non-being, by the possibility of his own death. The possibility of death makes man acutely aware of his finitude. It arises from the threat of nothingness, of non-being, of the contingent nature of human life. It fills man with despair because anguish is a threat to the very core of human existence: the human self. Without self, in which all human experience is centered, the individual is not truly human. Fears, motives, hungers, and the like — these are found in all animals; only man is capable of self-esteem, of value-bound experience.

The free-floating anxiety (*freischwebende Angst*) which the psychoanalysts have described so well, is similar to the anguish we are trying to describe, yet it lacks the psychic intensity and ontological character of anguish. The latter is not merely fear with no tangible source; it is the feeling of despair we all experience when we reflect on the state of our non-existence.

Some remarks on death. Anguish, anxiety, and despair are ontological conditions. They are immanent in human nature. Psychotherapy, therefore, cannot eradicate them, and if it did, it would destroy man's human nature. Psychotherapy can perform the supreme task of helping man to understand them as guarantors of his own individuality. The awareness of death as conferring a tragic dignity upon life can dilute, if not eliminate, its destructive hold upon men. Although one need not agree with Freud that the goal of life is death, it is wholly unrealistic to ignore it in the study of man. Every healthy human being has the lyrical impulse to contemplate, if he has not also witnessed, the lonely stillness of the moment of death — a strange silence which can be *heard,* for like death itself, it is the premonitory experience of non-being, of nothingness, of death.

The thought is here seriously advanced that a wholesome approach to death and the dread and loneliness associated with it, may have powerful religious bonds and implications. Reverence for life does not preclude a poetic regard for the dignity of death. Only to a paranoid mind, such as that of the Kwakiutl of Vancouver Island, is death the ultimate insult. Only to a life wholly deprived of value and meaningfulness can death hold a paralyzing terror. In the lonely moments when a man fearfully awaits the death of a loved one, he comes so close to life that life itself becomes tragically meaningful. This is but another way of saying with Whitehead: "Religion is what the individual does with his own solitariness." It is the moment when man is truly alone, with no one to share his guilt and desolation. Whitehead has put it with rare sensitivity and discernment. He writes:

> . . . The great religious conceptions which haunt the imagi-
> nations of civilized mankind are scenes of solitariness: Prome-
> theus chained to his rock, Mahomet brooding in the desert, the
> meditations of the Buddha, the solitary Man on the Cross. It
> belongs to the depth of the religious spirit to have felt for-
> saken, even by God.[11]

American life and psychology have both ignored the place of death in life. We tend to believe that interest in death is a sign of morbidity. We believe that people, especially children, should be shielded from exposure to its terrifying impact. We have not culti-vated what de Unamuno called "the tragic sense of life," the capacity to accept death with dignity, without undue pessimism; to come to terms with the inevitabilities of life. Only by assimilating the fact of death to the whole of life, can death be transmuted. Only then can we celebrate with Goethe the exhilarating thought that the end of life is not death, but life itself. (*Der Zweck des Lebens ist das Leben selbst.*) Although the fear of death may cause serious emotional disturbances, it is the fear of life, really, that is the source of most of our psychological ills.

Nevertheless, those psychologists to whom nothing human is alien, approach the subject of death with the same high seriousness with which they investigate the vital problems of life. Death, and the dread and despair which it generates, is an important truth, but the existentialist tends to make it too important. It is psycho-logically more sound to investigate joy and exultation, for like death, they too are neglected by contemporary psychologists. These have yet to write their Hymn to Joy.

Alienation

In the brief discussion of death we did not concern ourselves, except very indirectly, with its clinical nature. The psychological significance of death lies in the attitude we take toward it, not in death itself. For most people in American society death is the final separation. The solitariness of death is unbearable, and since re-ligion in America has been historically doctrinaire and sectarian, solitariness has not been one of its features. For this reason the

[11] A. N. Whitehead, *Religion in the Making* (New York: The Macmil-lan Co., 1926), pp. 19–20.

average individual, despite the promise of immortality made by his religion, finds the prospect of death unbearable. The alienation between life and death is intensified by the disturbing uncertainties regarding the outcome of our own lives. Since our education in the home and the school has not prepared us to reflect on the meaning of death and estrangement, we have not developed a rational understanding of their meaning in the lives of men. Had we begun to reflect on the nature of life and death, we would have discovered that, although reflection itself is an important source of man's uneasiness, it is also the means by which the breach between life and death can be effectively narrowed. Reflective thinking is inherently unsettling, and many have found that the most practical means for escaping anxiety is to stop reflecting. Accordingly, the reflective life of an increasing number of people consists of slogan-thinking, a form of mimeographed repetition of identical thoughts. The luxury of wonder, which we all possessed in our childhood, has given way to a comfortable parroting of standard ideas. If we wander too far from this herd-thinking, we become anxious and uneasy.

This totalization, this standardization of the human intellect, is an effective cause of the depersonalization of modern life. This depersonalization in turn is the source of much of the alienation that agonizes the modern mind. Thus, alienation is not the consequent of the human condition only, but even more a product of the nature of the social situation.

The socioeconomic origin of alienation was discussed in detail by Karl Marx, but his doctrinaire bias made his analysis undependable.[12] But alienation has a broader base and a wider implication than the Marxian economic interpretation would lead us to expect. In the bureaucratic framework of contemporary life, man perceives his world as fundamentally unfriendly, even hostile. Being deprived of his former certainties by the impersonal meaninglessness of the world, man distrusts it. Although bureaucratization is alleged to simplify human relations in an industrial society, it has vastly multiplied our daily problems. It has robbed man of social space and

---

[12] It is now a commonplace that Marx borrowed the concept of alienation from Hegel. Seldom mentioned is the fact that Hegel in turn borrowed the idea from Diderot; and as Burke has pointed out, Diderot undoubtedly borrowed it from its medieval source in the Church, where it referred to the transfer of church property to secular ownership. See K. Burke, *Attitudes Toward History*, 2 vols. (New York: The New Republic, 1937), vol. 2, p. 52.

forced him into the confines of an even greater impersonal system. Even our imagination is bureaucratized. Alienation is maximized when the estranged individuals suffer even more estrangement without knowing the cause of their suffering. In this state life is bereft of purpose and becomes even more impersonal. Everyone is spiritually dispossessed.

The pain of estrangement can be mollified by the enhancement of human relatedness. Contrary to a pervading cynicism, power and money cannot obliterate alienation. Relatedness cannot be created by fiat, and it cannot be bought. It is a form of sacrifice and commitment, not a business transaction.

The stranger. Marxists and existentialists alike have conceived alienation in too narrow terms. The Marxists see man too narrowly as an economic object, in which he is separated from his job, from the owner of the means of production, from the process of workmanship, and from his fellow workers. The existentialists, although aware of the role of the social situation in the alienation process, place a one-sided emphasis on its autochthonous nature. Regarded biologically, man is "an almost isolated figure in nature," as de Chardin has put it, whereas paleontology shows that "an animal form never comes singly."[13]

We do not deny a basic dichotomy in human nature, but we question its inherent quality. We believe that the separation of man from nature, man from other men and from himself, is fundamentally the convergent product of the human condition and the social situation. Alienation results from society's enslavement of the autonomous individual. It is a product of the unresolved struggle between freedom and control, individuality and authority. Our world is so constituted that practically everyone is a stranger in some areas of human endeavor.

As early as 1908, before Kierkegaard was rediscovered and before the fateful period of the First World War, Georg Simmel, the great German sociologist, contributed to a better understanding of alienation and estrangement, by his lucid analysis of the "Stranger."[14]

Although Simmel confines his description of the stranger to the person of the trader, particularly the Jew (because historically the Jew has been the perfect example of the "marginal man"), his analysis is relevant to the present scene. Modern man, who is more

[13] P. Teilhard de Chardin, *op. cit.*, p. 184.
[14] See G. Simmel, *Soziologie* (Leipzig: Duncker und Humbolt, 1908), pp. 685–691.

mobile than man was in any prior period of history, has only
incidental contacts with other men. His connection with other
people is tenuous, seldom organic, as it is in kinship or community
relationships. Lacking rootedness, the stranger stands apart from
others. He is truly *ex-static*, as the existentialists say. His separation
from his fellow men is a combination of abstract concern and indifference: these are the anonymous and impersonal qualities of
the alienated man.

Again, the detached, impersonal nature of his relations with other
men are responsible for that objectivity which is highly prized in
our anonymous mass society, including our science and technology.
Objectivity and remoteness, although highly useful in many present
activities, attenuate if they do not destroy, intimate and compassionate bonds among men. Objectivity prevents the growth of
sympathy, loyalty, and commitment to values, as well as promoting
impartiality and freedom from bias. The stranger takes pride in his
ability to stand apart from others and to survey the human scene
impersonally. That these traits are useful in facing the terrors and
brutalities of our times is perhaps true, but ultimately they destroy
the human bonds which alone, in the long run, make a humane life
possible. Instead of creating genuine individuality and independence, these characteristics frequently lead only to idiosyncrasy
and self-centered unconventionality. Following the existentialist,
we say of these traits that they are inauthentic and lacking good
faith.

The social situation of our time, we have seen, is one of conflicting values, a mood of pessimism, and a turbulence seldom
matched in modern history. In this situation alienation and
estrangement on a wide scale are inescapable. We are living on the
margin between conflicting ways of life, requiring of each of us a
vigilance and re-evaluation of meanings and ideals more radical
than heretofore. In the midst of all the talk about status, man has
no sure, no final, place in modern life. He is poised between two
worlds: the world into which he was born and cannot forget, and
the atomized world in which he lives but cannot understand. This
situation creates a degree of self-awareness to which modern man
is wholly unaccustomed. Although this self-consciousness is salutary from the perspective of long-term ethics and proactive personality, it is a constant source of anxiety, self-doubt, and estrangement. In the uncertain world devoid of clear-cut value-imperatives,
man does not move easily among other men; for to move easily
among them he must be one of them. He is of them, but apart

from them. In a world in which we are all more or less strangers we build barriers between ourselves. We are, in short, in the ambiguous state in which each of us attracts and repels at the same moment. And so we live as strangers in a world we did not make and which we feel helpless to improve or change.

Existential Guilt

In a world where we are strangers, no one truly loves anyone. Mutual trust is hard to establish in relations which are basically impersonal. This situation, and the added barbarities of our age, have generated widespread and unexpiated guilt. The grave violation of man's moral conscience is not a psychological state merely; not the easily understood guilt-feelings, but a profound condition of human nature. It is ontological, and cannot be transcended by means of psychotherapy or religious redemption. It is a part of human nature. No matter how man may *feel* about a destructive act, his guilt lies in its performance. It is inherent in the act itself. Thus man is guilty when he compromises truth, when he does not combat injustice, when he submits to evil, when he fails to actualize his potentialities. It is not enough, therefore, to describe guilt as a neurotic anxiety resulting from transgression. Guilt is not only a *feeling* of moral failure: it *is* a moral failure. It is not merely a form of psychological crippling, but a disordered state of being.

In psychology we have erred in reducing real, or existential, guilt to the level of a secondary effect. It is, however, a condition in which cause and effect are not crucial. It is a state of being that is *owned*, unlike neurotic guilt, which is rejected. It is not a symptom, but the condition of heightened sensibility which leads to constructive action; it is affiliation as opposed to estrangement; compassion as contrasted with self-seeking. It is rooted, not in the mores of our society, but in the self-reflecting human condition. It arises, not from the violation of moral prescriptions, but from the position we take in the moment of conscious choice. We are guilty because we can choose. Guilt, like choice, is an attribute of our human nature, a potentiality of human life.

Conclusion

It is a cause for sadness that modern psychology, in pursuit of the legitimate goal of scientific objectivity and analysis, should see fit to define human behavior in bland disregard of the human nature which is the sole reason for its existence. A psychology that dismisses the unique characteristics of man with ill-concealed contempt, is a dangerous doctrine, not a science of man. A psychology that is at once comprehensive and sensitive to the deeply moral and spiritual nature of human existence, must take seriously the predicaments of man in the human world. It must change, and when necessary reject, the comfortable notion that man can be fully understood within the framework of a controlled experiment. Man lives not in a laboratory, except figuratively, but in the clarities and confusions of his time and within the conditions of his human nature. Man faces two crises. On the one hand is the ubiquitous threat of personal invalidation, of engulfment by an impersonal mass society; on the other, is the terrible prospect of convulsive decimation, of possible annihilation. The time is not far distant when all psychologists will need to reckon with the morality and spirituality which, though not overtly identifiable, are the prime movers of man's being. Man is no abstraction, but a four-dimensional being. Although he lives amidst the fractionating forces of modern life, he is forever seeking to remain whole. Only in the interactive merging of the social situation and the uniquely human condition — in the awesome human predicament — can the essential nature of the human self be understood and its unity be restored.

In this chapter, as in this book, we are engaged in composing the joyous theme that man is his own maker.

4

Quentin . . . is faced . . . with what Eve brought to Adam — the terrifying fact of choice.

ARTHUR MILLER

The Burden of Choice

Guilt, we have argued, is ontological. It is characteristically human. Like dread and anxiety, guilt has its origin in the act of choice. When I choose, I incur an awesome responsibility not only toward myself but toward others as well; for when I choose I make a decision for all those in the orbit of my own behavior and experience. Since truth is a function of my immediate experience, whatever is true for me is true for all others, for we are all similarly constituted or resemble one another in our endowments. Human beings thus share a common burden, the *awe-full* responsibility of sealing their fate in the act of choice. Only another decision, equally fateful, can annul the consequences of a prior choice. The history of man is the record of his decisions and all their creative and destructive consequences. The burden of choice lies not solely in the choice itself, but in its inevitability. Even the decision not to choose, as Sartre remarked, is an act of choice. Man's helplessness in the face of uncontrollable events is the consequence, not of a lack of freedom, but because of it. In this condition lies the burdensomeness of taking an option, of fleeing *from* the freedom of choice. What rescues human life from passivity, from the tedium of the moment, is the "dreadful possibilities" inherent in man's choice.[1]

Because in his choosing man chooses for other human beings like himself, the problem of freedom turns out to be, to the discomfiture of the tough-minded psychologist, less a cognitive than a moral one. This is explained by the fact that every choice is based

---

[1] See W. Van Dusen, "The Theory and Practice of Existential Analysis," in H. M. Ruitenbeek (ed.), *Psychoanalysis and Existential Philosophy* (New York: E. P. Dutton and Co., Inc., 1962), pp. 24–40.

on a scale of values and has consequences for others, as we have already stated. The center of man's orientation has shifted from Descartes' *Cogito* to Jaspers' *ich wähle* — from "I think" to "I choose."

Since science is always a child of its time, it is inevitable that psychology, the most subjective of sciences, should increasingly reflect the moral and spiritual dilemmas of our age. Among these dilemmas is man's inner conflicts over his values, his deeds, and above all, his conscience. These, not his motives, his memories, his homeostatic hungers, are the living stuff of the human drama, the subject matter of proactive psychology.

Science, particularly technology, has multiplied the need and opportunity of choice. This fact is not a reason for complaint nor regret, but for the attitude of hope. Adventure entails anxiety and danger, but for the proactive mind it also promises the exhilaration of discovery and novelty. In the act of choice, man is able to look forward to a problematic future, rather than to the comfortable safety of a well-mapped past.

THE POSSIBILITY OF CHOICE

Any psychology that probes beneath the overt or public behavior of human beings is inevitably faced by the incontrovertible fact that they are profoundly motivated by their inner experiences. This subjective life has not been adequately described by the Freudian concept of the unconscious. On the contrary, the fully human quality of this inner life is not unconscious but conscious. It consists in the capacity and the act of choice. An act of choice is the overt expression of potential freedom, not of an undemonstrable unconscious trend.

This does not mean, however, that every choice is a clearly conscious act. Rather, it means that many acts are as yet not clearly differentiated. The burden of choice consists in the fact that alternatives are potential and unclear. Anxiety is generated by the realization that, although potentially the number of choices is unrestricted, the possibility of making the wrong choice is equally unlimited. In this lies the explanation of the fact that anxiety is inescapable, for it is an attribute of the human condition, a quality of freely choosing human beings. Man is a decision-making being who, in choosing, is faced by the terrifying possibility that the outcome of his choice is highly problematic. Although he may consult

his past for guidance, his choice is always an adventure into the
future. The healthy proactive individual is he who uses the "holy
insecurity," as Buber has described it in various places, as a means
toward constructive living.

Evidence of Choice

The romantic notion that man is free to choose whatever he wills
is an illusion and has no place in any serious discussion of the nature and role of choice in human behavior. At the same time we
must reject the false doctrine that freedom is merely the name we
give to acts for which science has been unable to find an acceptable
explanation. This view, which is representative of the positivist attitude toward uniquely human problems, has been expressed by
Skinner, for whom freedom of choice is a caprice, or "only another
name for behavior for which we have not yet found a cause."[2] Unacceptable also is the sophistry which carries water on both shoul-
ders by declaring that, although from a scientific point of view man
is completely determined, practically speaking, he can still act
as if he were in fact free. Finally, the sociological argument is also
unacceptable. While they are usually not dogmatically self-conscious in their argument, most sociologists by implication attribute
man's action to his environment. The criminal, for example, had no
choice but to behave criminally, for his behavior is the product of
a vicious and impoverished environment.

Have we, then, no grounds for freedom of choice? The answer is,
we have.

Direct experience. If we put aside our preconceptions, if we divest ourselves of the comfort of scientific orthodoxy, especially of
the need for scientific respectability, we can vouch for freedom of
action in our daily experience. Each of us knows by direct experience, of course, that we are driven to perform acts over which we
have no effective control. Each of us also knows that we engage
in acts which we *intended*, acts which we *meant* to perform. The
inwardness of man's experience tells him that he is not merely
driven in his acts but selects them on the basis of a goal which
he has himself established. His behavior does not simply follow
some internal or external push but precedes it by an act of reflection and evaluation. If we are not completely blinded by doctrinal
predilections, we can clearly see by simple introspection that each

---

[2] B. F. Skinner, "Freedom and the Control of Men," *Amer. Scholar,*
1955–56, *25,* 52–53.

of us is drawn toward something, that we can proceed toward it or recoil from it.

Our profoundest, our most significant, forms of conduct presuppose the freedom of choice. Guilt, regret, responsibility, and anxiety, all imply a measure of choice. They are warnings that something is amiss in our psychological organization, for which we must find suitable remedies. The remedies are alternative ways of behaving; they are selected answers to the prior warnings.

Conversely, every choice, as we have shown, involves some measure of responsibility, guilt, regret, or anxiety. Our guilt is the more powerful the more our act was the outcome of a deliberate choice, and less, the more we feel it was imposed upon us by accident or someone else's compulsion. There may be exceptions, but in these exceptions the guilt was more neurotic than fully healthy.

Experience thus persuades us to believe in the reality of self-determination, in the capacity of each of us to be an effective individual. Wisdom, if it means anything psychologically, is the recognition by each of us, that he is responsible for his own destiny. It means that we understand how much each of us owes to those free spirits who, through their conscious intentions, helped in the growth of human civilization; as well as how much we suffer as the consequence of the destructive acts of still others.

Rather than being a caprice, a mere whimsy, freedom of choice is a significant variable in the totality of obvious facts. Insight and wisdom should not be assigned to philosophy only, but to the science of man equally. In this fusion of wisdom with empirical fact lies "the reconciliation of freedom with the compulsion of truth." And in this way also "the captive can be free, taking as his own the supreme insight, the indwelling persuasion towards the harmony which is the height of existence."[3]

In this emphasis on direct experience as a source of knowledge regarding human freedom, we do not credit science less but the individual more. In this we are but giving the latest expression to the growing open-mindedness among scientists in denying the universality of mechanical determinism. This, and equally radical departures from orthodoxy, is no longer a cause for either alarm or ridicule. As we saw in Chapter 1, the universe described by many contemporary scientists is no longer closed, rigid, and fully governed

[3] A. N. Whitehead, *Adventures of Ideas* (New York: The Macmillan Co., 1933), p. 86.

by causal necessities. Randomness is not merely a function of intellectual limitation but a property of nature. The uniformities in the random behavior of events are statistical probabilities, not dynamic-causal laws. For this reason the experiencing person, relying on the subjective certainty of his immediate experience, may have a more veridical understanding of man's nature than the scoffing psychologist who describes it by means of statistical units.

This way of viewing man in his most human form, in the act of choice as it is revealed in his direct awareness, returns to psychology what a narrow scientism has denied it: the scientific validity of self-anchored experience.

Biological organization. The problem of organization is as old as science and philosophy. It is concerned with the logical or organic relationship of parts and whole. It could be demonstrated that a philosophical or scientific system survived or perished by how well it solved this ancient problem. For us the problem is important because the theory of biological organization throws light upon the related problems of choice, freedom, and purpose, with which psychology must reckon eventually.

In its very nature all organic life is a system. If it were not a system, it would be a mere collection of bits of matter. Protoplasm is a self-regulating system whose fundamental activity is direction toward a goal. Goal-seeking is not a superstitious or vitalistic explanation, but a scientifically defensible hypothesis. The behavior of every organism is influenced by the tendency to seek goals. All living stuff acts toward the consummation of a purpose. If its efforts are frustrated, if its goals are blocked, the organism will reach for the same end by some other route.

In the case of man this principle of goal-direction is normally a deliberate and conscious one. It is an attribute of the human self. Indeed, the mature self is the organized totality of self-regulations, of goal-directedness, of intentions in the process of actualization. This intentionality is an act of free choice among alternative goals, and an act of deliberation concerning the best means of reaching them. Operationally speaking, effective choice is the congruence of our intentions and their realization. This makes room, of course, for the all-too-human situation where anxiety, frustration, indecision, and failure are frequent outcomes of decision-making. But this situation is not an abrogation of freedom but its confirmation. Every choice, we have said, is subject to the limitations of the individual and the obstacles in the social situation. While man cannot bring to pass everything he chooses, he is free to make the effort.

The role of biological organization, of the tendency of protoplasm to move freely toward a distant goal, is supported by evolutionary arguments. Edmund Sinnott, a daring and imaginative biologist, holds that freedom of choice has an important survival value. The sense of obligation, the choice between right and wrong, are part of the evolutionary process, not useless by-products of the protoplasmic pattern. They are in the psychological sphere what pain, for example, is in the physiological domain. Pain is a signal of a bodily malfunctioning. It warns us that we need to take appropriate steps to rid ourselves of an infection, to remedy the malfunctioning. Taking the appropriate action implies that we are free to choose a course of action. If we are the determined creatures, the mechanical automata of orthodoxy psychology, it is indeed monstrous, as Sinnott points out, that "we should have to suffer not only physical pains but the more subtle ones of anxiety and remorse."[4]

Man differs from all other animals in his capacity of choice. In choice, also, lies his individuality and uniqueness. Modern geneticists are agreed that every human being is unique. They have amassed evidence showing that individuality is a fact, not a pious wish. This individuality, this uniqueness, has several sources. One of them is heredity, especially of blood groups. The enzymes and enzyme systems is another source. Biochemical research has strengthened the belief that there is a one-to-one correspondence between genes and enzymes, thus strengthening the scientific opinion that enzyme systems are responsible for human uniqueness and individuality. In the face of facts of this nature it would be strange if the freedom of choice did not play a significant role in man's effort not only to survive but to actualize his potentialities, to be more and more the individual that he can be and the goal-seeking being that he wills to be.[5]

We have called attention to the tendency of human behavior to be self-directive and goal-seeking, and to the freedom of choice as the uniquely human manifestation of this tendency. This means that the description of human behavior as nothing more than patterned responses to stimuli is, as we argued in Chapter 2, an unsupported simplification. What stimuli an individual responds to will depend on the goals he has chosen to seek. Each individual

[4] E. W. Sinnott, *Matter, Mind and Man: The Biology of Human Nature* (New York: Harper and Bros., 1957), p. 133.
[5] For a brief survey of the genetic aspects of man's uniqueness, see L. H. Snyder, "The Genetic Approach to Human Individuality," *The Scientific Monthly*, 1949, *68*, 165–171.

will choose to act in his own unique way. Freedom of choice carries with it the character of novelty, of the unforeseen, of the creative act pointing toward the future.

This mode of analysis has frequently been dismissed on the ground that it is teleological. However, it need not frighten us. Direction, purpose, goal-orientation are neither epiphenomena nor mystical injections into nature. They are, on the contrary, confirmed by many biologists, who attribute them to the fact of biological organization.[6] There is a growing tendency among geneticists and evolutionists to see purposefulness in nature and in both the structure and interaction of organisms.

Mystery lies not in the pervasiveness of purpose in animals and nature, but in the arguments of those psychologists who would deny it in human behavior. The problem is no longer whether purposive behavior exists, but to discover the factors responsible for its direction. Modern science and philosophy are replete with postulated forces designed to explain it, such as entelechy, *élan vital*, or noogenesis. Fortunately, we need not be detained with what is for the time being a highly speculative problem.

The new theory of evolution, a synthesis of Darwinian and neo-Darwinian principles, is unafraid to assign plan and purpose to man and nature. It differs from earlier explanations of purpose by not burdening it with the additional and difficult task of positing a "purposer." It argues for a creative natural selection as the directive factor in all evolution.[7]

A critical comment. Although we have cited Sinnott's remarks approvingly, we do not endorse the main trend of his argument. The views of contemporary geneticists and evolutionists, like Dobzhansky and Simpson, while making room for human individuality and purposive behavior, do not support the all-too-common tendency among publicists to use these views in defense of a new brand of theology. In Simpson's article, the point is made quite clear, that the scientist, *qua* scientist, cannot give an account of how the process of creative adaptation is initiated, for "of this still deeper problem the scientist, as scientist, cannot speak."[8]

Although a limited indeterminism is supported by evidence from contemporary natural science, as we demonstrated in Chapter 1, it

[6] See, for example, H. J. Muller, *Science and Criticism* (New Haven: Yale University Press, 1943).
[7] See G. G. Simpson, "The Problem of Plan and Purpose in Nature," *The Scientific Monthly*, 1947, *64*, 481–495.
[8] *Ibid.*, p. 495.

is dangerous to simply translate the phenomenon of randomness into human freedom. Dangerous also is the too ready conclusion that, since the generalizations of science are but statistical formulations, they cannot apply to individual behavior. What we have tried to establish so far is the conclusion that, if the natural scientist has reasons to doubt the universal validity of strict determinism in the relatively simple phenomena of nature, the psychologist has even stronger reasons for believing that there is a degree of freedom on the more complex level of human behavior.

Moral behavior. We make the simple claim that unless man is free to choose his conduct, moral behavior is impossible. Since man's first act of choice between good and evil, Calvinism and predestination to the contrary notwithstanding, moral behavior has been based on man's capacity to choose. Every moral act is postulated on the principle that man could have done otherwise than he did. When man could depend on his instincts — assuming he was a human being in that state — choice between modes of behavior was unnecessary, and choice was, from an evolutionary point of view, useless. It is characteristic of man, as man and not as animal, that he has no instincts to fall back upon in matters of moral conduct, but must rely on deliberate or conscious choice. Moral conduct is the area of behavior that belongs in human relationships and cannot be executed in the simple fashion in which an animal responds instinctively to the "right" food or the "wrong" course for averting destruction. It is impossible to account for the diversity of moral conduct in different societies if we assume that moral behavior is determined by instinctual mechanisms. Although moral behavior is culturally conditioned in every society, the fact of diversity implies the freedom of choice. Because men can seek goals of their own making they act on the basis of moral values or principles, for these are significant human aspirations. Man is not driven to be good, or honest, or compassionate: these are ends he strives for because they are humanly desirable. While they depend on education and enculturation, man can, and often does, choose to behave contrary to their prescription. Resistance to enculturation is an established fact. This holds for all forms of enculturation, whether moral or immoral, good or bad. Moral behavior is thus one of the highest, if not the supreme, manifestations of volition, deliberation, and choice.

The consequences of the foregoing analysis of moral conduct for the science of human behavior are enriching. For more than a century the prevailing psychologies have ignored the problem of moral behavior. This neglect is the natural consequence of a view of man which admitted only the sole or the combined influence of heredity or environment. Man was conceived to be the product of one or both factors, especially in early childhood experience. He could not modify his behavior in the light of his own purposes. He could not choose to transform himself in accordance with his image of himself as a perfectible human being. In this view the psychologist, either because of a strong bias or a lack of perceptiveness, was amply confirmed by man's fear of the consequences of his choice. We have said that every act of choice entails risks and anxieties. Men fear not only responsibilities but the consequences of their own acts. "*Escape* from freedom" is as much a human trait as the desire for it. But because they fear the responsibilities inherent in the act of choice, men have denied it in others as well as in themselves.

Furthermore, since psychology, like other sciences, is the child of its time, it could find no acceptable place for moral freedom either in the human situation or in itself. It required the despair and anguish of the twentieth century to shake enough psychologists out of their narrow concerns to perceive man as a being groping for ends and meanings in a world in which ends and meanings have been all but destroyed. The psychologist who ignores this fact is a victim of his own illusions. He has abdicated his true vocation, which is to find answers to the perennial question, What is man? for the humanly less important problems of how we know, learn, perceive, and remember. As natural science puts questions up to nature, so psychology must put queries up to man. Sad to relate, psychology has spent most of its efforts putting questions up to rats and pigeons, creatures which neither choose nor reflect upon their behavior. Freedom of choice, however, whatever else it might be, is nothing if not the expression of the human self in its totality.

Moreover, in a human situation that is completely determined, there can be no truths, moral or any other kind; for truth is an assertion — a deliberate assertion — about nature or the human world. So the determinist has placed himself in the inescapable paradox of asserting a deterministic world in which determinism is impossible because that world denies the possibilities of asserting truths.

And finally, since every choice implies a future — for we cannot choose the occurrence of events which have already happened — the freedom of choice affirms the proactive nature of man. Determinism is a necessary doctrine for explaining the antecedent conditions of behavior, for established habits and present memories; it is largely inadequate in explaining behavior evoked by aspirations and options directed toward the future. To the extent that a psychology investigates events in an emerging future, it is fundamentally a science of probabilities and uncertainties.

Returning now to the morality of free choice, it is not insignificant to point out that, at no other period in history has man been more confronted with the inescapable fate of all men: the fact that all men must choose. And nowhere else except in American society, where it is now least understood and appreciated, should this fact be more familiar, for it was in America that people as a nation chose the dignity of human freedom against bondage to an authoritarian past.

The profoundest myth regarding human decision tells us that man fell from grace when, confronted by the agonizing choice between transgression and obedience, between evil and good, chose evil. For this deed man has suffered from the beginning of time. Man's past doomed his future, somewhat in the manner in which many psychologists today would have us believe. But the evolution of man contradicts both the myth of religion and the tradition of psychology. "Man has risen, not fallen," writes a highly discerning evolutionist. "He can choose to develop his capacities as the highest animal and try to rise still farther, or he can choose otherwise. The choice is his responsibility, and his alone. . . . The old evolution was and is essentially amoral. The new evolution involves knowledge, including the knowledge of good and evil."[9]

The scientist's choice. In this mid-twentieth century there are neither scientific, philosophical, nor pragmatic justifications for the positivist's boast that science is wholly objective. Science has no single or official spokesman, as is true of professional societies, such as the American Medical Association, and it has no official doctrine. While the search for verifiable knowledge is its fundamental motive, it is characterized by diversity. Facts are important to it, but it is not, of course, a collection of facts; for if it were, a giant encyclopedia would do as well. No, science is in a sense all of these, but in a profounder sense, none of them. Science is the history of man's unhampered choices among competing views of man and nature. Every informed student of the nature and history of science knows that objective facts neither speak for themselves nor lead to a con-

[9] G. G. Simpson, *The Meaning of Evolution* (New Haven: Yale University Press, 1949), pp. 310–311.

firmable theory. On the contrary, science deduces facts from theory, and accepts or rejects the theory if it is confirmed or contradicted by the facts. There is nothing necessary or determined in the scientist's preference for one theory rather than another. It is not *dictated* by either fact or logical reasoning alone. Although it is false to conclude that on this ground scientific ideas are subjective, for they do contain empirical data; nevertheless, they are fundamentally constructions of the scientist's imagination. Science is not the impersonal activity of which we boast to our captive students. On the contrary, it is a personal and creative activity. Rabi, the renowned physicist, has described its essence by saying that it is "highly personal and yet universal."[10]

Clearly, scientific ideas are accepted by the scientist who creates them and by the scholar who adopts them, not only because their empirical or logical necessity compels them, but because each freely selects them. Apart from this free act of choice there can be neither a theory of nature nor a psychology of man. Accordingly, scientific knowledge like human life itself, is the marvelous expression of man's freedom of choice. Thus also, in science as in moral conduct, the basic attitudes are commitment and responsibility, both reflections of man at his highest and his best.

The scientist's act of choice is seen, finally, in his aesthetic preference among rival explanations. Frequently, neither logical necessity nor pragmatic considerations guide the scientist in his decisions. Quite certainly he is influenced by such apparently "useless" qualities as elegance and beauty. These must not be confused, as they have been by some writers, with the principle of parsimony or simplicity. This may have aesthetic value but adherence to it is largely dictated by the demands of economy. The basis of choice, while confirming the postulate of freedom, is heuristic rather than aesthetic.[11]

---

[10] I. I. Rabi, "The Freedom of the Scientist," in R. English (ed.), *Essentials of Freedom* (Gambier, Ohio: Kenyon College, 1960), p. 53. An extensive and discerning discussion of the above ideas is also presented by another distinguished scientist: M. Polanyi, *Personal Knowledge: Towards a Post-Critical Philosophy* (Chicago: The University of Chicago Press, 1958). For an engagingly written booklet on the same subject by a well-known mathematician who has written extensively on science, see J. Bronowski, *Science and Human Values* (New York: Harper and Bros., 1956).

[11] Another chapter of great length would be required for the delineation of the aesthetic nature of the scientific enterprise, by a discussion of science as an act of creation. There is abundant evidence, presented

INDETERMINISM AND FREE WILL

Clearly, freedom of choice is not the artifice of some misguided psychologists or religious apologists. It is not a means by which man's ego may be assuaged nor his shortcomings and failures be mollified. Man is able to choose, not because we want it so, but because experience, moral behavior, and scientific investigation have confirmed it. Human responsibility, which not even the most tough-minded can deny, is, on deterministic grounds, meaningless and impossible. In depriving man of the capacity to choose, we give him a primal innocence which he never had. The fall of Adam resulted from the exercise of a choice given to no other animal. This, then, is the meaning of that creative legend: Man is responsible for his own act.

It is sheer fancy to attribute the doctrine of choice to the machinations of priests and theologians as their justification of eternal punishment. Man, like his Edenian ancestor, was the author of his own punishment. Responsibility and commitment, two catalysts of human behavior, rest on man's capacity to choose a course of action. Anxiety and guilt, and similar consequences of choice, are proofs that the choice of alternatives is possible. Some evils of life stem, not from the capacity to choose, but from the freedom of the *will*.

The Doctrine of Free Will

There has been an avoidable confusion between the freedom of choice and the freedom of the will in modern philosophical and scientific thought. The confusion stems from the illicit process of identifying a psychological process, the act of choice, with a metaphysical being, the existent will. This misleading identification of choice — or shall we say, more justly, the extension of freedom of choice — with the act of will, is the heritage of German romanticism and objective idealism.

It would take us far beyond the limits of our restricted analysis to trace the problem to Kant's *Critique of Practical Reason,* where in its constructive form as free moral choice, it rightly belongs. Its influence on the German people took place largely through the philosophy of Fichte and Hegel and the poetic psychology of

by scientists themselves, that science is not merely the abstract representation of the external world, nor even its discovery, but in a real sense its creation. Reality is not there to be looked at and copied; its events are made and remade in the free act of creation.

Nietzsche. It is no exaggeration to say that the shift from the freedom of choice, for which Fichte himself spoke feelingly, to the freedom of the will, is largely of the latter's own making. At any rate, few philosophers would deny that the Germanic conception of freedom is Fichtean, unlike the Anglo-American, which is founded on the Lockean tradition.

The primacy of will. Like many thinkers of his time, Fichte was deeply moved by the political doctrine of the French Revolution. He believed that liberty is a natural attribute of man. In this respect the points of view of Fichte, modern existentialism, and our own proactive psychology, are in fundamental agreement.

A negative element, however, found its way, logically and inevitably, into Fichte's constructive thinking. Paradoxically, although an act of will was necessary to set thought in motion, once it was in motion it would follow a necessary course. Necessity thus became a product of the free will. Again, the only reality in Fichte's view, was the will. Opposing the will — or opposing the ego, which was the same thing — is the world of sense, of nature, of the non-ego. The will, because it is determined, imposes itself upon man and nature. The ethical man is he who automatically obeys the moral will. In this process man *opposes* or *dominates over* man and nature. Moral character can arise and develop only in opposition. In Hegel's philosophy, the notion of the free will as imposition and domination reached its logical climax in the belief that any force or being standing in the way of the will's free expression, must be stamped out or destroyed. The good life in the Fichtean ethics consists in the unconditional expression of the will, even if this entails, as it must, the negation of another's will, his domination, and subjugation. In effect this makes morality of immorality, for it sanctions the arbitrary and ruthless disregard of the rights and volitions of others. Since, in their national egocentricity the German people were taught to place themselves above all other societies and cultures, it was not difficult to take the final step in this destructive voluntarism, of believing in the primacy of the German State itself.

Is the answer to the question in the preceding chapter to be found in the Fichtean emphasis on the primacy of the will? Are the national self-centeredness and arrogance of the German nation, and the horrors of the Nazi era, true expressions of the German "character"?

The answer *cannot* be more than a speculative and inferential probability. No one has yet succeeded in demonstrating more than a tenuous connection between a nation's dominant philosophical trend and its national behavior. On the other hand, it is equally dubious that the general moral atmosphere of a time and place would bear no consequences in the lives of a people. It is plausible that more than a century of indoctrination in the mission of the German nation, supported in the conviction that the will is unconditioned, should have convinced at least the German rulers of the justice and inevitability of their own destiny. The Fichtean philosophy, particularly its exaggerated stress on the primacy of the will, was responsible for the *atmosphere* in which later events could occur, but not directly the events themselves.

In short, certainty in this area is impossible and conjecture is no valid ground for explaining the behavior of an entire nation.[12]

Nietzsche, who foresaw the danger in German provincialism, had a different attitude toward the doctrine of free will: he denied it. In his mind it was not only an illusion, but the foul invention of theologians to frighten men into submission to them. The doctrine of free will, he averred, was invented to impute guilt to men and justify their punishment. To make men feel guilty and warrant their punishment by God and theologians, these pious men fabricated the doctrine of free will. Since the concept of free will implies responsibility for one's acts, dependence upon God and the theologians is a natural consequence. If one failed, if one sinned, one deserved punishment, since one's acts resulted from the free exercise of one's capacity to will. Religion is thus responsible for the error of free will, for punishment and guilt. Christianity is no less than the "metaphysics of the hangman."

This negative view of individual freedom is no more reassuring than its necessitarian form in the philosophies of Fichte and Hegel. Man cannot choose between moral facts, according to Nietzsche, for there are none. Neither are there moral ends: these too are inventions. Choice and purpose have no effect on human conduct for, being imaginary, they can have no practical consequences.

Is an intelligent choice between the Fichtean and the Nietzschean views possible? In the Fichtean psychology absolute volun-

---

[12] For a single source bearing on the above issue, see J. G. Fichte, *Addresses to the German Nation,* in K. Francke and W. G. Howard (eds.), *German Classics* (New York: German Publication Society, 1913–14), vol. 5. A more detailed expression of the same view has been advanced independently by Northrop. See F. C. S. Northrop, *The Meeting of East and West* (New York: The Macmillan Company, 1946), Ch. 5.

tarism justifies any form of conduct, for all acts are determined by the force of will. The logical consequence is domination over, even destruction of, whoever and whatever interferes with the imperious demands of one's own will. In the Nietzschean view we end up logically in a moral paralysis. In the Fichtean view a promising freedom is destroyed by a remorseless absolutism, a destructive voluntarism. In the Nietzschean conception, a prefigured individualism is aborted by a boundless negation, a despairing nihilism.

Fichte's voluntarism contrasts sharply with Lockean freedom as embodied in the French Revolution, which influenced his earlier thinking. But the Lockean liberty was no match for the Kantian moral imperative. Post-Kantian thought was not a new venture, but a more uncompromising authoritarian ethic.

Nietzsche's nihilism compares strikingly with his libertarian emphasis on nobility and perfectibility. His vitriolic attack on institutional morality was an expression of what he had explicitly denied: man's capacity, through deliberation and choice, to create a life-affirming philosophy.[13]

COMMITMENT AND CHOICE

The point has been explicitly made, and the sense of our argument has clearly shown, that the problem of freedom, like many problems in psychology, would not our prejudices blind us to this fact, is fundamentally a moral one. Neither the antecedents nor the consequents of human choice are purely intellectual. Their vitality and urgency lie in their affective nature. They are basically feelings, sentiments, and passions. Choice is seldom motivated by coldly intellectual considerations. The enticing influence is an obligation, a responsibility, a commitment. These are matters in which we do not indulge light-heartedly, even though we may pursue them zestfully.

The Dilemma of Choice

How are we to deal with the fact of choice which is inherent in the human condition and the paradox that to be free is yet to be

---

[13] In justice to Nietzsche, it must be pointed out that not much is gained by calling attention to his inconsistencies. A systematic and logically coherent philosophy was the least of his aims. Indeed, he despised philosophy for its pretensions and its addiction to lifeless abstractions.

For Nietzsche's ideas about free will, see his "Twilight of the Idols," in W. Kaufmann (ed. and trans.), *The Portable Nietzsche* (New York: The Viking Press, Inc., 1954).

bound? How can we reconcile the anxiety of choosing with the exhilaration of having chosen?

Fichte and the idealistic tradition chose an absolutism which undermined the libertarian basis of the will. In abrogating the will of others, Fichte sowed the seed of freedom's destruction. Moreover, his authoritarian will precluded the possibility of universalizing intentional responsibility. The responsibly free person is one who acts not as he will, but as he must. Commitment and responsibility are the arbitrators of his decisions.

Although every man's choice is indeterminate by the uniqueness of his self, it is yet determined by his responsibility to the alternatives. Choice, like all forms of freedom, bristles with hazards. Even though man may be but dimly aware of the risks, he is yet besieged by anxiety or dread. In this lies the burden of choice. The burden is inherent in the act of choice, and is not an externally imposed limitation. The stronger an individual's commitment, and the more involved he is in his responsibility, the greater are both the hazards and the emotional rewards which they vouchsafe. Man takes risks because he believes that men are worthy of his love and that nature is sufficiently dependable to warrant its examination. In the first case he reaps the fruits of human relatedness, in the second, the joy of increased knowledge and understanding. We accept the accidents and failures in our choosing because they provide us with exciting opportunities for exercising our freedom and commitment. Both freedom and commitment give us assurance of the worth of our convictions and intentions.

The Limitations of Choice

Theoretically, choice is, within the limits of the possible, unlimited. Even the decision not to choose is, as we have stated, a choice. Practically, every man's choices are limited by his finitude. We have already rejected the romantic illusion of limitless freedom. Nevertheless, every individual can strive with all his energy, imagination, and skill to achieve whatever his potentialities permit. Freedom of choice is not a fixed quantity, but the attitude which men take toward their outer circumstances and their inner boundaries.

Man's biological make-up aids or hinders his freedom. Although man has ascended the ladder of evolution higher than every other animal, he is limited by his own imperfections. These imperfections vary from man to man as surely as do other characteristics. Men obviously differ in their energy potentials, endurance and stamina, vigor and health. Although one can always cite the situation where a man poorly endowed in these traits achieved success incommensurate with his physical imperfections, nevertheless, the pursuit of self-chosen ends requires uncommon strength and endurance. Initiative is largely a biological condition. The very act of choice demands a degree of sustained energy that varies remarkably among men. For some individuals inertia is the easiest road to security and well-being; for others, tension and energetic striving is a way of life.

Psychological conflict limits our capacity to choose. The problem of harmonizing impulse with intellect, of calming the turbulence within us, affects our daily decisions. Generally speaking, indecision is a mark of neurotic behavior. The neurotic is indecisive because he distrusts his inner experience. He perceives life as meaningless. He is paralyzed in the face of options and decisions, the victim of an impersonal fate.

Man's image of himself aids or inhibits his freedom of choice. Too many men and women are intimidated by the awareness of their limitations. They are crippled by their negative self-image. The image itself results in part from their conviction that they are victims of a blind destiny, of a fate over which they have no control. Those who doubt their capacity to choose will make little effort to risk the hazards of decision-making. As we said before, every act of choice is a gamble. For those men who will not risk a choice, life seems unalterable and they perceive themselves as utterly helpless within it.

Lack of knowledge is an impediment to free choice. This factor becomes more limiting as life becomes more complex. Contemporary life makes more demands on individual initiative than that of a century ago. Generally speaking, other things being equal, the greater one's knowledge and information and the understanding that normally accompanies them, the more numerous are the effective choices open to each of us. Although this intellectual condition may result in a multiplication of anxieties and conflicts, it also increases one's opportunities to resolve them.

The social situation, finally, particularly the cultural barriers, affect our freedom of choice. The situation of modern life, as we described it in the preceding chapter, is threatening enough to immobilize all of us. Choosing is at once easier and more difficult than before. If knowledge is power, then we have the means to solve our problems in the very act of creating them. Since through our knowledge we have made a nuclear war possible, this knowledge also tells us that there is no alternative to making it impossible.

Paradoxically, choice has become a necessity, our free act, determined.

CONCLUSION

Clearly, psychologists have been altogether remiss in banishing human choice to the farthest limbo of philosophy and theology. In this deed they have removed from investigation one of those vital processes that make us truly human. To say that man cannot choose is like saying that man cannot think, for in a larger sense all thinking is choosing. Man cannot choose not to choose, for in attempting it he would choose. In a world wholly determined, the scientist could not construct his theory, the composer could not create his symphony, the psychologist could not choose determinism, the psychotherapist could not practice his profession. The determinist's own assertions are proofs that man is not completely determined. No man in possession of his powers can escape accountability for his acts. He alone among animals, has the dreadful responsibility of choosing between good and evil, and he alone is conscious of possessing it. Every psychologist who denies man's capacity for choice must suffer the embarrassment of accounting for his indignation when others go counter to his own injunctions.

The freedom to choose is more than a logician's paradox. It is the root of purpose and meaning for each of us. In order to understand man it is more important to know what he chooses, what his commitments are, than to have detailed knowledge of his past performance. The healthy individual makes commitments and decisions. These are the freedoms that shape his own destiny, that set courses of actions regarding his future. This freedom is not the self-centered belief in a reckless indeterminism, but the liberty to pursue goals that lie within the limits of man's finitude. In the absence of choice man would not be human, for humanness consists in great measure of the capacity to prefigure ends and to realize them in action. Should man be incapable of decision and commitment, he would not grow. He would remain fixed at a psychological dead center. He will listen to his past and appeal to the insights of those who have chosen wisely, but in the lonely stillness of his decision-making, he will choose the life for which he aspires.

5

. . . freedom from external authority is a lasting gain only if the inner psychological conditions are such that we are able to establish our own individuality. . . .

ERICH FROMM

The Vision of Freedom

Freedom to choose, we have said, is a commitment to another's freedom and to one's own action. The power of choice makes the vision of freedom in action possible. We can understand another human being and impute our own dignity to him because as free agents we can freely share our own experience with him. Freedom is witness to the truth that human conduct has never been innocent. In the moment of his first choice, man became conscious of the free acts of others, either confirming or contradicting them. Freedom is the recognition that there are values in the world and that man must choose among them. Values join men to one another, yet preserve for each his sacred individuality.

There was a time when the psychologist could afford to disregard the problem of human freedom and leave it to the consideration of moralists and philosophers. This is no longer a justifiable attitude, and if the psychologist persists in his irresponsibility he will lose the freedom which makes his vocation possible. Today, freedom is besieged by a barbarism which has never shared its subtleties nor understood the roots of its durability. The liberalism of the Enlightenment is insidiously giving way to the fury and unreason of totalitarianism. The individualism of John Locke and John Stuart Mill has been gravely eroded by the collectivism of Stalin and Hitler. It is folly to deny this on the ground that both men are dead. So are Locke and Mill.

The totalitarian threat is not wholly an ideological one. Its immediate terror lies in our worship of the group. Today the

99

anonymous group tyrannizes over the daily lives of millions of people. Conformity and the cult of togetherness are not the fabrication of crisis-minded publicists; they are the realities of mid-century social arrangements, the actualities of *Das Man*, as the existentialists describe it, the facts of the anonymous mass society.

The critic who might complain that the best minds have already covered the territory of freedom many times may be answered by reminding him of the simple truth that freedom, like justice and truth, is continually revised in the light of the values and needs of the times. Every age demands thinking afresh about perennial problems. We can learn about freedom from our history books, but we cannot make it relevant and meaningful in our lives without rethinking and reliving it in the framework of our own personal knowledge. Every generation redefines and recreates the great store of enduring human values. Human growth does not proceed by inventions out of whole cloth, but by the revitalization of values in the light of new experience. And in times of great turbulence like the present, only this revision can promise hope of survival.

THE PSYCHOLOGICAL NATURE OF FREEDOM

In a nation with a long history of free institutions and individual liberty, freedom is taken largely for granted. We become conscious of it when it is abrogated, when it is circumscribed to meet a danger or a crisis, as in time of war. In normal times we guard it jealously against the encroachments of governments and communities. Some men fancy themselves so utterly free of institutional control that they justify revolt and destructive rebellion. Anarchists we have had with us since modern times, but theirs is less an expression of genuine freedom than a fanatical devotion to an unattainable ideal. A liberal state, firmly based on freedom and justice, will not deny them their rights, even though they are bent on destroying it. Their cause is an absurd one, for it would foster the very conditions that would make their ideal a logical contradiction. This situation should serve to remind us that limitless freedom is impossible and that effective freedom has been historically rare. Like the capacity to choose, which is bound by the circumstances of individual limitation, freedom is controlled by the mores and institutions of the social order which liberty itself vouchsafes. Although it may be true, even yet, that that government is best which governs least, it is arrogance, surely, to envisage all governments and all social arrangements as obstacles to individual freedom. Conceived either as individual choice or as political liberty, unrestrained freedom is an intoxicating chimera.

The Meaning of Freedom

Freedom may be defined either abstractly or by the form of its expression in human behavior. Human behavior, contrary to a dominant trend in psychology, is rooted in moral and philosophical beliefs. Freedom is a way of life, a matter of sentiment and conviction. It involves responsibility and the tension and anxiety that it engenders. Like individual choice, it subjects an individual to consequences which he may or may not be able to tolerate. In this situation some men would prefer to renounce freedom, to escape its terrifying possibilities. Still other men, those for whom freedom is the sole basis of a meaningful existence, are committed to the belief that, when all is said, genuine, viable freedom is not a static condition, but an endless transformation of basic human values in a continuously changing environment. The psychological imagination, joined with historical perceptiveness, is proof that we never see the past "as it really was." From this perspective, freedom is defined in the light of what it is becoming, what it will be. We may try to give it form and dimension, but in reality, it is never fixed. Fixation means stagnation, freedom on the way to degeneration and death. Conceived in any other way, freedom soon imitates authoritarianism, and becomes absolute. The freedom of responsibility and justice does not cater to cheap optimism; it does not promise the illusion of universal equality, nor the quietist's vision of a world without struggle and anxiety. Freedom is the moral courage to face the cataclysmic nature of our time. It is no longer a simple faith in "old-fashioned democracy," in which the happiness and welfare of the majority of people could be naively guaranteed.

On the other hand, freedom as here conceived, while eschewing the idealism of illusions, is no less opposed to the corroding cynicism parading under the banner of "science" and "realism." Neither one is the expression of a human nature facing the possibility of its own annihilation. Freedom in our age is not a set of conclusions, but a habit of thinking, feeling, and acting, with reference to a terrifying future.

Clearly, the concept of freedom, like the idea of democracy with which it is commingled, is not exclusively — not even extensively — a political term. It is a way of making life meaningful by giving it a purpose. Democracy as such is no sure guarantor of freedom, for our own democracy is replete with insensitivity to the values and liberties of groups and individuals different from ourselves. The freedom of which we are speaking provides the conditions in which every individual works toward widening the area of common and individual values and purposes, or in which every individual takes account of every other individual while retaining his self-affirmation and relative autonomy.

Individualism. Traditional liberalism identified individualism with independence, and it defined independence largely in negative terms. Independence meant apartness, privacy, and freedom *from* participation in the life of the group. It meant the absence, or relative absence, of *dependence* on others. In a simple and functionally less organized and rigid society, this kind of independence was both meaningful and possible.

In modern society individualism as independence is highly circumscribed. Conformity to groups and norms is an ever recurring pressure. Individualism as independence in thought and action is increasingly the power and prerogative of those who are not intimidated by the demand for conformity. Individualism, although more phrenetically pursued in intellectual discussions than in actual practice, exacts the heavy price of alienation and anxiety. It demands a degree of responsibility which modern man, intimidated by the fear of his neighbor's judgment, cannot sincerely claim as his own.

This is not to say or to imply that man has ever, in the few millennia of his history, been wholly free and independent. But the distinctive feature of contemporary individualism is that it is, as Fromm so cogently demonstrated, a negative condition of freedom *from* decision-making and independence.[1] It is much easier and less threatening for man to lose himself in the faceless mass society than to risk rejection by his group.

In their attempt to establish the thesis that modern man is in fact more free and independent than his compatriot of a generation ago, many writers appeal to a favorite device of the social scientist. They never grow weary of detailing the breakdown of tradition, the disorganization of the family and community, the increasing *anomie* in society. These are facts not to be denied. However, they are proofs of the cause of our alienation and despair as much as of our independence. They are evidence of the independence of the individual as a part-function, but not the freedom of the integrated

---

[1] See E. Fromm, *Escape From Freedom* (New York: Farrar and Rinehart, Inc., 1941).

individual. Moral responsibility is increasingly a function of the faceless group, not of the conscious and reflective person. The old arguments fail to credit the singular role of self-direction and self-control in freedom and individualism.

The sociological fallacy and the deterministic bias, as we have shown, have jointly denied freedom of action. But, freedom and independence are not properties which man simply owns, but habits of conduct which he assiduously cultivates. They are potential givens which, unless they are exercised, become atrophied.

The price of freedom and individualism is high: it demands self-control and moral vigilance. Every relaxation of self-discipline makes the succeeding resolution more difficult. The terrifying threats and confusions of our time make moral resolution and the freedom which it generates not less, but more, imperative. Unless men in democratic societies are ready at all times to practice this self-discipline, they are destined to lose what freedom they have.

This brings us around again to an oft-repeated statement. Significant human acts, acts which make a profound difference in human affairs, are acts of the human spirit. Instincts and drives, habits and reactions, are poor substitutes for the sustaining power behind resolutions, responsibilities, and commitments. It is these forces which engender and promote freedom in human relations. Each is an expression of faith in that which is not yet: a situation in which every human being, because he is human, may participate to create a world which, although not wholly free, is becoming freer.

Self-actualization. If the freedom of choice, because of its hazards and anxieties, is a burden; if the vision of freedom demands the unpleasant responsibility of self-discipline; why do men yet aspire for it? Why, if conformity, as we shall see, gives the promise of safety, do men nevertheless rebel and strive for independence? The answer is as old as the problem itself; only the language in which it is phrased, has the feel of novelty.

For all the emphasis on the externality of behavior in recent psychology, for all the panegyrics on the merits of social responsibility, man is first, not last, a self-affirming being. The center of his existence is neither nature nor society, but himself. Relatedness is surely strong, but it is a condition which man developed in order to render isolation and aloneness endurable.

Man seeks freedom, often in the face of grave risks, because in freedom he finds the initial promise of self-actualization. This capacity, not yet fully understood and even less legitimized by positivistic psychology, is the process of seeking to realize one's potentialities. All other freedoms aside, man *feels* most free and independent when, no matter what the obstacles may be, he can express his need for privacy, individuality, and autonomy. Just as the infant stimulates himself to increasing joy and activity by doing what is most natural to him, so the mature individual enhances his esteem and self-confidence, by affirming his own individuality. In aspiration and striving lie the vision of man's freedom. "Individualism," as Tillich so well phrased it, "is the self-affirmation of the individual self as individual self without regard to its participation in its world."[2]

Man seeks freedom because freedom is the way to self-validation or authenticity. Life as it is lived by all of us transforms persons into things, classifies them into general categories of which they are merely representatives. Those people for whom life is meaningless and the occasion for hopelessness and despair, have been brought to this state by the dehumanization of modern life. In order to transcend the nothingness of existence, man strives with all his being to maintain his individuality. His success in this process is measured by the freedom with which he maintains his individuality. The search for authenticity is the search for one's identity as a person. One proves his existence, or validates his individuality, by means of the courage to be himself. This self-validation through actualization of one's being, is a matter of moral integrity. It implies sincerity and the honest perception of one's being. It is what the existentialists call the authentic self. Thus the rebel who strikes at the social order is authentic, is actualizing his true self, has an increasing measure of freedom because, unlike the unwilling conformist who may be quite hypocritical in his adjustment, he has the courage of his convictions. He is authentic also because his choice to be himself is a personal responsibility. His conduct is purposeful because through it he realizes his own selfhood, actualizes his very being.

Freedom is thus a holistic blend of individualism, autonomy, independence, and self-actualization, cemented by the strong need for authenticity, self-validation, and being oneself as a total person.

The noetic urge. Freedom is both a cause and a consequence of the desire to know. In order to know one must be free, and in order to be free one must have knowledge. Our knowledge is in-

2 P. Tillich, *The Courage to Be* (New Haven: Yale University Press, 1952), p. 113.

adequate to determine the primacy of either freedom or the need to know, for both are powerful human needs. On inferential grounds, one may hypothesize the primacy of freedom, for in order to engage in the first act of knowing one must be free. However, since the intelligent discussion of each is possible without an answer, we shall not press the matter further.

The need for knowing manifests itself in curiosity and the search for meaning. Curiosity is a motivational concept over which heated polemics have raged. While it is found lower in the phyletic scale, man has up to now actualized it most widely and profoundly. A sure way to gain a reputation for banality is to take the trouble to point out that the great cultural achievements of mankind are products of a deep-seated curiosity. Man is by nature a dissecting, analyzing, and inventive being. He is lured by the puzzling, the inscrutable, the mysterious. One of the greatest pleasures, manifesting itself even in childhood, is the delight of discovery, of finding answers to questions. The great myths and legends, as well as the theories of science and philosophy, are outcomes of the impulse to investigate and explore. Man wants not bread alone, as Dostoevsky remarked, but answers to his questions.

No less imperious in its hold upon man, is the freedom to search for meanings. Man has, in the face of danger and punishment, sought for the meaning of his life. The grotesque notion, to which we have already called attention, that the hunger for meaning is a neurotic tendency, is contradicted by a wealth of facts. Like values, meanings make a life bearable. Those orthodox Jews in the concentration camps of Europe, who preferred starvation to the non-ritualized food served to them, may be judged fanatical by less committed persons, but their behavior was both free and meaningful within the framework of their religious values. The configurationist's proof that the human being has a natural tendency to organize his perceptions into a meaningful whole, cannot be dismissed on partisan grounds. It would be strange (a strangeness which is the skeptic's burden to explain) if the search for the meaning of one's life were not equally natural and compelling. The search for meaning is one expression of man's freedom: the freedom to know and understand. The appetite for meaning is an expression of the human adventure. Men who search for the meaning of things are persons in whom uncertainty and adventure vie with the need for safety and security. The latter states may be obtained through sheer inertia and passivity. Freedom, on the other hand, is achieved by means of risk and daring. Among the risks is the exploration of the unknown. If it is true that some men seek knowledge for its own sake, they probably do so because it gives them the freedom to explore the universe.

The need to know, the desire to find meaning in life, is thus another expression of the wish to realize one's freedom. Since freedom is not an abstraction but an act, we can remain free only by actualizing our freedom through its continuous practice. Through freedom and knowledge man creates his own life; for in the final analysis, the one important fact about the human being is that he is potentially the author of his own history. The fact that man may be disappointed in the end-product of this history, is proof that he was free to choose his attitude toward it.

THE SOCIAL CONTEXT OF FREEDOM

Although every individual is independent, autonomous, and unique, his freedom is circumscribed by the conditions imposed upon him by the social order in which he has his being. The notion of a completely autonomous individual, wholly unconstrained, is an absurdity which has never been seriously entertained by responsible thinkers. Even Rousseau's "noble savage" could live well and wisely only in a world designed by the great romanticist himself. Every person's values, even the most eccentric, have an admixture of social ingredients. Were this not the case, consensus and social order would be impossible. Only those writers who have been unduly impressed by the absurdities of life, will be embarrassed by the claim that no existence, and most particularly no personal existence, is possible in the absence of man's regard for and commitments to, other human beings. Men are loyal to group values because they intuitively know them as the fructifying fountainhead of their own ideals. No man has ever generated ideals in a social vacuum. In the wake of a virulent beatnik mindlessness, this is no longer a trite declaration. Freedom is social as well as individual. Only that man is free who lives in a society of free men. Only that freedom can survive and flourish which is sheltered by a free community — a *Gemeinschaft* in which mutual sympathy and respect for differences are guiding principles.

The Bane of Conformity

Society creates the climate in which freedom can arise and be protected, but it also produces the atmosphere in which freedom can be diluted, compromised, and destroyed. Consensus and allegiance hold society together, but when society does not respect the freedom and dignity of its members, it does not deserve their loyalty. Today the menace to freedom manifests itself in many forms, the most subtle and insinuating being the pressure for conformity. No single authority or institution is responsible for this condition; it is, rather, an aspect of the atmosphere of the time, of a terrifying fear of isolation and loneliness. When his behavior is a carbon copy of every person's behavior, modern man need no longer feel anxious and alone. Since selfhood and independence have lost much of their value in the contemporary world, the loss of personal identity is but a small price to pay for the safety of conformity. Whereas this surrender of the self was at one time resisted mightily, today it is a widespread phenomenon. Contemporary man feels no coercion in this matter for he has victimized himself by the illusion that, since no tangible authority demands his conformity, he is making his own decisions. The real threat to freedom, therefore, lies not in conformity itself, but in the false belief that man is acting freely. The man who does not feel coercion, who is unaware that he is submitting to group expectations, will not be energized to exert himself for something he does not miss.

Conformity also originates in a more obvious, but psychologically damaging, way. In a society like ours, where acceptance and popularity are highly prized, in which conformity is aided and abetted by the authority of adjustment psychology, people are terrorized by the fear of being different. Even though the wisdom of the ages is proof of the reality of differences, even though the facts of evolution and genetics demonstrate the existence of individuality, the tyranny of custom and psychology has intimidated man with the fear of deviance and maladjustment. The affirmation of the spirit, the pride in selfhood, cannot flourish in a world that ridicules and suppresses a mode of being that defies the rituals of convention. Man's malaise is due much less to vocational failure, even less to sexual deprivation, but increasingly more to spiritual frustration.

There are signs of rebellion against collective engulfment. Some efforts in this direction are salutary, while others are but expressions of a profounder sickness. The existentialist movement is its finest and most creative expression. However one may judge its excesses, existentialism has shown the European how he may come to terms with the nameless fears of a disintegrating society. His self, it teaches him, is constantly reborn by transcending the oppressive hegemony of the "collective will." Although this is the way of but a few, it has potentialities of becoming the road for the many. And as the American condition rapidly approaches in kind the European, what with the growing confrontation by collective crises and individual futility, existential thought and practice may point the way toward a new American individualism. Only a way of life akin to that of existentialism, to a proactive psychology that encourages self-affirmation and the courage to be oneself as an individual, has a fighting chance of saving man from the anonymity of compulsive conformity.

Much nonsense has been spoken about the beat generation. When we divest the beatnik protest of the froth and fury surrounding it, it is a disquieting manifestation of the emptiness of contemporary life. It is a symptom of the disease that it is designed to cure. It has neither drama nor poetry, as all genuine protest has, but only a loud whimpering in the dark. It is predicated on the proposition that noise-making and senseless exhibitionism are genuine articles. It has neither the courage nor the dignity of facing alone a world in the process of disintegration. It generates, but in the most idiosyncratic way, the very conformism it is trying to escape. It is a stunted impulse manifesting itself in bad faith. It is, in short, wholly devoid of nobility and greatness.

The upshot of the foregoing comments is that rebelliousness whose sole "purpose" is simply rebelliousness, has no meaningful connection with psychological freedom. Authentic protest is guided by responsibility to the institutions which one is trying to change. Honest rebellion against conformism is informed by a feeling of obligation to widen the area of freedom for everybody. Society itself confers or denies personal freedom; it is not the issue of wholly autonomous action by an individual. Freedom to choose, as we argued in the preceding chapter, always incurs responsibility toward others, not only oneself. In the absence of this responsibility, freedom is exploitation, empty of self-discipline. So obvious is this that detailed elaboration is unnecessary. Suffice to say, the person whose rights are protected by a free society is morally obligated to guard and enhance the freedom which sustains his own independence. In the absence of social responsibility nobody's freedom is secure.

If the phrasing of freedom is not in the psychologist's style, we must remind him that his own idiom has precluded its serious investigation. Freedom is a value that influences human behavior, and the psychologist who ignores it runs the grave risk of dwarfing the psychology of man. Of trivialities we have had enough in psychology; it is time to take seriously the very freedom that has made psychology a reality.

FREEDOM AND THE GOOD LIFE

Man finds the meaning of his life in two inseparable aspects of his total existence: his human nature and his social order. His nature we have briefly delineated, and will describe more fully throughout this book. The human world that gives direction to his life we shall discuss forthwith.

Man is not only an end in himself, but as Nietzsche phrased it, a bridge to an end that transcends his immediate existence. This idea has nothing whatever to do with a transcendent spirit, some entity existing beyond the stars. It refers to our becoming better creatures tomorrow than we are today. Man is a self-transforming individual. This is the meaning of Nietzsche's affirmation, spoken through the mouth of Zarathustra: "Man is something that must be overcome."

Man cannot perform this feat of self-transformation in utter isolation. It always takes place in the context of a living moral order. All too much of the history of man's effort to reach beyond himself, to improve himself, has been suppressive and inhibitory. Our morals and education, our religion and social practice, have been a massive negation of the spirit's desire to actualize itself. The social order in which these forces have operated has been largely a policing function. But the meaning of all we know about man as an individual and man as a participant, cries out for a world that will provide the conditions for self-actualization and for widening the area of common social purposes. Tradition alone, with all its provision for stability and conservation, cannot provide us with the guide to the good life in the nuclear age.

The good life and the fully functioning society are not fixed conditions. Freedom in the twentieth century can be realized only by means of a radical transformation of the encrusted traditions of liberty and democracy. Freedom must change from a mere slogan to a way of life; and a way of life — or more explicitly, a good life — can thrive only in a social arrangement where every individual is free to move in whatever direction will most enhance himself and actualize the values which are, or can be, universally shared.

The good life, and the moral order to which it is always fixed, are not accidental or adventitious: they are the heart and center of a fully human existence.

The good life, like the freedom from which it springs and which it in turn sustains, cannot be described well in the syntax of objective science. Like most of the ideas of proactive psychology, it is more easily, if less explicitly, presented in the idiom of literature and philosophy.[3] What follows is a brief statement of the psychological characteristics of the good life as it relates to the larger problem of freedom.

Commitment

We take it as self-evident that freedom and the good life are possible only in a society where every individual counts both himself and other individuals. Contrary to the universal American philosophy that every individual fulfills his purpose in the attainment of happiness, the men who have left a mark upon their fellow beings, have been individuals with the passion to leave the world different from what it was before they were thrust into it. The good life does not consist only in good living, desirable as this condition is. We have remarked in this volume and elsewhere, that pleasure and homeostasis are poor indications of psychological health.[4] People who have grown beyond the need for libidinal satisfactions, are motivated by the vision of freedom and the striving for previsioned ends. A characteristic mark of the goal as well as its seeking, is the uncertainty of its attainment. Goal-seeking is a process whose terminus is seldom guaranteed. The good life, and the proactive behavior which animates and suffuses it, is a life of improvisation as well as fulfillment. The proactivert approaches the challenges of life in the spirit of exultation.

Being thus freed from the compulsive search for happiness, the proactive individual can lend himself freely in the service of others. Freedom without commitment is licentiousness. The free man is capable of sacrifice as well as selfishness. The foolish embarrass-

---

[3] It is cause for curiosity and astonishment when one hears expressions of impatience with and even ridicule of the broadly philosophical language of personality theorists, in view of the fact that behavioristic psychology is at bottom an extended philosophical discourse, couched in the technical nomenclature of experimental science.

[4] See H. Bonner, *Psychology of Personality* (New York: Ronald Press Company, 1961), *passim*.

ment which our tough-minded psychologists experience — or affect — is a symptom of our moral shallowness and the extremity to which we are ready to go to avert our eyes from the moral intangibles. In a word of cynics it is much easier to be cynical and to make sophisticated jokes about the life that troubles us.

The reality of the self is validated by its participation in the world of other selves. *Ich und du* — I and thou — together form the continuum of human existence. Apart from another, I am only an object, never a complete person. The alienation of which existentialists have written so movingly, is not due solely to the partition of the individual, but to his separation from other individuals. Although his very uniqueness estranges each person from every other person, each cries out for the completion of his personality in a union with other selves. The person is a person because he has a world of other persons by which he is both separated and united.

Commitment is thus the attitude which impels a man to affirm and transform himself as a person *and* to transcend himself in the act of affirming the selves of others. Moral responsibility is the free participation of each in a social order which belongs to all.

Education

The building of oneself beyond the limits of mere self-centeredness, is aided and hindered by the process of socialization. Although each of us learns the norms and values of life in the primary institutions, particularly the family, contemporary man's selfhood and the intellectual powers which inform it, are increasingly patterned by the more formal process of education.

Conformism, the increasing surrender of personal freedom, and the decrease in genuine rebelliousness, are greatly facilitated by the American school system. Education, despite its emancipation from the cruder and harsher discipline and indoctrination of an earlier period, is an imposition rather than an evocation. In school, the freshness of youth is often exhausted, and its curiosities are dulled. Education today is, as it was when John Dewey described it more than forty years ago, "the art of taking advantage of the helplessness of the young."[5]

Clearly, this attitude, this mode of imposing one's own will upon another arbitrarily, is contrary to the spirit of democracy and free-

[5] J. Dewey, *Human Nature and Conduct* (New York: Henry Holt and Company, 1922), p. 64.

dom. Democracy is a way of life — at least this is what we believe — which aims to develop individuality and originality in people. But in an education that is primarily conservative, that aims to propagate the *status quo,* neither genuine individual freedom nor creative commitment to new values, can flourish. If "progress" has, nevertheless, been widespread and rapid, much of it has been adventitious and accidental, not the result of a system of ideal objectives.

The adjustment psychology on which much of our educational philosophy and practice are based, must take a large share of the responsibility for the conservative and restrictive character of education. This psychology confirms and reinforces the modes of belief which are fixed by individual habits and past customs. It is easier to live in fixed routine than in the anxiety of experiment and improvisation. There is something ironic about this condition. Despite the multiplicity of customs brought about by the wider sphere of human relationships into which men have entered; despite the extended range of choices which life has opened for each of us; education still indoctrinates the growing youth with the moral rightness of things as they are. We give lip service to self-determination and freedom to choose one's own life, but we praise and reward the life that fits well into the old ruts.

From the standpoint of freedom and the good life, there is more in this condition than the constriction of individual growth, horrendous as that in itself is. It imperils the very basis of freedom. If the end of education is the transmission of custom and the social adjustment of individuals, then the dangers of totalitarianism are constantly present. Collective authority can easily replace the moral authority of the responsible individual. Indeed the "responsible individual" is easily persuaded by the pressures of a deified collective authority. The step from the legitimate assertion that education always transmits the ideals of a former generation, to the belief that it *should* in fact do so, is a small and easy one. "Education for freedom" is easily corrupted into education for conformity. This is not a paper dragon created for the joy of slaying it. In the era of the deep economic depression of the 1930's, it was widely discussed by respectable educators. Education as the expression of the "common will," of the "social organism," is easily translated into the *will of the state.* It happened in Germany, the nation most responsible for the doctrine of academic freedom.

Clearly, then, although participation in the life of the other one, transmission of the settled customs of the past, and protection of the life of the social organism are legitimate ends of education, they are not in themselves guarantors of egalitarian democracy. "Eternal vigilance" is as necessary in education as it is for the life of the state.

Individualism

Education and the larger process of socialization are perpetually opposing the self-assertions of the individual. Yet, there is no real incompatibility between the ends of society and the goals of the individual, once the purposes of both are sympathetically accepted. The individual who labors toward self-development eventually transforms society. In actualizing his potentialities he advances the self-renewing tendencies of the social order. Although modern field theory has made popular the idea that the whole determines the activities of the parts, the fact is that the individual also helps to modify society. As a "center of high potential," to use Lewin's own terminology, the individual is free to make constructive innovations. If these centers of high potential, these self-affirmations, are uncommon, it is because the cultural authority of society and education destroys them. Both school and society are geared to the production of practical skills, rather than versatility and creativeness.

The tyranny of the group. The school is not alone in making man apprehensive about the fate of his individuality. All communication is, of course, deeply social. But communication with others in the group is more than a social pastime: it is a form of communion between individuals in which each can realize his inward tendencies.

However, neither education nor socialization encourage communication as communion. On the contrary, both dictate the kind of behavior which the group considers acceptable. The "science" of group dynamics, although potentially productive of self-fulfillment, can quickly descend to the level of group-exaltation.[6] In this connection, group dynamics not only confirms the excesses of adjustment psychology but often exceeds them. This is particularly evident in those quarters in which group participation and group-belongingness have been made into all-embracing principles.

We do not deny the superiority of the group over the individual in certain kinds of activities. Indeed, we have ourselves paid extensive tribute to its effectiveness. The cause for anxiety lies in those excessive and unsubstantiated claims that are bent, unwittingly —

[6] This situation is discussed extensively in H. Bonner, *Group Dynamics: Principles and Applications* (New York: The Ronald Press Company, 1959), especially Ch. 18.

sometimes deliberately — on destroying individualism itself.[7] The perversity of the anti-individualistic argument is compounded by the dogmatic assertion that individualism threatens rather than advances the values of individuality.

The advocates of group-determinism and anti-individualism facilitate and promote the very conditions which they profess to deplore. The seeker of freedom and self-validation is forced by the tyranny of the group to flee from the imprisonment of group-belongingness or, having been deeply wounded by its repressiveness, to indulge in destructive compromises.

The emphasis on every side of us — in the home, the school, the church, and in that most insensitive of all modern relationships, the peer group — the soil for self-actualization and individual authenticity is barren or wholly non-existent. Yet, all the conditions of contemporary experience point unequivocally to the fact that man's most desperate longing is not group-relatedness, but self-fulfillment. Man does not seek merely the happiness that a group can provide, but more profoundly the dedicated search for himself. Man is truly his own foundation. Take away this foundation of selfhood or individuality, and man has left only the skeleton of his existence — the happiness which material life can abundantly afford him.

The good life, then, is that condition in which the social arrangements promote the wholeness of the individual and the unity of society. Although we describe it as a condition, it is never static. It is a process in which the goals of the individual and the aims of society, though never fully identical, are moving toward a common fulfillment. Since it is a process, the fulfillment itself has no foreseeable terminus. The good life is conceived as a "set of intelligent improvisations, as a meeting of unexpected elements at every step."[8] It is never a finished thing. Only a life that sustains and maximizes what Tillich has called "the courage to be," both as an individual and as a social whole, can be fully meaningful. The courage lies in the individual's strength to bear the estrangement that self-affirmation begets, and the humility of affirming his dependence on the society that guards and promotes his freedom to be himself.

[7] D. K. Benne, one of the most ardent exponents of "groupism," explicitly states that a democratic methodology of social changes "must be anti-individualistic." See D. K. Benne, "Democratic ethics and social engineering," *Progress. Educ.*, 1949, 26, 204–207.

[8] H. Bonner, "The Proactivert: A Contribution to the Theory of Psychological Types," *J. Exist. Psychiat.*, 1963, 3, 323–328.

CONCLUSION

There are two extreme views regarding the nature and role of freedom in the life of man. The radical existentialists, represented chiefly by the nihilism of Sartre, argue for the complete autonomy of the individual. The conscious presence of another person, to use Sartre's well-known example, limits one's freedom. The moment each is aware of the other, the freedom of both is curtailed or ended. Each is denying the liberty of the other. Accordingly, all relatedness, by its very nature, not only destroys freedom, but produces alienation and conflict. Genuine love between two people is thus impossible, for it is bound to be either sadistic or masochistic: sadistic because it denies the freedom of another, and masochistic because it denies oneself all opportunities of self-expression.

The other extreme on the continuum encapsulates the individual in the fixed relations of the human group. The relatedness which it generates provides the security and approval which all men need, but at the cost of genuine individuality.

Clearly, then, the first argues for what is in effect an impossibility; the other, for the absolute supremacy of a mindless collectivity.

Now, there are apologists for both views, who criticize the more "liberal" writers on the subject of freedom by accusing them of compromise with popular opinion, of currying the favor of the traditionalists in order to gain a wider acceptance of their watered-down egalitarianism. This is an emotional view of the matter, based on a projection of suspicion upon those who refuse to join the true faith. It is an intolerance which blinds some writers to the incontrovertible fact that there are no absolutes in human relations. Complete autonomy and absolute collectivization are dogmas unsupported by history and impossible of attainment. If in some future utopia either condition should come to pass, each will immobilize individual and social action.

6

Man is always what he is yet to be; and the true human is the one whose face is toward the future, whose life is yet to be made.

GEORGE F. KNELLER

The Lure of the Future

We begin our discussion by noting the obvious fact that only dead things have no future. All living things, and most profoundly human beings, complete themselves in the future. The human traits of freedom, responsibility, and commitment, it should now be clear, all imply a tomorrow. Every time we make a promise we are positing a future. Man is, indeed, as Nietzsche said, "the animal that can promise." Other animals can adjust themselves to the oncoming acts of another, but only human beings can assume obligations regarding the future. All that we have said in this book thus far, confirms the belief that, to use Emerson's phrase, men "live always in a new dawn." This proactive direction makes man a self-affirming, self-renewing, and self-transforming individual.

It is interesting to note that Rokeach, in his "quantitative" study of the role of the time-orientation in behavior, found what he interprets to be a relation between the "closed mind" and future-directedness. Moreover, he found a correlation between future-orientedness and anxiety.

The matter hinges largely on the question of interpretation. For example, Rokeach interprets the future-pointed attitudes of his subjects "in terms of a greater intolerance of ambiguity and a greater need for closure." He also found a high rate of anxiety in the future-oriented subjects.[1]

Yet all that we have said in this book challenges in a most funda-

[1] See M. Rokeach, *The Open and the Closed Mind* (New York: Basic Books, Inc., 1960), pp. 366–375.

mental way Rokeach's main conclusion. For instance, nothing is more characteristic of the proactive individual than openness to experience. To a person who is always in the process of becoming, closure, completion, and similar conditions, are abhorrent. He dreads fixity and rebels against the terrible inroads of ossification. His life is, as we said before, an improvisation, not an attainment.

It is very significant that none of the mental cases reported by Ellenberger, was future-oriented. The future was especially meaningless for the manics and certain psychopaths. Their behavior was fixed and incapable of fulfillment; they were people "without tomorrow."

"Openness to experience," as Rogers calls it, is a characteristic mark of the healthy proactive individual. Because he lives in an open, unstructured world, the proactivert is subject to more anxiety, but the very openness of his being permits him to absorb his anxieties in a constructive movement toward the future. Rokeach himself has found this condition "specific to creative men." Although this may appear more abundantly in creative persons, it is a trait specific for all in whom the forward thrust is fundamental.[2]

Although anxiety is never easy to assimilate, and although it is present in all people, when it is fully understood and one's attitude toward it is acceptant, it is a way of confirming one's individuality. Anxiety is a sign that we care, that persons and events are important to us. Since the future is never made, but always in the making, it is false to say that future-directed persons fear ambiguity and seek for the safety of closure and completion. On the contrary, the very opposite characterizes the healthy and proactive-individual. He is lured by the untravelled road.

TIME AND THE FUTURE DIMENSION

A marked characteristic of contemporary science is that it takes time seriously. The processes of growth, development, evolution, and goal-direction are predicated on a temporalism that stresses the future mode. Process pervades both science and life. In its most developed form, temporalism identifies being with process, as we shall see, or being-in-becoming. This way of conceiving time as

---

[2] For Ellenberger's findings, see H. F. Ellenberger, "A Clinical Introduction to Psychiatric Phenomenology and Existential Analysis," in R. May *et al.* (eds.), *Existence: A New Dimension in Psychiatry and Psychology* (New York: Basic Books, Inc., 1958), pp. 92–124.

process has received its greatest impetus from the neo-Darwinian, or synthetic, view of evolution.

The Triple Modes

If time is process, then it is extremely artificial and arbitrary to make a sharp demarcation between the past, present, and future. A sound psychology is one that aims to integrate these dimensions into a single process or continuum, perhaps stressing one or another according to need, interest, and individual predilection.

The past and the present are always somehow apprehendable. We can recognize the past in the form of our private histories. We can recall events in the past, or others can furnish us with them. In this sense our past lives in the present. The past is memory.

The present, too, we can comprehend, for it consists of ongoing events external to ourselves, and of our sensations, feelings, and perceptions.

The future, however, seems to be a dimension of a different order, yet is not. It is difficult to apprehend because we do not experience it as something of the moment, for it is that in the process of becoming which is not yet. Nevertheless, it exerts a powerful force upon us, for much of our present behavior is elicited by the future. We strive for things ahead of us, and are not driven solely by events behind us. Even our past is redefined in the light of the future. The future can modify the effects of the past. This is a fact of common experience and is attested to by every successful psychotherapy.

Ordinarily, we do not comprehend this fact because, by force of habit, we conceive events under the aspect of *completeness*. However, completeness can hold only for past events and, perhaps, for immediately present ones. Because we think of events as finished, the future can have no meaningful existence.

The future is to be described, then, as the process toward completion, but it is never the finished thing. When the process is applied to the human personality, it means the act by which the individual is perpetually seeking self-completion and self-actualization. The future can never be actualized in the present; and yet, without a future there can be no present, for time, we have said, is a continuum, a processual manifestation of the three temporal modes of experience. Whitehead, who devoted his career to the study of time as process, has made this clear. "Cut away the future," he said, "and the present collapses, emptied of its proper content. Immediate existence requires the insertion of the future in the crannies of the present."[3]

The future is thus immanent in the present; it is to the present "as object for a subject."[4] In this sense it is logically and ontologically correct to say that the future is part of the nature of things. The present may be said to determine its own relationship to the future. Psychologically, this is manifested in anticipation and intentionality. What place the future may have in the life of a person will be determined by the stand or attitude which he takes toward it.

However, it would be a mistake to believe that because past, present, and future are intertwined, they mutually determine one another in a causal sequence. If they were causally dependent, freedom would be impossible. As we have already pointed out in Chapters 1 and 2, of two events neither can belong to the past of the other. This independence of events, one of another, is the "preservative of the elbow-room within the universe," and provides each event "with a welcome environment for irresponsibility."[5] The elbow-room saves the universe from becoming completely mechanical and keeps things running smoothly.[6]

The psychological meaning of time. Any psychology that aspires to describe and understand man in his living totality, must aim to synthesize the three modes of time into a unity, a process of being-in-becoming. To the amnesic person who cannot reconstruct his past, the depressed psychotic who cannot anticipate the future, and the psychopathic individual who lives completely in the specious present, life invariably is without meaning. As Ellenberger has concluded, on the basis of extensive psychiatric practice, life can be meaningful only through the subjective feeling of time. "Distortions of the feeling of time necessarily result in distortions of the meaning of life." In the stream of psychological time the future is particularly important. Only in the anticipated future can man compensate for and correct the distortions of the past and the present. It

---

[3] A. N. Whitehead, *Adventures of Ideas* (New York: The Macmillan Company, 1933), p. 246. For an interesting experimental study of the future dimension, with important relevance to psychology, see R. Bergius, *Formen des Zukunftserlebens* (München: Johann Ambrosius Barth, 1957), especially Part III.

[4] A. N. Whitehead, *op. cit.*, p. 250.

[5] *Ibid.*, p. 251.

[6] See S. T. Bornemisza, *The Unified System Concept of Nature* (New York: Vantage Press, Inc., 1955), pp. 3–4.

is tomorrow that we hope to correct the errors of yesterday; it is in the future that we hope to succeed, expiate our guilt, and realize the perfection of our children. *La vita comincia domani* — life begins tomorrow — is a bit of folk-wisdom espoused by distinguished minds as well. Men who devalue the future for its ominous threats are wholly blind to its creative opportunities for averting the danger itself. Dangers there are in any time fixation, a fact which but argues for the need of synthesis of the temporal modes. As Ellenberger, following Israeli, has pointed out, an individual's interest in the future may be constructive, cataclysmic, or paranoid.[7]

Yet, all in all, fixation on the past, with its paralysis of present action, the obsessions and compulsions that are glued to the present, inhibiting that novelty which alone can cure or dispel them — these and many other forms of ineffective and abnormal behavior far outweigh in seriousness the anxieties and fears generated by the future. They inhibit man's capacity for self-actualization and becoming. The future alone promises self-actualization and the opportunities for correcting the errors of the past. Gebsattel, in explaining the past-fixations of the compulsive individual, or his patient's obsession with pollution, has shown that his trouble lies in being "nailed to the past.'" The patient cannot eliminate the fear of pollution, because "this would call for the very condition of one's openness for the future," a change of position away from the past toward the threatening future. Yet, until the patient succeeds in transcending the past, and despite all his defenses against the future, he is destined merely to repeat his crippling behavior. He cannot become, for becoming is the process of passage into the future. He cannot become well without overcoming his past. "The past must be dropped, like stool," says Gebsattel, in analyzing the obsessive dread of pollution by the obsessive-compulsive (anankastic); "and the healthy life, which is directed toward the future . . . continually deposits the past, leaves it behind, thrusts it off, and cleanses itself from it."[8] The compulsive cannot face the future because the future is always a summons to action and choice. The sick person, in his fear of being himself, of actualizing his potentialities, distorts his potential uniqueness beyond recognition. He is sick because his self-activity is weak or atrophied. Self-activity,

[7] See H. F. Ellenberger, *op. cit.*, p. 107. Israeli's discussion is found in N. Israeli, *Abnormal Personality and Time* (New York: Science Press, 1936).

[8] V. E. von Gebsattel, "The World of the Compulsive," in R. May *et al.*, *op. cit.*, p. 178.

or becoming, is the authentic sign of psychological health, of movement toward self-perfection.

On the other hand, the present-oriented person is scarcely more fortunate. He is in the paradoxical position of trying to achieve "happiness" or "adjustment" in a moment that does not in fact exist. His confusion and disorientation spring from the frustration of trying to live in an instantaneously given present which has no reality. What is immediate in temporal experience is not the present, but the feeling of duration. The immediate present is at best an ill-defined dimension, and in trying to live in or adjust to it, one's conduct is equally vague and ill-defined. In Whitehead's well-known assertion, "There is no holding nature still and looking at it."[9]

The healthy, creative individual lives in the process of becoming, and this requires a future for its actualization. Man grasps the notion of becoming because he is himself becoming; he apprehends the future because as a proactive being, he is lured forward by it. Man, we have said, is not a passive reactor to stimuli or situations. He is a seeker of future ends. He is not fixated on a single temporal dimension, but unites all of them in himself. His style of life is, nevertheless, an expression of a dynamic forward thrust. The sick individual, on the other hand, as we have elsewhere remarked, "regrets his past, abhors his present, and dreads his future. He is caught in a state of suspension, and he can move neither backward nor forward. Fear and boredom are the terrors of his life."[10]

Evidence from Evolution

When man becomes conscious of human history, he is aware of time. When he becomes conscious of time as duration, he is aware of the proactive nature of time's arrow. When he becomes conscious of the foreworld as the direction of the human adventure, he is aware of life as the creative advance into the future. Growth, development, and evolution have the same fundamental meaning. The referent of development is the individual — the ontogenetic dimension; whereas the referent of evolution is the plurality of individuals — the phylogenetic dimension. Both imply an end or purpose. Synthetic evolution justifies the belief that life is tending in a general direction — forward — although it cannot inform us

[9] A. N. Whitehead, *The Concept of Nature* (New York: The Macmillan Company, 1926), pp. 14–15.
[10] H. Bonner, "Idealization and Mental Health," *J. Individ. Psychol.*, 1962, *18*, 136–146, p. 145.

of the specific nature of the forward thrust. Evolution is neither haphazard nor reversible, but always directional. This directional evolution is due to what Simpson has called "creative natural selection." Genetic systems may arise through creative natural selection that could never have emerged under the influence of mutation and random combination of hereditary factors. Thus, although natural selection does not produce the raw materials, it is nevertheless creative, for it creates the integrated organism.[11]

Like the forward thrust of time into its future, evolution is the elaboration of novelty, a maximization of reality, in which new elements leap constantly into existence. Like life itself, evolution is that improvisation of which we have already spoken, an exercise in creation on an enormous scale. Judging by the stage it has reached, there can be little doubt that it is moving in the direction of maximum individuation. As every moment of time differs from all others, so evolution, in the long perspective of its onward pulsation, gives rise to an infinite variety of events. Evolution, like the rest of reality, is incessant movement, change, life. Evolution, like life, is the movement of the past thrusting itself into the future, with novelty insinuating itself into the process.

The process of evolution thus illuminates not only the nature of living things, but throws a shining light upon man's effort to transcend and transform himself. It is no mere "unfoldment" of potentialities, as an earlier interpretation averred, but the individual's response to the challenges of his world. In the enormous vastness of time as it strives forward in its unending movement toward the future, man is, indeed, "the ascending arrow of the great biological synthesis," to borrow Dobzhansky's beautiful phrase. Although this conception of man is scientifically undemonstrable, it is at the same time compatible with the great and productive ideas of synthetic evolution. It is a "fundamental vision" of man moving into the future.[12]

The Role of the Past

A basic tenet of proactive psychology is that the past, present, and future are the fused dimension of an ongoing temporal process. We have affirmed that human beings differ in the dimension around

---

[11] G. G. Simpson, "The Problem of Plan and Purpose in Nature," *The Scientific Monthly*, 1947, *64*, 481–495.

[12] See T. Dobzhansky, *Mankind Evolving* (New Haven: Yale University Press, 1962), Ch. 12.

which they orient their lives. We believe that it is characteristic of the healthy, growing individual, to point his life toward the future, even though it is embedded in the past. We repeat what we said earlier, only dead things have no future. This observation may be applied to living persons. Those individuals for whom inertia is safer than the adventure of growth, are largely driven by the past.

It is a familiar fact that this tendency is especially strong in the old. The attitude is encouraged and intensified by the present worship of youth, even though many young people are as fixated on the past, or are as impelled by habit and the need to play safe, as the aging individuals themselves. This is a paradox of our time. While there are no other people who are as ready to discard the past and embrace the innovations of the present and emerging future, as we are in America, in our personal lives we are timid about tomorrow. Americans have yet to learn that despite the darkness of the past and the ominousness of the future — both of which we have detailed in earlier chapters — there are substantial reasons for confidence in the future. Proactiveness is an expression of growth, quite apart from chronological age.

Again, fixation on the past is characteristic of those who see no hope in the future. This attitude has been common in human history, and is exceptionally strong in minority and subject peoples. Having no status in a group, people return in their minds to a former period which they invariably idealize. This has been the story of people who have had no acceptable place in society, who reverted in their aspirations to a Golden Age in the past. It has been the story, too, of persecuted people, who were able to find comfort in apocalyptic religions and exotic cults. For these people the future holds no promise, and they are enabled by their worship of an idealized past, to avert their eyes from an unpleasant future.[13]

It can be said truly that all men guided by a long-term ethics, are dedicated to the future. Interest in and dedication to human welfare imply a profound concern for what will happen tomorrow. Concern for the humanization of man — for the enhancement of his opportunity to exercise his impulses and capacities for the enrichment of human life — are predicated on the belief in a future in which wrongs can be righted, defects can be modified, and errors can be

---

[13] We are not here concerned with the concept of immortality, which is a future-oriented condition. We focus our attention entirely on the human and social situation as it is lived in the world of known reality.

corrected. The highest type of human being feels responsible for the welfare of humanity. He is a self-determining individual capable of projecting his present conduct into the indeterminate future. This self-propulsion of the individual into the future, is a trait of proactive man and a postulate of his moral life. The psychologist who denies or neglects this self-determination toward the future, has both a low and false estimate of the creative nature of man.

And so, although the past can make the future easier of achievement, by the accumulated knowledge and wisdom it puts at man's disposal, by itself it can never be crucial. As past, it remains but an idea that has not yet actualized its purpose. Purpose always lies ahead, never behind. In order to actualize its potentialities it must step outside itself, extend its power beyond the moment, and realize itself in future action. The backward look, the regression to a former epoch, the safety that comes from custom, habit, and authority, are the paths to quiescence and death. The growing person has that matchless daring which has been the moving force in the great leaps forward in art, science, human affairs, and ordinary life.

The perspective of history. It is noteworthy that even the historian, with whom we normally associate the backward look, is not by any means fixated upon the past. Arnold Toynbee, who has spent a half-century in studying the past, is convinced that human affairs become intelligible only when they are seen as a whole — in the flow of time from past to present to emerging future. He sees all life, whether it be the world of the Mediterranean, the Italian Renaissance, or the death of the European community in 1914, as a more or less integrated whole. To him, history is not a collection of morsels, each minutely described and catalogued, but the movement of events in a larger whole. Although as a scholar he has the greatest intellectual stake in the world of the distant past, he cares a great deal about the emergent world of the future.[14] It is safe to assume that a similar passion for the unity and connectedness of time in history animates the scholarly lives of most historians; for who is in a better position than they to see in perspective the interpenetration of the past, present, and future in the lives of men.

---

[14] This concern for the vast movement of history is embodied in his multi-volume work published over a period of many years. See A. J. Toynbee, *A Study of History*, 10 vols. (New York: Oxford University Press, 1934–54).

The holistic view is as valid and productive in the study of history as it is in the investigation of the personality of man.

The Ironic Element

One's past can hold no surprises, for it is already completed; one's present is too immediate to cause more than a fleeting emotion; but the future can be full of astonishment and wonder. Human life is replete with examples of men who set out to search for one thing only to find something quite different. This principle of irony is usually attributed to the novelist Walpole, but it is of much older origin. This irony has been barbarized by the word *serendipity*, after Walpole's *Three Princes of Serendip,* who searched for one thing and found another. Goethe, in his *Wilhelm Meister,* likens Wilhelm Meister to Saul, the son of Kish, who, while searching for his father's asses, found a kingdom. Similarly, Nietzsche conceived life as a set of improvisations in which a goal, even when partially achieved, is lost sight of and new efforts toward the future are initiated. *Ich habe meine Gründe vergessen,* he wrote; "I have lost sight of my original aim." The search for goals, the expectation of tomorrow, is an intentional change made by the proactive individual with a view to seeing what will happen. If the results are different from those he expected, the proactivert will make the most of them. The irony of the future dimension lies in the fact that the ends we reach are often different from the goals for which we aspired. There is no evidence that the exploring ardor of Columbus, while searching for the far East and discovering America, was dampened at the unexpected turn of events. The human adventure rarely reaches its intended end.

At the same time, man's history demonstrates that ideas, innovations, the great forward movements of civilization, were born when men's aspirations outran their actualization. Man is the dreamer of dreams which find their realization only in a dubious and unpredictable tomorrow. The essence of all things unrealized is that their actualization may be disappointing. The stuff of all adventure is the courage to reach beyond the safe limits of the present and the changeless immortality of the past. Without adventure into the uncharted future, civilization sinks back into decay. Although the cynic is quick to show that there is a worm in every flower, the proactive individual knows that, with effort, he can realize perfection by successive approximations. Since he knows that the future can never complete itself, and that the end may differ from the ideal, man can, nevertheless, enjoy the whole world of life and thought and beauty, and these are inexhaustible.[15]

The irony of the future thus lies in the fact that, while man makes promises to it, it does not reciprocate. The future is ambiguous and uncertain. It is devoid of closure and completion. It is an adventure by which timid souls are terrified. It generates that creative anxiety by which men have always nerved themselves to surmount their self-inflicted limitations. It makes man self-affirmative without causing him to be self-willed.

THE WORLD OF VALUES

Nowhere in the temporal process of the human adventure does the future mode obtrude itself more sharply than in the world of values. Whether one defines a value as an interest, a preference, a collective norm, a hedonic satisfaction, or a *summum bonum*, it is always an *ideal* to someone. An ideal is invariably a state toward which we strive, a state of perfectibility, a thing in the process of becoming. An ideal cannot be satisfied, but only be the object of our striving. Whether the value for which one strives be the ideal of a full stomach or the perfection of one's being, each is psychologically the expression of anticipation. Anticipation, as we have said, is the envisioning of the future, of that which might be but is not yet. Accordingly, values cannot be understood — nor can they, indeed, exist — apart from their becoming, apart from their actualization in the future. And the greatest of all the values, the value that is basic to all values, namely, the freedom to be and to choose, is predicated, as we have shown in Chapters 4 and 5, on the temporal dimension of the future. The world as it was belongs to the past; the world as it is, to the present; and the world as it is coming to be (and in moral terms as it ought to be), to the future. The future, in brief, is the open sesame to whatever of himself each person can project into it.

The Place of Values in Psychology

It is sad to reflect on the fact that psychology, which has a greater stake in the problem of values than any other discipline — greater even than that of ethics — has deliberately excluded them from serious considerations.

The exclusion of values from psychology is based on an obsolete

[15] See H. Bonner, "The Proactivert: A Contribution to the Theory of Psychological Types," *J. Exist. Psychiat.*, 1963, *3*, 323–328.

conception of the nature of science. Claiming that science must exclude private or subjective knowledge, psychologists, in their determination to be scientific, have rejected values as legitimate objects for scientific investigation. Their reluctance to study values is increased by the disagreements regarding the nature of values, from ancient times to the present.

However, in view of the fact that nothing in the whole repertoire of behavior as truly embodies the humanness of human nature as values, their continued neglect in psychology is wholly unjustified. It is no longer practical nor sensible to study man exclusively by what he has achieved at any given time. In order to understand him in his fullness, we must also see what he is trying to become. Values do not exist *per se*, but as the striving of the human self. They are *qualities of persons*, not conditions of independent existence. If psychologists have seen fit to ignore values, it has been partly justified by their concern over the philosopher's tendency to give them an independent ontological status.

Values, then, are ends to be actualized and fulfilled, not conditions to be endured. Indeed, as we shall try to show in a later chapter, values show us man as striving toward perfection, toward actualization of himself. Perfection itself cannot be a static state, but a process of becoming. If striving for virtues is arduous, it is because they do not lie around to be appropriated. The facts of history and psychology are proofs that the chief ends of life are not given, but are values that each person must create himself. Although he will build his values partly on those of the past, he will transform them in the light of his character and in terms of future possibilities. Values are important in psychology because they make for significant differences in human relationships. If this were not so, man's centuries of struggle to actualize his values would be vastly more inexplicable than it is.

Psychology, then, must take values seriously, not only because values tell us what *ought* to be (a situation understandably outside the realm of science), but because they inform us about what *is*. Values are as real and indisputable as the descriptive facts of science; and they are more supremely relevant to human behavior than the homeostatic drives by which positivistic psychology has tried to replace them. Even if one reduces all values to "mere" appreciation, this affective process is nevertheless profoundly human and must be fully acknowledged. And in view of the markedly humanistic character of modern science, the distinction between factual description and personal appreciation, is wholly indefensible.

The most damaging consequence of the arbitrary separation of fact from value in psychology, is that it has emptied life of its dynamic content. Values are the silent and hidden potentials of behavior which men are perpetually trying to actualize. As such, they are important data in the science of psychology.

An increasing number of psychologists, aside from those with whom we have long associated an interest in human values (such as G. W. Allport, C. R. Rogers, and G. G. Thompson), are recognizing the role of values in human behavior. Students of perception and cognition know that these processes are influenced by the values and expectations which people project into them. Group dynamics has demonstrated that job-productivity is affected by the scheme of values which the worker carries around in his head. Every counselor of youth knows that one of the most crucial things in planning and pursuing a vocation, is the knowledge of the kind of future each person is trying to build for himself. Values lie in the realm of the possible, in the future of the human career. And finally, the conviction is daily increasing that psychotherapy, insofar as its fundamental objective is to aid the individual to find his authentic self, to actualize his potentialities, is successful because it unites with him in his helpless groping to find the meaning and value of his own existence. Client-centered therapy, existential analysis (*Daseinsanalyse*), and logotherapy, bear witness to the crucial role of values in the process of becoming a healthy person.[16]

The meaning of these observations is clear. If psychology is going to take man seriously, if it is going to transcend its self-imposed exclusion of his truly human attributes, it will have to dedicate itself once more to the study of human ideals. This task it cannot perform within the positivistic framework, for this framework is the very source of man's trivialization. Psychology must widen its horizon to permit us to view man as a self-directing, freely-choosing, value-creating individual. Anything less is a denial of that which is more.

Not least, psychology must rid itself of the pretense of disinterestedness. If it were attainable, it could serve as an evocative ideal, and so along with other ideals, act as a spur to psychological

---

[16] The literature on the newer psychotherapy is enormous. The following are suggested for a good introduction: V. E. Frankl, *Man's Search for Meaning: An Introduction to Logotherapy* (Boston: Beacon Press, 1962); R. May *et al.* (eds.), *Existence: A New Dimension in Psychiatry* (New York: Basic Books, Inc., 1958); C. R. Rogers, *On Becoming a Person* (Boston: Houghton Mifflin Company, 1961).

investigation. But in the realm of psychology, as in the natural sciences, it is an impossibility. Many natural scientists, as we have shown, admit this limitation. In psychology, it is a false and self-impairing idea. It presents us with a view of man as much less a person than an object to be investigated. Granted, man is no demigod, but neither is he a mere specimen. Like Prufrock, in T. S. Eliot's neglected poem, man refuses to be classified. Even though life has no meaning for him — or is it because of this? — Prufrock is horrified to think that, like a bug mounted on a collector's board, he has no real identity, but is merely like a stuck bug among other bugs. A proactive psychology is fully cognizant of the fact that every man, however much he is like other men, is unique and irreplaceable. Man joins in chorus the anguished cry of de Unamuno: "I do not want to let myself be classified."[17]

In conclusion, let it be said emphatically, that psychologists took the back road instead of the main highway, when they separated the study of human behavior from the process of human living. Human life is the pursuit of the possible, and the possible lies in the future. The future is never finished, but always in the making. It is, as someone has said, an infinity of unredeemed possibilities. There is nothing mystical or mysterious in this forward directedness; it contains no idea of man's "destiny," but of his opportunity. Destiny implies a push from behind, a determined fate, rather than a future of unlimited opportunities. Even one's history is not a fully deciding factor regarding one's future. History is the totality of other people's choices, not my own. These choices may serve as cues, not as guides, to conduct. Only my own decisions, born and matured in the crucible of my own experience and value-schema, can serve as a fit paradigm of forward movement in my own life. Nietzsche was right: only he who is building himself a future is fit to judge the past.

Conclusion

A psychology that neglects the future mode of the temporal process cuts itself off from the fullness of human nature. It limits itself to what has been, and neglects what will be. It has erred in believing that because becoming, self-actualization, striving for

17 M. de Unamuno, *Plenitud de Plenitudes y Todo Plenitud!* in *Obras Completas,* 5 vols. (Madrid: A. Aguado, 1951–52), vol. 3, p. 506. For Prufrock's plight, see T. S. Eliot, "The Love Song of J. Alfred Prufrock," in *Collected Poems,* 1909–35 (London: Faber and Faber, Ltd., 1943).

ideals which lie in the future, are literary and philosophical ideas, they have no place in scientific psychology. This is a prejudice, not a fact.

It is a fact of profound importance, that those people who made significant contributions to human civilization were essentially non-historical, people whose eyes were focused away from the past and in search of novelty. The ancient Greeks were the supreme examples. They were innovators, not copyists. They were adventurous, and they found excellence, not in a narrow reverence for older forms, but in the envisioning of the new. All creative work is characterized by the fact that the ideas which inform it are in the future, ahead of their actualization. Human personality, like a work of art, is always not quite. Anticipation of the future, although it generates anxiety, also brings pleasure. Anticipation of the future gives conduct its novel content, its individuality. Anticipation is the energizing element in the creative urge, the urge toward fulfillment in the future, the creative stage in the process of becoming a person. The voyage from the past through the present to the future, is the passage from stale abstraction to sheer repetition to emerging novelty.

In the perspective of biological evolution man, unlike all other animals, has broken forever with the past. The evidence from biology points unmistakably to the fact that man has not exhausted his possibilities. Psychologists must take the responsibility of seeing time in perspective. Although man has put the past behind him, he has not outgrown it. The vision and lure of the future are based on a true appreciation of the past and the present. We have grown accustomed to reading of biological mutations. It is now time to give serious attention to novelties in the human personality. Proaction, self-transformation, and self-actualization, are the novelties of human behavior. Although man cannot yet modify his genes, he has increased the number of the chromosome sets. Although man cannot produce geniuses at will he has the capacity of transcending those limitations which are not fixed. He can and does transform himself in the stream of his own becoming. In positing the primacy of self-fulfillment man is, through a long-term ethics, affirming the self-fulfillment of others. And in the end, the act of fulfilling himself as a person, is the only thing worth having.

7

*For only in the process of Becoming does the
form of life complete itself and the "eidos" of the
person become realized.*

V. E. GEBSATTEL

Being-in-Becoming

Πάντα ῥεί (panta rei) — all things flow — was the way Heraclitus,
of Ephesus, phrased it 2500 years ago. This truth has neither
tarnished nor faded in the long interim. However, there is a marked
difference in its modern meaning. Change takes place, the philosopher believed, according to a fixed law — the Logos, or divine
reason. But ours is the easier task, for we shall talk about becoming
in an entirely human context. Man's being, we shall show, consists in his becoming. What a man does depends on what he is;
yet, what he is depends on what he does; so that as Bergson said,
we are continually creating ourselves.[1]

All reality, then, and most profoundly the reality of the human
person, is a tendency, a potentiality, a becoming. The becoming
of a person involves the intrusion of the past into the present and
its transformation into novelty as it moves into the future.

A psychology of being is an important step toward a psychology
of the growing and self-actualizing person, but it is not enough.
Being is essentially a static concept; it implies that experience is
fixed and unchanging. The realization of being is not a process,
but implies the impossibility of further becoming. It is a situation
in which we can "predict" every act of behavior, for it has already
been achieved. Prediction and testing can be made only of that
which is "in being." However, the human person is in a constant
process of becoming, and as such cannot be adequately measured

[1] See H. Bergson, *L'Évolution Créatrice* (Paris: Librairie Felix Alcan,
1925), p. 7.

empirically. From the standpoint of a proactive, dynamic psychology, being must be defined as process, as *being-in-becoming*. Only in this way can we conceive man in the process of growth. Static psychology of being perceives man as the creature who has an overriding need for adjustment and accommodation. However, it is a commonplace that, basic to all achievements, is man's profound dissatisfaction with things as they are. The great moments in the history of human psychology, from Plato to the contemporary growth theories of human personality, have described human nature as always in the process of becoming. The view of man as a proactive being is nurtured in the belief in that which is not yet. It believes that, in a real way, what gives every person his being, his personality, is the person himself. Each creates his reality, his being in accordance with his vision of who he wants to be: *Es ist der Geist der sich den Körper baut.*[2] Each of us is a being in the process of becoming. Every act that we perform is, in William James' poetic idiom, a turning place where we can catch reality in the making.

STABILITY AND GROWTH

Everything that we say in this book cries out against the overwhelming tendency in all positivistic psychology to describe man entirely in the language of homeostasis. Man as a concupiscent animal, as a learning machine, as an adjustive mechanism — all these are but partial descriptions of the human being. The drive-reduction strait-jacket is so inclusive that even creative behavior is caught in its self-negating shackles. Thus a recent attempt to account for creative thinking would have us believe that it is related to *reward*. Thus the teacher is admonished to reward original thinking when it is produced in children, on the valid assumption that behaviors that are rewarded tend to persist.[3]

Encouraging children to think along novel lines is obviously

[2] It would take us beyond the limits of the present discussion, but it is important to call attention to the fact that American society is rapidly growing into a "becoming" culture, away from a "being" culture. See F. Kluckhohn, "Value Orientations," in R. R. Grinker (ed.), *Toward a Unified Theory of Human Behavior* (New York: Basic Books, Inc., 1956), pp. 83–93.

[3] See E. W. Eisner, "Education — The Role of Reward," in a paper given at the Education Conference for Gary School Personnel, as reported in *Tower Topics*, The University of Chicago, February 1964.

an important feature of all good education. But the reinforcement of original ideas tells us nothing about their origin. The view applies to creative thinking a principle that works effectively in the realm of learning and remembering somebody else's ideas, but does not account for the origin of new ones.

Homeostasis: Its Value and Limitation

One of the great dangers inherent in the current mechanistic approach to human behavior, is the exaggerated importance it attaches to the principle of equilibrium, or homeostasis. The static condition of modern psychology can in large measure be traced to this important idea. Its supremacy in the psychology of motivation has been pernicious, for it has reduced all human striving to the individual's effort to eliminate the discomforts inherent in his pursuit of a goal. That this is true of animals, and often of human beings, is certainly demonstrable. As a universal principle, however, it is insupportable and persists in psychology because it is consistent with its reactive and hedonic presuppositions. From this point of view, human life in all its aspects is the repetitive process of disequilibrium and repose. If a novel adjustment should creep into the process the result is but a readjustment to a new situation. The individual is really not projecting himself into an uncertain future, but responding to the past in a new setting.

Homeostasis is a physiological concept. It refers to the tendency of every organism to retain a "steady state" of energy, temperature, chemical organization, etc. When these features of the total physiological process are maintained in balance, the organism is healthy; when they are seriously unbalanced and no compensatory adjustments are available, it is sick; and when the interactive energies are completely disorganized, it is dead.

This marvelous arrangement of parts and functions to maintain the health and life of the organism, cannot fail to impress the sensitive spirit, be he scientist or untutored individual. Yet, it has nothing to do, except as an imaginative analogy, with the proactive life of the psychological individual. As a mode of describing the adjustive and protective impulses of the individual, the homeostatic analogy is convenient and useful, and it fits well the excessive demand for simplicity and economy. However, as a model for constructive behavior, it is wholly inadequate. It can tell us much about the nature of being, but next to nothing about the process of becoming: of man's hopes and dreams, aspirations and longings, dedications and commitments. Homeostasis is a static concept which conceals and distorts the essence of psychological growth and becoming.[4]

The Role of Tensions

The principle of homeostasis and the adjustment psychology to which it is intimately related, has its psychological analogue in contemporary motivation theory. Its extreme expression is found in the concept of drive-reduction. The theory of drive-reduction in behavior has been applied most widely to the learning process. According to this view, we learn because we are trying to satisfy desires, reduce tensions, and "seek" rewards. A drive is a stimulus to action, and when there is no drive, there can be no learning. But the drive alone is insufficient: in order to learn, the individual must respond to a selected stimulus; and for the learning to be more than momentary, it must be reinforced, or rewarded, for when there is no reward, the response will not be repeated. Furthermore, an act is repeated because it reduces the tension inherent in the drive, or need, and this reduction of tension gives pleasure to the individual. The pleasure itself is a reward, so that the individual repeats his response in anticipation of further pleasures or rewards.

The adequacy of the drive-reduction theory extends to the human personality only if we assume that personality is an organization of responses. It has value in giving us a partial view of the human personality, namely, a view of its external manifestations. It makes no provision for the proactive, self-affirming man, who is not only driven by hunger and other deficiencies, but as much, and often more, by the inner needs of love, beauty, reverence, and self-actualization.

But the theory is also self-contradictory. It holds that tension-reduction is pleasurable and hence reinforcing or rewarding. At the same time, it maintains that the reduction of tensions cannot strengthen the link between the selected stimulus and the response-induced tension, for this strengthening would cause the tension-reduction to reinforce the tension-producing response. Paradoxically, tension-reduction would increase tension!

Aside from this theoretical and logical difficulty, the theory of drive-reduction denies the constructive value of psychological ten-

---

[4] Perhaps neurophysiology can itself dispense with the homeostatic principle, for recent advances in brain physiology demonstrate that activity is inherent in the organism. The concept of equilibrium in this view is superfluous. See M. Arnold, *Emotion and Personality* (New York: Columbia University Press, 1960), vol. 1.

sions. The healthy human being is not as fearful of tensions and anxieties as reactive and adjustive psychology would have us believe. Proactive or humanistic psychology is finding increasing evidence in support of the view that man is not wholly — or even largely — a seeker of stability and quiescence. Peace of mind is a state desired by the less energetic, less healthy, less adventurous, and less self-propelling individual.

The healthy, proactive individual is able to cope productively with the world. Being motivated by ideals as well as by hungers and deficiencies, the healthy individual is perpetually "on the go." Ideals, like all human sentiments, are not like drives that can be satisfied, for they do not complete themselves. Ideals are not need-reductive, but tension-productive. Animals may indeed be driven by homeostatic needs, but human beings create and intentionally strive for their own ends. The proactive person is not disturbed by anxieties, although he has more than the average individual's share. In his dedication to the task of surpassing every moment of himself and every instant of reality, creative tensions are the catalysts of his forward movement.

There is no more difficult psychological process than the act of self-transformation. Yet, self-transformation is the end of all psychological growth, and the object of all creative psychotherapy. The healthy individual is not satisfied with changing only in the form of repeating what he already is, as the Freudian view would have us believe. Rather, he grows in the sense that he moves toward the values and ideals to which he has committed himself. This is the view of health derived from the practical work of Adler, Rogers, Frankl, and the far-flung representatives of existential psychology and psychiatry in Europe and in America.

It would be sheer folly to deny the destructive nature of many tensions and anxieties. The world is full of individuals who, while neither psychotic nor neurotic in the technical clinical sense, nevertheless suffer from crippling hatreds and anxieties. Psychosomatic medicine has established a close connection between unresolved tensions and physical illness. It has even found associations between types of personality and physical diseases. Thus, to take the most simple example, ulcers are found most frequently in tense, over-ambitious, hard-working, and repressive individuals, who find no satisfactory outlet for their frustrations and resentments.

At the same time, there are individuals with similar characteristics for whom tensions and anxieties hold no terror. They are able to direct their tensions into productive channels and face the problematic future with exultant anticipation. Many psychologists prefer not to take these individuals into account, for they challenge and even contradict the assumptions of drive-reduction and adjustment psychology. Non-Freudian and non-positivistic psychology and psychotherapy have demonstrated beyond a reasonable doubt, that the healthy human being is characterized by tension-sustainment and tension-inducement. Only neurotic tensions, which by definition are defensive and personality-impairing, are to be classified as abnormal and destructive. Only a life that contains strong elements of forward-directedness, and therefore of unknown and unpredictable events, can be said to be fully human. Healthy existence is not a comfortable state of homeostasis or inertia, but of striving and becoming. Growth is no mere unfoldment of inherent traits, but a creative transformation. This entails change, movement, and transcendence of the *status quo*. By its very nature, novelty disturbs and makes for *dis-ease*. This is the elementary meaning of the word disease. Mental disease, or serious dislocations in one's relation to the world, is basically a fear of the future, an impairing timidity regarding the actualization of one's potentiality.

Estrangement

In Chapter 3 we described in some detail the nature and source of alienation. Our concern there was largely with the separation of man from man, owing to the totalization and impersonalization of modern society. We showed that the depersonalization of modern life causes man to perceive the world as unfriendly and hostile. The meaninglessness of life generates mutual distrust, and most people become spiritually dispossessed.

Alienation, particularly self-estrangement, is also a condition in which man is separated from himself. Here the acceptant relation of the self to itself — the *Seinsverständnis* of existential psychology — is weakened or destroyed. This is not, however, the loss of the feeling of being, but of the sense of becoming. Its severest form is found in schizophrenics and compulsives.

The compulsive individual is immobilized by indecision and the incapacity of initiating action; or, having begun an act, is unable to carry it through to completion. He may enter his automobile, but having entered it, be unable to start the motor. He may even forget why he entered the car initially. Although he seems to be moving ahead in time, he is actually standing still. Completion of a task implies the process of becoming, a preparation to act in the emerging future. Self-actualization is here completely blocked, being fails in becoming. The person lives in a state of rigidity, unable to move forward. He is paralyzed by his past, and so cannot create for himself a future. To paraphrase Gebsattel's remark, the compulsive, not being master of time, is its slave.[5] Being a slave to his past, he is doomed merely to repeat it. Being begets more, yet the same, being, but is incapable of forward movement, of becoming. The person who is bound to his past cannot effectively participate in the process of becoming. He can affirm neither himself nor another, for affirmation is a potential act, the process of becoming. Since he cannot do either, he is estranged from himself and from others. Being bound to the past, that is, to his fixed habits, he moves away from both himself and others. The living of oneself and another is not a moment, not a being, but a process of becoming.

The neurotic person is profoundly deficient in the process of becoming an authentic person, of actualizing his potentiality, of self-acceptance and of entering into the self of another. Instead of actualizing himself, instead of freely exercising his spontaneity, he bogs down in a compulsive process of trying to *appear* other than he is. He constructs false beliefs regarding himself which he then must defend against exposure. Being more concerned to have others believe that he is perfect than striving to become better, the neurotic individual is the picture of insincerity. Self-deception is self-estrangement, the inability to accept oneself as a limited human being. Having no sense of himself as a person in the process of becoming, he is depressed by the defects of his being. He must continually reject and deny himself as he is, in the hope that people will accept him as he thinks he is. Since this deception is full of risks, and can never result in more than a fleeting success, the neurotic person is in a chronic state of tension. He remains at a psychological dead-center, repeating his mistakes and incapable of unimpeded growth and creative becoming.

The estrangement from self and others is maximized by the fact that every neurotic has only the vaguest conception of his temporal orientation. His life is not only without meaning but it lacks the resources for making it meaningful. He lives by values which he thinks others want him to accept, seldom by his own. He has only

[5] V. E. von Gebsattel, "The World of the Compulsive," in R. May *et al.* (eds.), *Existence: A New Dimension in Psychiatry and Psychology* (New York: Basic Books, Inc., 1958), p. 185.

the vaguest self-image, and may even disown his own feelings. In many cases he may be so fully alienated from himself that he cannot accept his own body. He rejects it by means of neglect, thus presenting an appearance of untidy disarray. What is more natural than to renounce that for which you have no love and cannot approve. When self-feeling is blunted, we cannot measure our capacity for becoming. We can experience neither joy nor sorrow, for these are expressions of spontaneity and growth.

In this validation of his false self, the self that he wants others to think he is, he plays a continuously diminishing role in his own becoming. Since he cannot accept himself as he really is, he has no springboard, no initial base, from which to project his life into a propitious future. In this objectifying of his inner life, the neurotic has thrown away his inner resources, leaving him only the empty feeling that he is nobody himself. The feeling of unreality which is characteristic of most neurotics, is a hazy manifestation of self-rejection. The *Seinsverständnis,* the acceptance by each of his selfhood, becomes highly *impersonal,* devitalizing, and dehumanizing. This is the root of that blunting of feeling and perceptiveness behind the facade of pseudo-joyfulness, excessive exuberance, and false-imperturbability, that are the hallmarks of every dwarfed and stunted personality.

The subject is too vast to pursue further. It may be summarized by saying that the person in whom the force of becoming has been blocked or hindered, is a person without a sense of direction. His lack of direction results in anxiety and often in a compliance to directions imposed upon him by others. Self-reliance, initiative, and responsibility for his own actions are grossly impaired. He is not a determining agent in his own life.

Becoming and Proactive Psychology

Clearly, our stress on temporality in this book, especially on the future mode, is justified when we examine the process of being-in-becoming, the process of growth and coming-to-be what one is able to become. Becoming, like the flow of time itself, is not a mere immersion in the temporal stream, but a condition of growth or development. The future is not empty, merely because it is not yet; on the contrary, it is full of possibilities. Insofar as existence, or being, consists in its becoming, becoming is like the future dimension itself, the primary phenomenon of nature, both material and human. "The primary phenomenon of the original and authentic temporality," we agree, "is the future, and the future in turn is the primary meaning of existentiality. . . ."[6] In the process of becoming, each man can cleanse himself of his past, rectify his mistakes, and attentuate the guilt of having failed to actualize his potentialities. Becoming thus bestows upon each of us a special elegance and grace, that dignity which comes to us from the knowledge that we are not victims, but architects, of fate. There is something sad in the bondage to the past and the constant leaning upon the person of another for one's fulfillment, in the failure to actualize one's inner strengths, the strengths which are realized in the process of adventure and in the encounter with becoming.[7]

Becoming, we have said, is the process in which being grows and becomes actualized. It cannot be studied by orthodox empirical methods. This fact is a challenge, not a disappointment. In conventional psychology we are afraid of the obscure and intangible, and so we are doomed to deal with the surface of life instead of its inwardness. We are so strongly biased in favor of the mensuration technique that we neglect those features of the human person which can be probed, for the time being at least, only in the language of art, imagery, and metaphor. Much of the penetrative power of psychoanalysis and existential psychology lies in their bold and imaginative use of literary and poetic conceits. Life at its core is not a visceral process that can be encapsulated in a formula, but a suffering and enthrallment. The depth of the human spirit reveals itself most elementally in joy and tragedy, not in learning and memory. That "tragic sense of life" of which de Unamuno spoke feelingly though obscurely, that anguished gratuity which he sensed in the finitude of life, he could express only in the language of feeling. Yet the truth of man's suffering and uniqueness is not marred or compromised by his affective idiom, but is supremely enhanced by it.[8]

---

[6] L. Binswanger, "The Case of Ellen West: An Anthropological-Clinical Study," in R. May *et al., op. cit.,* p. 302.

[7] We believe that empirical investigation would reveal that children, who are not yet overburdened with crippling habits, who are still full of wonder and openness to experience, provide testimonial to the indestructibility of the *open self*. Studies bearing upon the durability of the children evacuated from bombed London in the 1940's, and young survivors of the Nazi concentration camps, are provisional confirmation of this hypothesis.

[8] See M. de Unamuno, *Del Sentimiento Trágico de la Vida,* in *Obras Completas* (Madrid: A. Aguado, 1951–52), vol. 4.

On Becoming Oneself

In describing the neurotic facade of the individual whose becoming has been blocked, it was stated that he is immobilized or stunted in his forward movement by the compulsion to appear different from what he is. His defense of the self prevents him from actualizing his potentialities and makes him inauthentic and insincere.

However, the overwhelming evidence from proactive psychotherapy, the mode of psychic aid which stresses fulfillment and renewal, leaves no doubt in one's mind that the primary striving of the individual is toward increasing self-affirmation and self-validation. The impulsion toward health is the striving to become oneself. In the "loving" relationship between the person in distress and the helping individual, the former gradually renounces the facade behind which he concealed himself and becomes increasingly independent. Becoming means change in a forward direction, away from the past. In psychotherapy the individual dares once more to become himself, to transcend the crippling power of his inauthenticity, his insincerity. The fearful, harassed, and ingratiating individual, bent on wheedling for love and acceptance, soon discovers that he can achieve his goal most securely by becoming himself, rather than by being what he believes others desire him to be. There are fewer despairs more unbearable than the desperation of failing to become oneself.

Here again, the insights and discoveries of existential and individual-centered therapies must be acknowledged in validation of the view that a constructive forward thrust is deeply embedded in every individual. Psychological sickness consists in the blockage of the process of becoming oneself. Having witnessed the process of change from helplessness and despair to independence and self-confidence in the psychotherapeutic setting, we are deeply impressed by the powerful urge of every individual to extend himself beyond the inhibiting present. And this holds for group therapy as well as individual treatment.[9]

Potentialities

The supremacy of the concept of homeostasis has interfered, as we have shown, with the vision of man as a self-transforming

[9] The growth toward independence is sharply evident in group psychotherapy, where an individual may rapidly show a reduction of timidity and ingratiation in the presence of other individuals who may even be censurious and disapproving.

individual. The emphasis on being is creating a similar difficulty. Being is a static concept which leaves no room for the process of growth.

Growth and becoming free the human individual to realize his inner potentialities. The healthy individual is free to deviate from former modes of behavior. This is the meaning of growth and becoming. Becoming is thus the process of actualizing potentialities, of fulfilling one's own being. Any interference with this process may lead to stunting or neurosis.

The affirmation of one's potentialities is not a self-centered denial of the potentialities of another person, but the courage to be oneself as a person, to use Tillich's phrasing. Self-affirmation is the healthy assertion of one's own individuality, one's capacity for becoming different from what we have been.

We believe that Goldstein is much closer to the truth than the advocates of homeostasis, when he affirms that the fundamental tendency in the healthy human organism is self-actualization.[10] In the language of potentiality and becoming, this means that the healthy individual is deeply motivated to live out his inner potentialities, and to fulfill himself as a person. Creativity, as we shall see in Chapters 10 and 11, is not confined to special abilities, such as those in art and music, but is characteristic of the healthy proactive individual. It refers to man's impulse to achieve optimal performance and to deal productively with his environment.

The person who fears his own becoming, who seeks safety in sameness, stability, and routine, denies his own capacity for growth. He is motivated by the drive for self-preservation, which conventional psychology has thoroughly exploited in its description of the adjusted individual. With Goldstein, we believe self-preservation is the neurotic style, not the way of the proactive individual. Self-preservation impairs the possibility of "further ordered activity." We have already rejected the Freudian and behavioristic argument that life is directed by the need to release tension. Indeed the healthy individual enjoys the "pleasure of tension." Potentialities are unrelieved tensions, and insofar as becoming is the process of externalizing potentialities, it is a tension-inducing as well as tension-reducing event.

Becoming as the process of externalizing one's potentialities is tension-inducing for still another reason: it is difficult, because it is

[10] See K. Goldstein, *The Organism* (New York: American Book Company, 1939), p. 197.

never completed. It is a continuous process of facing novelty, uncertainty, and ambiguity. To meet a constantly changing situation requires both imagination and courage. It is not the way of the timid or the faint-hearted, but that active state of mind which is always eager to explore the outermost limits of the human adventure. It is not a life, but a living; not a finding, but a seeking. The neurotic individual maximizes his illness in failing to actualize his potentialities. No one, of course, achieves the fullness of his being, and in this failure each of us stands guilty before the process of becoming. But the neurotic person's guilt is acute because he is more greatly remiss. Immobilized by the fear of moving forward, he remains unproductive, his hidden powers lying dormant and unutilized. Guilt results from the failure to actualize one's potentialities, from failing to live up to the fullness of the being with which we are endowed. In failing to use his capacity of becoming, the individual stands in debt to himself, a debt that he cannot honor because, in denying his becoming, he has no resources left. He is empty, void of all power and will. This is neurotic guilt, and it differs from productive guilt, the guilt that impels us to use our potentialities, in that neurotic guilt is repressed and denied. Confronted guilt, as some existentialists call it, leads to a creative use of one's basic endowments.[11]

The Self as Being-in-Becoming

In a long chapter on the self, the writer argued against the conception of the self as a mere learning process described in terms of an individual's expectancy. In its place, he suggested that the self can be described more meaningfully by considering the individual's *intentions*.[12]

The self is not a being, but a process; an enduring, but constantly changing individual. It is not a set of conditioned or learned responses merely, but more significantly, a mode of action directed toward the future. "It is directional as well as reactive; future-oriented as well as adjustive."[13] Murphy has phrased it well when he described the self as *something to be realized*.[14]

---

[11] The concepts of self-indebtedness, and repressed or "unconfronted" guilt, are analyzed at length by the Swiss psychiatrist, Boss. See M. Boss, *Psychoanalyse und Daseinsanalytik* (Stuttgart: Hans Huber, 1957).
[12] H. Bonner, *Psychology of Personality* (New York: The Ronald Press Company, 1961), Ch. 16.
[13] *Ibid.*, p. 464.
[14] G. Murphy, *Personality: A Biosocial Approach to Origins and Structure* (New York: Harper and Bros., 1947), p. 539.

The important process of self-enhancement clearly argues for the self as a becoming. Self-defense is a static condition, the preservation of equilibrium. Self-enhancement, on the other hand, refers to man's aspirations, and human aspirations, we have stated, have no fixed terminus. It is well known that when the healthy individual has reached an intended goal his standard of performance is raised higher. His level of aspiration increases as he strives forward toward a goal. Although the term "level of aspiration" was introduced by Tamara Dembo, the process was described by Goethe, Nietzsche, and William James.

Clearly, then, man desires not only safety and security, but the exultation that comes from adventure and the search for novelty. He has been known to abandon security for the risk of achieving greater fulfillment and a higher level of self-integration. The facts of creative psychotherapy are proof of the self-propulsive nature of the human organism. They show that a self that lacks the wish and the energy to move forward is a sick self. The healthy individual knows that although death will eventually put a quietus upon his forward striving, while he lives, he does not permit himself to sink into stagnation. Healthy psychological life is one in which a continual change of tension impels the individual to actualize himself in a constant process of becoming more and more what he has the capacity for achieving.

A fascinating aspect of this becoming is that the person who *cares* for the becoming of another person is himself swept along by the other's self-actualization. Parents who are more concerned with their children's self-affirmation than with their own egotism and vanity; or therapists who exult more in the startling growth of the impaired individual than in the heightening of their own professional reputation, can give us testimonials to a mutual growth and becoming. Each is directed forward by the becoming of the other. It is this mutuality as well as the sacrificial nature of creative human relationships, that lends to self-affirmation its other-mindedness.

"Measurement" of Becoming

The tough-minded positivist quickly grows impatient with the subjective nature of the foregoing description. However, although we are not easily troubled by his criticism, and although our intentions are less "scientific" than the attainment of a humanistic grasp of man's inner nature, it is possible to confirm the validity of the process of becoming. In the discussion of the self-anchored methodology in Chapter 1, and of Stephenson's centrality-of-self technique, we briefly indicated the dependability of these modes of procedure. Every individual reveals his inner self in the statements which he makes about himself. Every conversation, every interview, every transaction between persons in psychotherapy, is part-descriptive of the individual's inner tendencies. Every statement is a self-description, an indication of how the individual perceives himself as a person. Thus, the individual may say, "I am afraid of women," "I don't trust men," "I think I am intelligent," "I like privacy," or "I am terrified of loneliness."

Using Stephenson's method called "Q-sort" technique, one may present many self-descriptions on cards to a person and ask him to sort them out in accordance with their descriptions of himself as he perceives himself at the moment.

Carl Rogers used this technique with clients before and after therapy. The clients' sortings were then intercorrelated. A high correlation between two sortings indicated little or no change, whereas a low correlation indicated a marked degree of change.[15]

Becoming, when measured as a change in an individual's perception of himself as a person, is a real phenomenon, not the philosophical reflection of an undisciplined observer. Existential thought, proactive psychology, and scientific method thus find congruence in a humanistic view of man as a being-in-becoming. This congruence characterizes the scientific and humanistic approaches at their best — the best, however, which is still not widely understood. Helen Sargent, as reported by Rollo May, has put the matter trenchantly when she said, "Science offers more leeway than graduate students are permitted to realize."[16]

CONCLUSION

The process of being-in-becoming is the fusion of two aspects of existence which have intrigued scientific thinkers from the beginning of science, in the teachings of Thales and Heraclitus, namely, the being of Thales and the becoming of Heraclitus. The uninformed individual will object to this integrated process on the ground that, not being observable by means of the senses, it is not

---

[15] See C. R. Rogers, *On Becoming a Person* (Boston: Houghton Mifflin Company, 1961), Ch. 11. For a detailed description of the "Q-sort" technique, see W. Stephenson, *The Study of Behavior* (Chicago: The University of Chicago Press, 1953).

[16] R. May (ed.), *Existential Psychology* (New York: Random House, Inc., 1961), p. 37.

an object of scientific investigation. This objection is contradicted by the entire history of science. The process of becoming, like potentiality itself, though unobservable is a bona fide phenomenon. Both are legitimate concepts in contemporary quantum theory. Indeed, we are indebted to quantum theory for having once more legitimized the concept of potentiality, of the power of becoming.

Being-in-becoming is not, however, a mere abstraction, but a living, ongoing process of human growth. It is not a "force" or "drive," or a similar mechanistic concept, but a holistic process. It does not describe the merely adjusting person, but the self-affirming individual. There is danger in the orthodox view of buying homeostasis and adjustment at the price of the growing human being.

In conventional psychology, both psychoanalytic and behavioristic, the individual is almost entirely described in the framework of pleasure-seeking, tension-reduction, and survival. In proactive psychology, on the other hand, man is seen as the seeker after values which he sets up himself. From this point of view, more important than tranquility, security, and survival is the individual's desire to fulfill himself as a unique person. If man should ever destroy himself as a unique self, he will do it by blocking himself off from encounter with growth and novelty.

The healthy man knows that he cannot rely on his past, for there is no certainty that the future will resemble it. Indeed, what he learns from the past is that the future cannot be like it. And so he meets the future exultantly, instead of remaining in bondage to a psychological dead-center.

As one reflects on these matters in the light of orthodox psychology, one has the uneasy feeling that the normal person whom it describes and praises in the standard literature, is but the ordinary, inauthentic individual who conforms to the standards and norms of life and psychology, so that we fail to see him as the drab and crippled individual that he is. Truly, many psychologists are facile in deluding themselves and the public with honorific words and technical abstractions.

Finally, mild and moderate neurotic symptoms are the lot of every one of us. Generally speaking, when our interest is in the study of neurosis, knowledge of a person's past is of value; but when our interest is in psychological health, the individual's past recedes into relative unimportance, and the future, toward which he is becoming, transcends all bondage to the past. What is broadly called creativeness or productiveness, results when the individual frees himself from rigid habitual sets and actualizes his

inner potentialities. In this sense all creative behavior is a process
of becoming, be it in the form of artistic production, scientific
investigation, or the making of one's character.

And so we return once more to the beginning: there is no such
thing as holding nature still and looking at it. While each of us
may want to crystallize some fleeting moment, it passes on. In this
lies the poignancy of all life, the moment that cannot, though we all
long for it, be immortalized: *Erwart' nur Augenblick, du bist so
schön!* ("Stay, O moment, thou art so fair!"), as Goethe expressed it.

8

Love is the only way to grasp another human being in the innermost core of his personality.

VIKTOR E. FRANKL

Love and Sensibility

Love and freedom have a paradoxical relation to each other. Love is the giving of oneself to another, an act that implies limitation of one's self-affirmation. At the same time self-actualization, the realization of one's inner life, can be achieved only through communication with another. Alienation, while never completely transcended, because of every man's uniqueness, is made bearable by man's relatedness to others. Through love, through sensibility, or the power of comprehending another person sympathetically, the unique and solitary individual can at last surmount the psychic wall that separates him from the being of another. The creative power of love lies essentially in this vitalization of the lonely individual by creating for him another individual. Through love and sensibility each individual is enabled to participate in the subjectivity of another person. They create for two individuals a common bond of feeling and comprehension, a "we," or *coexistence*, as Martin Buber has called it. In love, two individuals see the world separately, because each is unique, yet they share it in common. Each dignifies the other by sharing with him his precious personality. Each rescues the other from the indignity of anonymity by personalizing him. The man of sensibility relates himself to the other, not as subject to object, but as person to person. Love so conceived is neither a function nor a reaction, but an act of concern, *Sorge*, or αγάπη (*agape*).[1]

---

[1] This is the language of existentialism which describes most sharply the meaning of love. *Sorge* is Heidegger's term, and it means to care, or take responsibility, for another person. The psychiatrists Binswanger and Boss use the term in their respective writings. *Agape* is a Greek word which describes selfless concern or devotion.

The Loving Encounter

Love, we have said, is neither a function nor a reaction, and the stimulus-response paradigm reduces it to absurdity. Love is not a mere reaction to another person, although it has reactive components. It is a searching, a reaching out, for the person of another. It is an encounter with the other "as he is." For this reason we use its adjectival form, as Fromm does in his *The Art of Loving*. But even in this form, the term does not convey the act of *engagement*, or *encounter*, with the inwardness or subjectivity of another person.[2] The loving encounter is free of manipulation and exploitation. Man's sensibility, his sensitive regard for the dignity of the other person, impels him to participate in the latter's being without trying to change it. Change, nevertheless, there will be; for the mutuality of an encounter absorbs something of the life of each, so that each is to a degree modified by the other. This tempering of one by the other, as well as the attenuation of the loneliness induced in man by his uniqueness, is an eloquent testimony to love's creativity.

Love and Solitude

Man's alienation, we have frequently said, is immanent in his nature as a unique being. His aloneness, his solitariness, is an attribute of his being, not a deliberate isolation or separation from his fellow human beings. In love, as in religious devotion in its profoundest meaning, man is at once bound and forsaken. He loves himself in his aloneness and participates in the being of another. Love is the fusion of that which is mine and that which is another's. Being-as-oneself is united with being-as-the-other. My aloneness is thus limited by my loving encounter with another, and the dread which solitude induces is mitigated by the other's concern for my own being. The widespread loneliness and boredom in contemporary life are due to a weakening or break of the encounter in which each person validates and dignifies the subjectivity of the other, making it "real" and "objective."

The reality and objectivity of love, clearly, are not conditions that empirical or positivistic psychology can establish. The loving encounter is not a causal relation between two individuals, but an affective experience that is immediately felt. It is an invocation, an

---

[2] The term encounter (*rencontrer*) as we think of it, is frequently used by Marcel. See G. Marcel, *Du Refus à l'invocation* (Paris: Librairie Gallimard, 1950).

entreaty, a summons to share in and care for the individuality of the other.

Love and Selfishness

It is to Fromm's great credit that he has pushed through the wall of prejudice to call attention to what every loving person knows to be an indubitable fact, namely, that self-love and love of others make an indivisible whole. Selfishness and self-love are widely confused, but they are not identical. Although the selfish person does not love others, neither does he love himself.[3] His behavior resembles the neurotic insincerity which we discussed in the preceding chapter. The highly selfish person must at all times appear to be unselfish. He thus engages in pseudo-altruism, practicing self-abnegation in the eager hope of being mistaken for a self-sacrificing person. However, he is never convinced by his own practices, as witnessed by the fact that his "selflessness" earns him neither love nor spontaneous acceptance.

"Love thy neighbor as thyself," is not the mystical utterance of an oracle, but a stubborn fact of life. It affirms the great truth that self-hatred and self-renunciation are destructive forces that make love of others impossible. Much pious nonsense has been uttered concerning the "evil" of self-love. Freud's concept of narcissism has been invoked in establishing the negative effect of self-love. Let it be said in defense of Freud's doctrine that narcissism at a certain stage of life is normal, and is an integral part of Freud's libido theory, not an evaluation of the libidinal process. Freud's error lay in quantifying psychosexual energy, and in contending that the more libidinal energy is invested in another, the less the person has left to confer upon himself. Love of another deprives one of love for oneself, and vice versa. This libidinal calculus becomes absurd in light of the fact that love is a manner of relating oneself to others and to oneself, not an economic transaction. It is a psychic encounter between persons, not an expenditure of quanta of energy. It is an active concern for the growth of another person, in which the existential "I" is transformed into the coexistential "we." Love is, in short, the acceptant relation of the self to itself and to others.

As is true of every bold and original thinker, Freud was not altogether consistent. This is fortunate for psychoanalysis, for it redeems Freud's concern with libidinal investment from being but

[3] See E. Fromm, *Man For Himself* (New York: Rinehart and Company, 1947), Ch. 3 and 4.

another shallow description of "animal" selfishness. Freud, no less than the existentialists and ourselves, recognized the sacrificial nature of love, not only its neurotic selfishness. Readers of Freud's ideas are often misled by his dramatic description of the vigor of libidinal striving, and fail to grasp his intention of showing that genuine love is concerned with the well-being of the loved one. And yet, in fairness to his many readers, it must also be stated that Freud's concern for "productive love" was more often implied than expressly affirmed. At any rate, it is not an integral part of his libido theory.

However, the haunting question persists: Was Freud himself deficient in the loving encounter? Freud did not display in his own human relationships a humble acceptance of others. His intolerant relations with his early colleagues is well chronicled. His relations with his wife were largely those of indifference and superiority. Ernest Jones has informed us well in this regard, describing it not as a defect, but as consistent with the mores of the European society in Freud's day.[4] Compared with such profoundly compassionate men as Mohandas Gandhi and Albert Schweitzer, Freud occupies only a secondary position.

It is not difficult to find evidence in the lives of men of character and achievement, of the important role of self-love. President John F. Kennedy placed great importance on it in his interesting study of several distinguished Americans. They did what they did, he said, not because they "loved the public better than themselves,'" but "precisely because they did *love themselves* — because each one's need to maintain his own respect for himself was more important to him than popularity with others . . . because his conscience, his personal standard of ethics, his integrity or morality . . . was stronger than the pressure of public disapproval. . . ."[5]

Self-love, then, is not selfishness, but that high respect for oneself which is the mark of the healthy, self-confident, and loving individual. As with so many human characteristics, self-love is a trait of character; the belief in the rightness of one's own self-image.

Love and Guilt

Paradoxically, love is at once the most fragile and the most durable of human feelings. Although it is the most perdurable of

---

[4] See E. Jones, *The Life and Work of Sigmund Freud*, 3 vols. (New York: Basic Books, Inc., 1953), vol. 1.
[5] J. F. Kennedy, *Profiles in Courage* (New York: Pocket Books, Inc., 1963), p. 203.

experiences, it can be mortally wounded. Tenderness is by its very nature vulnerable. No *ad hoc* argument designed to defend its alleged imperishability, has been altogether successful. Even when it survives all the vicissitudes of life, it can be haunted by guilt and unfulfillment. There is no justification in the *post facto* argument that, when love failed, it was not "genuine" love initially. It is precisely because love is the deepest encounter between individuals that it is also the source of the most tragic of human sorrows. The loneliness and despair of unrequited love have been life's most tragic events and the stuff of its most magnificent art.

These, however, are love's more dramatic moments, not its prosaic recurrences. The loving encounter is essentially a call by the other that I heed his entreaty, that I answer his wish to be a part of my own experience. It calls for an openness of myself to the openness of the other self, of a mutual participation in each other's inner experience, in active acceptance and confirmation by each of the other.

But this fragile exchange between two persons is hampered, and easily destroyed, by *egocentricity* and *insensibility*. Although self-love is not to be identified with selfishness, and although it is essential to genuine love for others, when it becomes the inability to free myself from my own subjectivity, its outward direction is seriously blunted. I cannot then introject my own subjectivity into the subjectivity of the other. We are cut off from each other as persons and sink back into factitious objects.

Egocentricity. This self-centeredness is quite different from Freud's concept of narcissism. That condition, we saw, is described in quantitative terms, the condition in which the narcissistic individual cannot love another because his libido is invested exclusively in himself.[6]

In egocentricity as it is here understood, I close the door to the subjectivity of the other. I am blinded to the other's subjectivity by my refusal to accept the other as a person in my own world. I shut him out from my selfhood; I make him an object for manipulation and control. Self-centeredness feeds on domination of the other. It is a power-relationship, not a mutual sharing of subjectivity. Nothing destroys the tenderness of love more quickly and lastingly, than the subjection of the other person to the status of a thing. Love is

---

[6] We have translated Freud's word, *Besetzung,* quite literally, as the process of *investing* the libido in oneself.

a mutual encounter, we have said, and in the absence of mutuality, it becomes a state of indifference, unconcern, and insensibility.

Self-centeredness destroys love also because it does not nourish trust. When I reduce the other person to an object of manipulation, I create fear within him. When he is afraid, he must be vigilant and on guard against my exploitation. He cannot accept my proffer of love at face value. Instead, he weighs it in the light of its possible curtailment of his precious freedom. Love, freedom, trust — these are inseparable qualities in every creative encounter.

Insensibility. The loving encounter is broken also, we have said, by insensibility. Insensibility is not only an absence of feeling for the other individual, but a moral irresponsibility toward him. When I fail to make the other's subjectivity my own, relatedness to him is impossible. There is no loving encounter between us, but merely an unfeeling symbiosis. We are each to the other not as a united self-process, but somewhat like a fungus adhering to an alga. Each is indifferent to the being of the other.

In this connection we cite Sartre's well-known analysis. According to this writer, I become aware of the other person when I discover that he is looking at me. The other person's stare (*le regard*) makes me conscious that there is another person in the world and that in his look he is making an object of myself, thus destroying my subjectivity. Thereafter, there is nothing left for me to do but to outstare him, to subjugate him and make him the object of my attention. I can regain my subjectivity only by preventing him from outstaring me in turn.[7]

Although Sartre's fascinating analysis accounts for the initial engagement of two selves, it scarcely goes beyond the impersonal interest of a subject in an object. The more one stares at the other, the more he makes of him an object to be manipulated. Neither "owes" anything to the other; neither shares with the other a feeling that is more than a sharp awareness of the other's embarrassment, as each contemplates the other's discomfiture and determination to control him. The relationship is one of mutual insensibility, an absence of responsibility and mutual concern.

Egocentricity and insensibility are sources of moral guilt. We are guilty because in our engagement with another self we have shown indifference and egocentricity, the two powerful inhibitors of productive love. We are guilty because we failed to actualize the great reservoir of potential love that is characteristic of the human

[7] See J.-P. Sartre, *L'Être et le Néant* (Paris: Gallimard, 1943).

species. We are guilty because we have denied our sociality; for when we think of man, we think also of other men, of whom we are representatives. We are guilty because in manipulating the other person to our own advantage, we are promoting ourselves at the price of the other person's subjectivity. We have turned a human value into an impersonal fact.

Man has the quality of being other men, the quality of togetherness implicit in the "I and thou" relationship, the *ich und du*, of Buber's coexistentialism. When man denies this quality in himself, he denies his humanness and the humanness of other individuals, and implicitly, of humanity itself. For this nihilism, man is alienated from himself as well as others. He is guilty because in this negation of humanity he has affirmed nothingness, or non-being, as the primary existence. No greater hate has man than to affirm himself by destroying the self of another. The price of human manipulation, indifference, and insensibility is alienation, guilt, and hate; and as Congreve put it, heaven has no rage like love to hatred turned.

Love and Self-love

We have already made clear that love and self-love form an indivisible unity. Like all paradoxes, the paradox of love is made meaningful when we transcend its conventional meaning. Every loving encounter has implicit in it a dependence on the other person. This dependence consists in the anticipation of love from the other person. This anticipation is an entreaty to the other person that he validate my own subjectivity, that I am worthy of his concern and care. I am seeking to find myself, to validate myself, in the person of the other individual. I desire to complete myself in the other's acceptance of me as an authentic person. I need him in order to forestall a threatened loneliness. In entrusting myself to him, I am counting on his fidelity to myself, on his trustworthiness. I know that my own selfhood is not completely autonomous, but exists only in a field of other selves. The other person's self is open and accessible to me, as I am open and accessible to him. My self-actualization and self-fulfillment are dependent on the freedom of others to actualize themselves. I know that if I deny the freedom of the other to achieve his selfhood, I am universalizing the process of negation. I thus love the other person in order to safeguard my own freedom and independence. Insofar as this is a matter of fact, a completely selfless love is a human impossibility. Love and self-love are interdependent.

THE SEXUAL ENCOUNTER

It is difficult to maintain one's poise when confronting the subject of sex, for it is encapsulated in hoary tradition, religious dogma, and romatic sentimentality. Like hunger and thirst, it is at once primal and universal; but unlike either one, it has been mutilated far beyond the limits of good sense. In Western society, particularly in America, it has been discussed as *Sex*, a psychobiological state that seems to be leading an isolated life of its own. Psychologists, as relative newcomers to its investigation, prefer to call it sexual behavior; and as if to compensate for their belated efforts, they have published handbooks and encyclopedias — a forbidding amount of labor on a relatively simple subject. Thus, to mention the latest and in some ways the most formidable effort, we cite *The Encyclopedia of Sexual Behavior*, a two-volume publication on every conceivable aspect of sexual behavior, ranging from abortion to venereal disease, some of which has little or nothing intimately to do with sex as a mode through which two people participate in each other's subjectivity.

In the empirical thoughtways of contemporary investigations, be-they those of Kinsey, the biologist, or the above-mentioned compilation of two psychologists, sex is largely a measurable output. It is not our intention to disparage these efforts, for as informative descriptions of sexual *behavior*, these and similar publications have an important educational value; and insofar as they help to dispel in the reader the superstitions and tribal misinformation with which he is generously supplied, and give him a feeling of confidence in his own sexual encounters, they are of inestimable practical value.

The Dogma of Sex

Freud has been both praised and maligned for his views of sex in the life of man. The purists who identify sex with evil have blamed Freud for the loosening of sexual morals and the degeneration of contemporary life. The "liberals," who believe that sexual practices are individual preferences, have credited Freud with promoting sexual sanity and the sexual emancipation of the individual. The first is contradicted by Freud's own observation that sexual repression and frustrations are the prices that man must pay for the growth of civilization. The second is weakened by the fact that the changed outlook on sexual behavior was accelerated, if not initiated, by the moral upheavals of the first World War and its disturbing aftermath. There is, however, a third explanation, as undramatic as it is true. This explains the change as a consequence of the generally skeptical and debunking spirit inhering in the modern way of living. In the face of these observations it is more plausible to credit Freud with creating a more enlightened moral atmosphere — in itself an achievement of the greatest significance and magnitude.

When we speak of the dogma of sex, therefore, we do not refer to its physiological and social attributes in the life of society, but to its place in the psychic economy of men. Specifically we ask, what is the nature of the sexual encounter, and what do our answers tell us about human nature?

We must dispose at once of the unwarranted but widely believed charge that Freud's conception of sex was that it is mostly sensual, having no concern with the welfare of the sexual partner. However, what makes his view not fully acceptable is the pan-sexualism which it established. In this, Freud committed the particularistic error common to monistic accounts of complex behavior. In Freud's view, libido, or psychosexual energy, is the motivating influence in all behavior, from the love of a parent for his child and the lover's attraction to his mistress, to the transference-relation between the therapist and his patient. There is no indubitable criterion in this view for distinguishing the qualitative differences among the sexual modes. In trying to distinguish them one is troubled by the uneasy feeling that Freud's view explains far too much.

We remain unconvinced, for neither moral nor aesthetic reasons, but on the ground of universal experience. Should someone advance a valid argument to prove that sex is the most carnal of human acts, we would be ready to accept even this most radical statement with that sense of triumph which accompanies every important discovery. But neither fact nor human experience support the belief that we are all driven by libidinal energy manifesting itself in different modes of expression. Pan-sexualism, however much it may be hedged by self-confirming arguments, retains a basic implausibility. Love is manifested in a variety of forms, of which coitus is by no means the least laudable. On the contrary, it is one of the great life-affirming experiences of mankind. Like every loving encounter, the sexual engagement of two persons is a supremely binding psychic activity. In the sexual encounter each person enhances the life of the other, greatly enriching the resulting community of persons.

Sexual love is never self-sustaining. For its full actualization, it is dependent upon other human activities. Isolated from the rest of life, as it is in the Casanovas and Don Juans of the hedonic disposition, it withers and dies. Sexual love and nothing else quickly becomes nothing else. So perishable a moment as the ecstatic sexual engagement needs for its sustainment, not greater sexual energy, but an expanding universe of other vital interests. Sexual love is an attainment, not a "given." It is the tender giving of oneself to another and his loving absorption into ourselves. Like other forms of love, it unites self-love with love for another. Only in this way can the sexual embrace transcend the momentary ecstasy of the libertine and act in the service of a growing psychic community. Psychotherapists and marriage counselors have found that promiscuous sexual relations are unsatisfying and even harmful, not because they are "immoral," but because they are furtive, secretive, and divorced from the rest of the lovers' experience. Sex thus leads a life of its own, without a meaningful relationship to other important events. Sincere sexual love, in or out of marriage, is the expression of a profound affinity between two persons who are separated by their psychic uniqueness. It is the harmonious intermingling of physical and psychic feelings, the experience of an inward rapture. Its sanction is affirmed neither by custom nor religion, but by the goodness of the encounter itself.

Thus, while man shares with other creatures the physiology of the sexual process, he differs from them profoundly in the superb blending of physical and psychic attributes in every loving encounter.

In this conception of the sexual encounter there is no artificial separation of the spiritual and the carnal. This is a theological divorcement which is arbitrary and indefensible, contradicted by psychological evidence and the noblest human experience.

Love and Marriage

With typical worship of "know-how," we in America have transformed the art of love into the science of marriage. Marital experts can now tell us — or so it seems — not only how to pick a mate but how to keep him by using effective coital techniques.[8] We do

---

[8] See C. Adams and V. Packard, *How to Pick a Mate* (New York: Dutton, 1946); A. Ellis and A. Abarbanel (eds.), *The Encyclopedia of Sexual Behavior* (New York: Hawthorn Books, Inc., 1964).

not impugn either the scientific merit or the practical helpfulness of the unending flood of information. Our reaction to it is of a different order: we are distressed to know that man, the brightest of all animals, has not the imagination to cope successfully with the problem of sexual intercourse. We are disturbed by such pat generalizations, for instance, as to say that there is a positive relation between the success of a marriage and the quality of premarital instruction.[9] Although this kind of information may help to dispel the romantic illusion that marriages are made in heaven, they give man no hint of the fact that success or failure in marriage is a function of the total personality. "Adjustment in marriage" is largely a function of a healthy personality "adjusting" himself in life. When all is said, when all the techniques of sexual adjustment are exhausted, the fact remains that marriage, like the loving and sexual encounters themselves, are the joint responsibility of two persons engaged in the serious business of building a community life.

It is disturbing also, that the purveyors of marital instruction should believe that a verbal description of the techniques of marital relations should make for skill in their application. Like every other skill, the skill of sexual relation can be acquired only by practice. Logically, this implies that people should practice the techniques in premarital intercourse. At this, most of the marriage counselors throw up their hands in a chorus of denunciations. In this they are right, of course, since the mores of American life prohibit it. Yet, the implication is there, and it cries out for explication.

The upshot of this line of argument is that the sexual encounter is confused with extraneous, even though consequential, aspects of marital love. Sex is inadvertently abstracted from the rest of the loving encounter by special preoccupation with means, rather than with the end which the means were designed to achieve. Like the principle of historical irony, of serendipity, the goal for which we aim is not the end which we finally reach. The surest way not to achieve happiness, whether in love or the whole of life, is to consciously seek it. Love, like the rest of life, is a process, not an achievement, a growth, not a static condition. It is the fusion of one's whole nature in the nature of the other person. It is a powerful argument against the juvenile belief, so ingrained in our ro-

[9] See, for example, G. Seward, *Sex and the Social Order* (New York: McGraw-Hill Book Company, Inc., 1946).

mantic conception of marriage and happiness, that success in marriage lies in the personal contentment which the marital partner provides. It is an expression of that domination over the other person which we have shown to destroy mutual respect and trust. It deprives the other of his freedom while making oneself a slave of the other's whims.

Finally, the excessive intellectualization of love and marriage, implicit in the attempt to make it more rational than it is, breeds a false confidence in its mastery and a hypocritical denial of its emotional nature. This is as dangerous as the danger which it is designed to combat, namely, the Cinderella complex which leads us to believe that love is a dispensation from heaven, instead of a human creation. The lines by Pope, in his Essay on Man, are fittingly apropos:

> The ruling passion, be it what it will
> The ruling passion conquers reason still.

LOVE AS A CREATIVE ENCOUNTER

In several places in this chapter, we have either stated or implied that love is a creative encounter. Following Fromm, we have also described it as "productive" engagement. The meaning of each term is in no way mysterious. It means that the loving encounter is always directed outward toward the person of another. It involves that sensibility of which we have spoken, which creates a world for the other one, and in this creative act toward the other one, I am conferring his being also upon myself. Love, then, is creative because it produces a world each for the other. I am no longer alone, and he is no longer a world unto himself. Each of us has given something of himself to the other, and the meeting ground is now our shared and common existence.

To be creative in human relationships is to open myself freely to the wants and needs of another person, and to take into myself the other person's being unconditionally. What I give to him and receive from him is not some isolated emotion, trait, or disposition, but himself as a whole being. Love does not fractionate and partition; it unites and builds. It does not reduce the other person to something else, but with reverence accepts him as he is and as he is coming to be. Love is not blind, but a source of insight.

Love as a creative encounter is the expression of care, responsibility, faith, and sacrifice.

Care

This word we have already defined as the act of concern for another individual. It is an important example of what we have called productive anxiety. The person who cares for another individual is concerned with the latter's well-being. He worries about him, and in his anxiety for him is able to enhance the other person's existence. It is not the same as responsibility, for one may feel responsible for another out of duty, rather than because of a deep feeling of solicitude. In caring for another person we transcend our self-concern and become concerned largely with the welfare of the other. We validate and confirm the selfhood of the other person when his existence becomes our own existence, our own concern.

Care is thus at the opposite pole from indifference or insensibility; and we cannot accept Boss' all-inclusive meaning of the term, that care embraces hate and indifference as well as love and sensibility.[10]

Care, or anxiety for another's well-being, can be neurotic or creative. Neurotic concern is based on the absence of full trust, or on selfishness. The neurotic worries not about the other, but about himself. In his indifference and insensibility he fears that he may be losing the other's love, or he resents its insufficiency in the other. He dreads the other's demand upon him because he is in actuality making unreasonable demands of the other person.

Healthy concern for the other person's well-being involves a form of anxiety that validates one's own existence. The parent, for instance, who cares for his child is anxiously concerned for him, but his anxiety makes for a sense of viability. Self-awareness is always intensified when we feel most deeply alive. Life takes on an inward delight because we know that in caring for the other one we have enhanced and intensified his own being. Life is enriched also because in caring for the other we are giving ourselves to him without asking anything in return. The sense of aliveness is not nourished by tranquility and repose, but in active concern for the other's well-being. Care is that creative encounter of persons which vouchsafes their mutual sensibilities and their common concerns.

In proof of the claim that care denies hatred and indifference, we

---

[10] See M. Boss, *Psychoanalyse und Daseinsanalytik* (Stuttgart: Hans Huber, 1957).

call attention to the most provocative fact of its nature: in its fullest condition it impels one to sacrifice every concern but the concern with the other's existence. It transcends the separateness and estrangement that our uniqueness engenders, to effect a union of each with the other. If belongingness means anything, it can mean only the union with myself of that other to which I belong. The belongingness is no external captivity, for my choice of or devotion to the other is a spontaneous act. In love one is not a slave, as the cynic never wearies in telling us, but a free individual. Love and care are means for the liberation of the human spirit, not for its enslavement. In love and concern each man can overcome that widespread ailment of the human spirit: the partitioning of each into part-responses and the separation of each from the other. In this surmounting of a crippling limitation, love displays its creative nature: it is the creator of a human community.

Responsibility

Care and responsibility, although related, bear only a partial resemblance to each other. In responsibility I hold myself accountable to the other. In contrast to care which is typically spontaneous, responsibility is a cognitive act. It is a moral decision which I make in relation to another individual, an act of conscious choice. The difference can be clarified by an example.

If in the darkness of night and in somnolence and fatigue, I instantly rise to minister to my crying infant, I do not so act because of a moral consciousness of the possible cause or consequence of his behavior, but purely because he is a life for which I deeply care. My pity or compassion alone provoke my action, with no thought of where my moral responsibility lies.

My sense of responsibility to him, on the other hand, involves an action based upon knowledge or rational choice. I may decide to inquire into the cause of the infant's distress, and I may reflect on the consequences of my failure to respond. Should I be swayed in my action by the current doctrine of child rearing, I might respond or not respond depending on what the doctrine teaches. I may decide to let him cry because the lesser evil of his discomfort is better than the greater evil of implanting a destructive habit. In either case, my act is determined by the responsibility I bear toward him in the light of my knowledge and intelligence. The act may be a product neither of care nor compassion, fundamentally, but may be largely based on my understanding of the situation. Indeed, the decision may even be used to justify and rationalize an absence of genuine care. Care, on the other hand, cannot be rationalized, for it is primary and unconditional, the spontaneous engagement of one life in the life of another.

We trust that we are not belaboring the issue if we point out that care is an intrinsic, and responsibility an extrinsic, regard for the well-being of another person. The man of compassion does not invent a metaphysic to explain or justify his conduct. It is only when he casts an anguished look on the meaning of his act, that his care is transformed into responsibility. Responsibility is care rationalized.

The distinction between care and responsibility is not evaluational; for love, we have said, is a comingling of different qualities, particularly of care, responsibility, faith, and sacrifice. These do not form a hierarchy, and to value one above another is to destroy the organic unity of the loving encounter. In loving someone we do not judge him; on the contrary, we confer upon him a personal existence; and in this conferment we reveal our own loving personality. This is the meaning of Meister Eckhart's profound observation, that a man is what he loves. In loving another, I *am* that other, and the other *is* myself.

Sacrifice

We return to the quality of *agape*, the selfless devotion of one person to another. All love which transcends the exclusive desire for self-fulfillment by the other, is sacrificial. When I love another person deeply, I do not measure my encounter with him as a mere transaction. I do not concern myself with my own comfort, my own reward. Sacrificial love is not an asking but a giving. It is unconditional, for it depends upon nothing else but its own power to enhance and fulfill the being of the other. It is an act of one's total being, one's entire selfhood. It is a love in which self-love is temporarily negated. As such, it is also rare. It demands a degree of selflessness with which our limited human nature does not amply provide us. It is a condition of being, nevertheless, which we can attain by successive approximation. It is a process which consumes the whole of the loving person, leaving him with no concern for himself but wholly devoted to the other. Like all great moments of life it is perishable, and must be endlessly renewed. Sacrificial love by its very nature, therefore, is fragile and in constant need of a reassuring faith.

Its fragility is attested to by its vulnerability to pathology. The mother who completely indentifies herself with her offspring, for instance, and establishes an absolute dependence of one upon the other, is an oft-recurring unhealthy condition. Both the mother and the child are psychologically damaged by this relationship, for neither can grow into an independent personality.[11]

Having said this, we must, nevertheless, stress the fact that there is no great love that is not founded on sacrifice. By means of sacrificial love man lifts himself and others above the indifference, unconcern, and insensibility which beset our lives, both individually and collectively. Man is drawn, by the very imperfection of his love, to the self of another, and to sacrifice his individuality for the greater individuality of the other. The fragments of the world, its unique selves, can be united only by the selfless concern of each for the other. The paradox of love is that it demands mutual self-surrender, yet in this self-surrender each lives his life in the other, and each gives to the other his freedom. Sacrificial love means self-renunciation and supreme commitment to another individual. Much of the joy of love comes from sacrificial care. One feels most alive, as we have said, when one cares or sacrifices for another. When the self-sacrifice is mutual, one person is able to comprehend the other person in the depth of his being. Each comprehends the other "mystically," rather than rationally. Love reveals the secret of the other person, and in this revelation each transcends his aloneness and creates a community. Self-sacrifice leads us away from self-absorption. It places the other person inside my own life-sphere as a co-equal.

Faith

Care, responsibility, sacrifice — these are vital and dynamic qualities of human love, but they depend on faith for their fulfillment. Faith is the unconditional belief in the sanctity of the human person. It is the unconditional belief that the other individual has an unconditional belief in myself. Each has a complete and absolute trust in the being of the other. Faith strengthens the unifying power of care, responsibility, and self-sacrifice. Love vouchsafed and perpetuated by faith brings together what by its very nature is separated, namely, every individual as a unique person. Faith is care, responsibility and sacrifice in their fullest expression.

[11] This state is called *symbiotic psychosis*. See M. Mahler, "On Child Psychosis and Schizophrenia," *The Psychoanalytic Study of the Child* (New York: International Universities Press, Inc., 1952), vol. 7, pp. 286–305.

We do not speak of faith in its doctrinal meaning. Psychologically, it is always the attitude of *personal* trust. Although it is related to loyalty and fidelity, these are situational nuances of it, but not faith itself. Hope as expectation regarding another's well-being is also a manifestation of faith, but is not identical with it. Faith is the necessary condition, not only of love, but of life itself. In love we live proactively, with reference to each other's future, and we act on the assumption that each can help in the growth and becoming of the other. Love's self-transcendence would be impossible, or being possible, would be short-lived, without faith. This faith which suffuses love is the immediate intuitive trust of one self in another self. It is responsible for that experience of unity-in-difference, of going outside oneself and living for another self, which poets and mystics have penetrated more profoundly than psychologists. In loving faith I open the fullness of my spirit to the needs and wants of another spirit. I impart, or make accessible, to the other all that I am and hope to become. In the absence of faith, love soon becomes selfishness; and in its more extreme form, as we have seen, it becomes the insincerity which is found in all neurosis. The neurotic cannot accept others at face value, but distorts them in the light of his own fears and animosities. He distrusts others because he has no faith in himself. His inability to love is a function of his inability to establish genuine trust for other people. His sexual life suffers for the same reason. He is incapable of relating himself warmly to his sexual partner because he cannot treat him as a person, but only as an object. The productive sexual encounter is always based on mutual trust and acceptance. Bad faith leads to and is nurtured by exploitation which mars the spontaneous goodness of the sexual relationship. Few human relationships are more delicate and subtle and lead to more recrimination and hatred, than the sexual encounter. Sexual compatibility, like other human compatibilities, depends upon one's unconditional adaptation to the person of the other.

CONCLUSION

When he sheds his cloak of professionalism and the pretense of total impartiality, every psychologist knows, of course, that men love, sacrifice, and revere. When he penetrates the thick wall of self-consciousness, embarrassment, and affectation, in the presence of a human experience of which only the poet sings freely and passionately, the psychologist will be less hesitant in writing about the most noble of human sensibilities.

Love, care, sacrifice, and faith are man's most treasured sentiments. They deserve the psychologist's devotion, for they are facts about the nature of man. The psychic anemia which characterizes man in our empirical formulation does not describe his dynamic nature. It is love, with its moving qualities of care, responsibility, sacrifice, and faith, that moves men and impels men to move mountains, and so moves life on to greater perfectibility.

The sickness of modern man is not pathological in the clinical sense. It consists of a spiritual anguish in which man, although living his sexual life with accelerated abandon, is increasingly incapable of establishing durable affections. Not much, either inside or outside his disturbed interior, is fully meaningful. He finds it more difficult to attach his loyalty to himself, to others, and to noble ideals. In this predicament he turns sentiment into sentimentality, or hope into cynicism. For this tragic condition, there is only one cure: self-actualization and fulfillment in self-affirmation, in the loving encounter, and in human solidarity.

9

Alles Leben ist Streit um Geschmack und Schmecken.
("All life is a dispute over taste and tasting.")

FRIEDRICH NIETZSCHE

Style of Life

Although man is conditioned by the world in which he lives and is molded by its powerful influence, he emerges from the enculturation process as a relatively autonomous and liberated individual, living his own life in accordance with his own potentialities. Every personality actualizes itself in the unique stance the individual takes toward the living of his life, which is his personal style. Personality is a way of striving toward self-perfection, and this striving is the individual's style of life.

This style is an expression of man's creative potentiality. It bestows on his life whatever meaning man can formulate in the light of his experience and endowment.

Conventional drive theory is not very helpful in explaining man's determination to confer a unique meaning on the nature of his own life. There is no *drive* for meaning; yet man seeks it more powerfully at times than he does his own physical survival. It is "nonmotivational" in the sense that it is the striving, not by an isolated mode of existence, but by the total individual. Although it is used in the service of adjustment, it is fundamentally not a coping mechanism, but rather it is the process of self-affirmation.

The style of life is never fully made, but always in the making. It does not reveal itself in a specific form of conduct, but in its general direction. Alfred Adler, to whom psychology is most indebted for the concept of style of life, was explicit in his emphasis on its processual nature. According to him, a person expresses the meaning of his life — or more correctly, its goal — quite vaguely, so that we must intuit or divine it from its actualization in each individual's conduct. This is of necessity the case, because the modes of

striving are as numerous as the individuals themselves.[1] This indefiniteness fits well our constant stress on the openness of the proactive individual, his uniqueness, and his being-in-becoming.

At the same time, the indefiniteness of the life-style is repugnant
to the empiricist who demands a strict rationalization of human behavior, even when the rationalization transforms man's viable conduct into a statistical abstraction. But style of life is a fact of
human sensibility, and is not confirmed by reason exclusively. It
follows neither rules nor regulations, for like all human impulses
and creations, it is inconstant in its consistency, conflicting in its
harmony, and manifold in its unity.

STYLE OF LIFE: ITS NATURE AND SIGNIFICANCE

Uniqueness scoffs at classification and routine; and style of life
as an expression of individuality defies every effort to place it into
an intellectual strait-jacket. It can be described meaningfully only
indirectly, by a kind of intimation, not in mensurative language.
It is not a mechanical adjustment to one's environment, but the
manner in which each person creates his own life. In this manner
of creating one's own life, we are, as Berenson phrased it, functioning according to our own nature, not merely responding to a
world outside.[2] For this and other reasons, conventional psychology's description of behavior as an individual's structure of responses, is untenable. By means of his individual style of life, every
person perceives reality uniquely, not as mechanical reactions to
external reality. Every person experiences the world individually,
even though his sensorium is physiologically like the sensorium of
every other individual. Our experience of the world is not a set of
responses, but a set of uniquely determined self-attitudes. In this
formulation we are again in accord with Adler's stress on the
uniqueness of every individual's perception of psychological reality.[3]

---

[1] See A. Adler, *Der Sinn des Lebens* (Wien und Leipzig: Rudolf
Passer, 1933).

[2] For a thoughtful and wise discussion of creating one's life, see B.
Berenson, *Sunset and Twilight* (New York: Harcourt, Brace and Company, 1963).

[3] It is both difficult and unnecessary in a book of this special scope
to trace Adler's ideas to their specific sources. This is the more difficult
in view of the fact that Adler redefined his position so frequently that at
times he seems to be superficially inconsistent. For the American reader,
we recommend Adler's *The Science of Living* (New York: Greenberg,
Inc., 1929).

Rise and Development of Life-Style

We have shown, in different places in this book, that the study of personality may be approached from two perspectives. From one point of view, man is described almost exclusively as an adaptive or adjustive organism. He is conceived in the framework of problems and the manner in which he seeks to solve them. His behavior is stimulus-bound and habitual. This is the approach of the functionalist tradition, both psychoanalytical and behavioristic.

From the other point of view, man is not only an adjustive, but also an expressive organism. This view holds that even adaptive behavior is performed by each individual in his own *particular way*. It asserts that behavior is not entirely social in character; not the skillful or effective playing of expected roles, but expressing oneself as he is. Every behavior of the total person bears the stamp of his own individuality, his own style of living. While it is born in the framework of social roles and expectations, it is steadfastly modified in the light of the individual's values and intentions. Every healthy person strives for greater individuation and self-actualization. This individuation takes place in the form of a fairly consistent life-style, or mode of individual orientation. No matter how fixed his environment may be, the individual will transcend it and, within variable limits, establish his own direction within it.

While it would be folly to deny the origin of this direction or life-style in childhood, it is a mistake to conceive it as entirely bound to the individual's past. This seems to be the mistake made by Adler himself, and it partly negates his own contribution to the subject.

We have said that "it seems to be the mistake" made by Adler. One cannot with certainty say what Adler's position really is. He speaks of it in terms of "a fixed law of movement" in a person's life.[4] It develops in childhood, indeed, but it changes as the individual's potentialities become more fully actualized. Actualization of potentialities cannot be a "fixed law," for it is the creative transformation of the individual's past.

Adler unwittingly implies as much, when he holds that it is impossible to predict what uses the developing adult will later make of his own past. Being an open personality, as we believe man is, his future, while he lives, is never closed. It cannot be predicted because the connection between the past and the future is not completely determined. Adler should have foreseen this, since he was

---

[4] Adler, *Der Sinn des Lebens, op. cit.*, p. 7.

one of the first psychologists, outside the existential fold, to deny universal determinism. Functional autonomy is characteristic of the style of life as it is of human motivation. But with characteristic inconsistency — or a later and legitimate change of mind — Adler asserts that once the early pattern is established we can predict an individual's subsequent behavior. But then, as if to confound the reader further, Adler assures him that the more healthy the individual is, the more is he able to redirect his behavior along new lines. Unless Adler himself believed this, he could not have justified his belief in the capacity of the individual to create his own personality. From our point of view — and Adler concurs in this — an individual is not a passive respondent to stimuli, but is a self-transforming person. His creation of his personality, his actualization of his potentialities, always takes place in a unique way, namely, in accordance with the individual's style of life. When we speak of potentiality, however, we are not concerned with inherited powers — for we can seldom determine what they are — but with the *manner* in which each individual actualizes them in his own life.

The style of life, then, is not a biological mechanism, but a proactive self-direction. While it develops early, it is subject to all the changes that characterize the total personality. It is not a fixed frame of reference, but an aspect of the total being-in-becoming.

In this regard Adler, who was no mere imitator of Freud's psychology, makes Freud's mistake of imputing to childhood experience a disproportionate influence. In this respect Nietzsche and the proactive psychologists are much closer to the facts of human experience. Nietzsche, a most inconsistent philosopher, was yet the most radical and obstinate defender of the changing and creative style of life. Life is, indeed, a dispute over taste and tasting.[5]

Style of Life in the Making

French literary critics like to tell us that *le style est l'homme même* (style is the man himself). This statement is true as well of an individual's style of life. We recognize a man by his pattern of intentions as we identify a writer by his literary form. We know that most writers of distinction transcend the influence of their masters and develop a style of their own. So patent is this truth that many writers discourage, or hold in contempt, the efforts of

[5] See F. Nietzsche, *Also Sprach Zarathustra*, in *Friedrich Nietzsches Werke* (Leipzig: T. G. Naumann Verlag, 1906), vol. 7.

teachers to mold the stylistic endeavors of children and youth. Teachers can give helpful hints to incipient writers, and the latter may gain practice by imitating a literary model; but when all is said, the style of writing, like the writer's personality, is distinctly his own. A writer may bend his material to his literary form, or modify his style to fit the needs of his subject-matter, but in the end his style tends to prevail and substance submits to a characteristic mode of expression.

Style of life, like style of creative functioning, is not a clearly defined activity, nor is it fundamentally cognitive or intellectual. It is a comingling of both potential and actual forms of being. It is constantly changing and growing. The psychic basis on which it is built is a sustained faith in its dependability. Living trustingly by the elemental wisdom of his style of life, the individual will make fewer grave and fatal errors, for in living by his authentic selfhood, he has fewer neuroses to defend.

A style of life, then, calls for an openness of self and a capacity to face ambiguity that are present in every healthy individual. It is at once a guide for living and an allurement to improvisation and experiment. Style of life, like style of creativity, is a process of becoming, an act that is never wholly finished. Every time I begin creating, whether in art or life, I must begin at the beginning, and I cannot predict the outcome. Max Weber, the American artist, stated it superbly, when he said, "In carrying on my own humble creative effort, I depend greatly upon that which I do not yet know, and upon that which I have not yet done."[6]

Academic psychologists, by and large, have not shown much interest in the problem of "style" of personality. With such notable exceptions as G. W. Allport, C. R. Rogers, and some of the "perceptualists," those who have given their attention to the subject have been too atomistic, despite their interest in finding unity in human behavior. Thus, to mention one of the earliest, Cattell's work on the persistence of percepts once established, shows that stimulus generalization is the source of unity and consistency of personality. This is undoubtedly true, but it ignores, even contradicts, individual uniqueness.[7]

---

[6] Quoted in C. R. Rogers, *On Becoming a Person* (Boston: Houghton Mifflin Company, 1961), p. 23.

[7] R. B. Cattell, *Personality: A Systematic Theoretical and Factual Study* (New York: McGraw-Hill Book Company, 1950); and by the same author, *Personality and Motivation: Structure and Measurement* (Yonkers, N. Y.: World Book Company, 1957).

The perceptual and atomistic view is right in holding that every individual tends to perceive the world in a characteristic way; but it is mistaken, we believe, in maintaining that the way can be standardized. This criticism applies with considerably less force to the researches of Klein on "perceptual attitudes."[8] He recognizes that, although the adaptive properties are common to all perceptions, each individual, nevertheless, uses, or organizes, the properties in his own unique way.

The chief weakness of Klein's analysis is his tendency to cast his conclusions in a homeostatic framework. As we conceive style of life, or style of personality, it is not basically an adaptive mechanism, but the unique forward thrust of the individual, his idiosyncratic way of directing his life and building his personality. We lift style of life out of the closed context of adaptation and equilibrium, and place it in the broader framework of productiveness and creativity.

In this manner we render the concept of style of life more flexible than Adler's and the perceptualist's views permit. If style of life is as inflexible as these writers describe it, then we have no valid basis for distinguishing it from the tyrannical superego of Freudian psychology. A person's style of life, we believe, consists of those goals and intentions which best fit his own nature and which permit him most effectively to fulfill and actualize his own selfhood. Style of life means living in accordance with our innermost needs, not merely in the interests of our defense mechanisms. Genuine, authentic, and healthy behavior, by its very nature "deviates" from what is common to all individuals. The person described in these terms can safely tolerate idiosyncrasy and ambiguity in others and in himself. Paradoxically, his very individuality confers upon each person a special kind of consistency and unity. It is by his uniqueness that we learn to know him, rather than by the traits which he holds in common with members of his species, and with the behavior patterns of his cultural group.

The individual's life-goals are the concrete expressions of his style of life. Although they are "concrete," they are not, as we have already said, highly specific. They endure, not because they are fixed, but because they are changeable. Psychic durability is always a function of change, of the capacity to continually redefine our basic purposes. Success or failure in achieving their actualization modi-

[8] G. S. Klein, "The Personal World Through Perception," in R. R. Blake and G. V. Ramsey (eds.), *Perception: An Approach to Personality* (New York: The Ronald Press Company, 1951).

fies both the purposes and the means for attaining them. By means of our style of life each of us can make of his life a work of art. Whether the life each creates for himself is good and beautiful or ugly and bad, will be determined by the quality of his life-style. Just as there are great artists and small ones, so in this most difficult of all the arts, the art of life, there will be in the style of life forces which make for growth or inhibition, for development or decline.

The reader must be struck again by the ambiguity of our formulation. There are two kinds of people who are repelled by the indefiniteness of our analysis. One is the positivist with a low tolerance of ambiguity. The other is the fervent moralist for whom a guide of life is only a set of rules for making another individual over in the former's fixed image. For the positivist, a style of life, if he tolerates the idea at all, is a set of habits originating in childhood and strengthened or modified by means of later reinforcement. For the moralist, life has no style at all, but is the mechanical obedience to a rigid set of commandments. The positivist does not see, and the moralist does not know, that vitality in human behavior is precluded by inflexible habits and rigid formulas. A prime condition of effective and self-enhancing conduct is the self-corrective quality of the individual's way of life. Life, we have said on different occasions, is an adventure full of risks as well as satisfactions. Without the quality of flexibility, a style of life can be nothing more than an inhibiting "set," or an abject slavery to artificial formulas.

Flexibility in the style of life does not mean chaos and indecision. It has a strain of consistency, but not a fixity. On the contrary, even while it changes it serves as a regulative principle. Its being consists in its becoming. Every healthy individual guides his life by a selected motive which takes precedence over all the others. He is the man who maintains his integrity in the midst of change, his individuality in the face of external pressures to conform.

This way of describing the nature and role of a style of life reminds us again of the creative role of solitude and aloneness. When we say that the healthy individual retains his integrity in the midst of change, we are acknowledging the ancient truth that man's character, although in danger of disintegrating in the absence of productive human relationships, is also formed in the cleansing stillness of his solitude. Goethe, to whom we find ourselves returning constantly for depth of insight, described the force of solitude and relatedness eloquently thus:

Es bildet ein Talent sich in der Stille:
Ein Charakter im Stromme der Welt.

(A talent is produced in solitude:
A character in the stream of life.)

The couplet is particularly apropos because it confirms the soundness of our emphasis on the fact that a style of life, like life itself, is more than a guide to conduct; it is the art of creating one's own life. In short, the style of life is the set of ideals which a person selects from many possibilities, and to which he pledges his loyalty, above all other sentiments. In this way man conforms freely to one expectation: his image of himself.

We thus combine in our view of style of life the stability of self-consistency and the productive impermanence of becoming. The proactive man grows and changes, but in the process of change he always selects his own way to direct it, overcome it, or utilize it.

DIVERSITIES IN STYLES OF LIFE

The moment we go beyond his purely biological nature in our study of man, we are confronted by the fact that he is a proactive individual. The moment we transcend the ready-made conventions of man's culture, we are struck by the propulsive nature of his individual life. Man is that creature who, with the help of his biological and cultural heritage, creates his own outlook on life. Although each of us reacts to the same "objective" world, each of us imparts to it his own meaning. We assume that there is a veridical world "out there," and we know that the social world is constantly pressing upon us its own preferred patterns of conduct; but in the end, every individual tends in some degree to follow his own predisposition. Some individuals are more dependent on objective conditions; others can more freely modify their behavior in response to them. But the significant thing about both forms of behavior is that in each the individual acts on the basis of his inner cognitive structure, his subjective style of life. Each is, in various degrees "field-independent."

In this observation we are critical of workers in the area of motivation who make an unwarranted and sharp distinction between flexible and inflexible, "field-independent" and "field-dependent," individuals. They posit clear-cut "cognitive styles," thereby committing the errors of both Adler and the perceptualists whom we have mentioned.[9] These distinctions have pedagogic value but not the strict scientific validity which the authors seem to attribute to them. The force of tradition regarding the persistence of perceptual or cognitive style — a tradition that existed long before the advent of rigorous experimental work on perception — predisposes psychologists to perceive more persistence and fixity than exists. The "styles" found in the above-mentioned investigations are the extreme, and hence probably the exceptional, forms of behavior.

Bearing this criticism in mind, it is legitimate, on purely heuristic grounds, to hold that there are tendencies toward similar, and therefore general, life-styles.

Patterns of Life-Style

We have remarked before that, although man's behavior is always in part a product of his biological and cultural heritage, what each individual selects from it to make his own is largely an individual predilection. In proactive psychology the crucial question is not what one inherits from his parents or what the customs of society demand, but how one uses one's native powers and what one appropriates from his cultural surroundings. This individual use and appropriation Adler fittingly calls the "creative power" of the individual. By means of this creative power the individual is able to direct the forces in his life along selected lines. This direction is what we both mean by style of life.

The style of life differentiates individuals from one another; for it describes the unique way in which every individual directs his own life, interprets the meaning of his experience, and transforms himself into a work of art.

Described in this way, we feel that every individual possesses proactive qualities. They are human characteristics, not special gifts. Like intelligence, or a "musical ear," they are distributed differentially in the human species, but are never completely absent. This is so because human beings are not mere structures of part-reactions, but more or less integrated wholes. Whether a person strives mostly for material wealth or the well-being of others is determined largely by the meaning he gives to life as a whole. "Meaning of life" is not some ineffable value, but a powerful directive force. In order to understand a human life, therefore, it is more important to know a person's interpretation of his experience than his drives and intellectual powers.

[9] See especially H. A. Witkin *et al.*, *Personality Through Perception* (New York: Harper and Row, 1954).

If we remember that every individual selects from his native equipment and his social surroundings all that is consistent with his dominant trend, then we are not amiss in declaring that styles of life divide themselves into real but vague categories. We are mindful of the fact that classification of persons into types easily results in distortions of their individual personalities, and we make no effort in this book to present a typology of persons. Classifications in psychology can never be more than temporary and useful expedients. Nevertheless, the tendency to see similarities and resemblances, and the need to give to every object and experience a local habitation and a name, is also a human characteristic. Although the healthy individual is always sensitive to the dignity and autonomy of other individuals, as an observant and reflective person he identifies them by their dominant dispositions, by their styles of life.

There have been many type-descriptions in the history of psychology, but none has received universal approval. It may be said that the best way to describe an individual's dominant trend is to think of it on the basis of the value systems which characterize a time and place, and from which every individual chooses and transforms those qualities which are most in harmony with his need to actualize and fulfill himself as a person. This approach is in complete agreement with our stress on the fact that style of life is the meaning which each individual gives to the world, and the hypothesis that proaction and self-actualization are in varying degrees autochthonous human traits. Thus, while the paths of life are "there" for anyone to chose, every individual assimilates those values which are in greatest harmony with his unique being. Style of life thus becomes style of personality: the expression of sharable values in a uniquely personal way. Path of life and individual choice fuse to make a genuine *Lebensform* — the integration of the objective and the personal worlds into a meaningful style of life.[10]

And finally, style of life is not a *reaction* system, but a personal *construction*, or creative activity, in which the values of one's com-

---

[10] No English word conveys the essence of style of life as well as the German word *Lebensform*. This word combines what is common and unique in a way of life. For this reason Spranger's value-oriented life-styles are still among the best attempts to formulate dominant personality trends. See E. Spranger, *Lebensformen: Geisteswissenschaftliche Psychologie und Ethik der Persönlichkeit*, 6th ed. (Halle: Max Niemeyer Verlag, 1925). There is an English translation of the 5th edition by P. Pigors: *Types of Men* (Halle: Max Niemeyer Verlag, 1928).

munity are recreated and transformed into an individual way of life. *The noetic style.* The individual who directs his life according to the noetic style is repelled by the open world on which he must confer a degree of closure. Although he looks upon life and the world as intellectual problems, his aim is to find answers to his questions. He cannot tolerate ignorance in himself, and is moved largely by rational arguments. He views life with the cold eye of the intellect. Spranger describes him as the *theoretic* man. The noetic individual cannot tolerate ambiguity and non-rational explanations, and he values truth and reason above all other values. When we say that he cannot tolerate ambiguity we are affirming that both life and the universe are considered as ordered totalities, and that he cannot endure chaos and disorder. His knowledge must be precise, objective, and certain. He is ruled by logic and the "law" of necessity. In the "pure" form, the noetic individual is moved by ideas and a strong determination to control his emotions and reduce his physical desires. Intimate associations are difficult for him, for his interest lies in abstractions not persons. The center of his life is his own intellect.

This life-style is an extremely narrow one, especially since it is largely devoid of passion and affect. Even the intellectual interest is characterized by immoderation. In his pursuit of truth — truth as he sees is, of course — he is insensible to social life, and unconcerned with community. What interest he may have in the social world is largely one of contemplation, seldom of participation and reform. Social sympathy is atrophied, or of a low order. This is seen in the fact that the noetic person views people in the cold light of impartiality and objectivity. However, they are not in his mind objects to be manipulated, but subjects to be contemplated. He prides himself in his capacity to judge human nature, but his judgment never permits him to apprehend men in their human reality, but always in the light of a rigid theory. Since he must always find a reason for everything, he does not easily accept people as they are, but must seek a more "basic" explanation of what may really be a simple and obvious cause.

Accordingly, his judgment of people is often deficient. Because he views them in the light of abstract principles, seeking to explain them by means of universally valid generalizations, he is well-nigh blind to their uniqueness. Since objective validity is his highest criterion, he distrusts his own intuitions. Since the being of another person can be grasped only in the sympathetic "living" of the other person's life, and since the noetic approach lives more with abstractions than persons, he may see sharply the meaning of isolated behaviors, but only dimly the pattern of the whole.

The mystic style. At the other end of the value spectrum stands the individual for whom the meaning of life is not contemplation but salvation, not a restless inquiry, but a tranquil blessedness. He is the completely religious individual. His selflessness is not the sympathetic merging with the community, as in the case of the other-minded individual, but the union with a deity. The mystic is found in certain monastic orders, in some of the religions of the East, and in occasional ineffabilities of some contemporary sects.

Generally speaking, this style of life is, outside the above-mentioned groups, rare in Western society. The unstable and conflictual nature of contemporary life neither respects nor rewards the mystic's search for unity with the God-head. Accordingly, it exists in our society in the mild and inoffensive religious denominations, whose doctrines are always anchored in the safe haven of secular belief and activity. Where the true mystical way of life exists in the contemporary world, it is either a sporadic activity or an escape mechanism. The best example of the latter is the fad of Zen Buddhism in America.

The style of sympathy. It is unfortunate that Spranger's idea of *Mitgefühl* has been crudely translated as *social attitude*. This is the more true in view of the fact that he explicitly excluded rational elements from *Mitgefühl,* and stressed the impulse of an individual to give himself to another, and to place himself in the life of the other individual. The style of sympathy is no anemic social relatedness, but a powerful feeling of compassion and sympathy — a feeling-with-and-for-another (*Mitgefühl*).

The man of sympathy and compassion is the man of love and sensibility, whom we described at length in Chapter 8. He is lured by the other person in a loving encounter, in a psychic engagement with and care for his well-being. Although there are degrees of compassion and sympathy, even at its lowest ebb it is no mere social interaction, in which each modifies the behavior of the other, but a relatedness in which he participates in the other's joys and sufferings. In its highest intensity, as we saw, it means care, responsibility, faith, and sacrifice. Mere sociality does not describe this style of life, and the term social attitude only remotely suggests, if at all, the psychic interpenetration that exists in love and compassion. Only the main body of sentiments which we discussed in the preceding chapter adequately describes the meaning of the compassionate way of life. Anything less describes not sympathy, but gregariousness.

The authoritarian style. This mode of self-expression is at once more explicit and inclusive than Spranger's political attitude. The term political is too narrow, and suggests what Spranger did not fully intend, namely, a Machiavellian political attitude.

The authoritarian life-style is characterized by the quality of domination, and may range in degree from crass manipulation of people to the more refined need to be superior to everybody. In the latter form it is often a neurotic manipulation, a compulsive drive to be always on top. The "typical" authoritarian individual relates himself to others by means of power-attitudes. He lives by his own *Machtmoral,* as German writers have described it, or by his own "power morality." While he may or may not be motivated to exploit and manipulate, he cannot brook opposition and is intolerant of anyone or anything which challenges his own style of life. His mind is closed in the sense that he feels uneasy in the presence of novel conditions, for the new is always potentially threatening to his rigid pattern of attitudes. He must impose his values upon others, because he has little or no trust in the basic decency of human nature. He would make men better — which is to say like himself — by imposing rigid standards upon them. He is, therefore, prone to insist on the use of religious doctrine to compel men to be moral and good. He preaches this doctrine, not for its inherent moral ideals, but because, in his inability to tolerate ambiguity, he considers it to be self-evident and therefore absolutely certain. He lives most naturally by rules, and these rules he needs to impose upon others, lest they disturb the safe and dependable world in which he lives.[11]

The aesthetic style. Spranger's is still by all odds the most lucid and economical discussion of the aesthetic attitude.[12] Quite clearly, the person who views life aesthetically sees it by means of the categories of form, beauty, and symmetry. He evaluates life primarily by the individual standard of fitness, not by means of abstract or utilitarian categories. Life for him, therefore, as for all proactive persons, is individual and unique. Like the artist Weber, the aesthetic individual depends less upon what he knows and does,

[11] At the present time, the definitive study of the authoritarian way of life is: T. W. Adorno, E. Frenkel-Brunswik, D. J. Levinson, and R. N. Sanford, *The Authoritarian Personality* (New York: Harper and Row, 1950).

[12] See E. Spranger, *op. cit.,* Part II, Ch. 3.

than upon experience in the making — that is, life as it is "originally" (*ursprünglich*). This attitude is found not alone in artists and other "creative" people, but also in many scientists who impose upon nature the form of their own inner life. It is found in the scientific work of the poet Goethe as well as in the mathematical investigations of Pioncaré and the physical theories of Einstein. In his relations with others, he is limited by his individualism, and often by his eccentricity, for his openness to people is marked more by empathy than by sympathy, more by a genuine enjoyment of them, than by the impulse to help them. In short, his life is integrated by love of beauty and aesthetic harmony.

The utilitarian style. This is the way of the "economic" man, most broadly conceived. The person who lives by the utilitarian style approaches objects, people, and human experience with an eye for their utility. All values, whether as truth, beauty, or morality, are meaningful only if they promote the material life. People are perceived as producers and consumers, and if they are neither, are merely adventitious creatures. God is the giver of useful gifts, and religion is the sanctifier of work, efficiency, and thrift. In its purest form, the utilitarian life-style prefers utility, especially material riches, to all other values, for only they can render life meaningful and pleasant.

The proactive style. The proactive style of life is a unique integration and intensification by each individual of those values which are creative in the sense in which we have been using this concept. It incorporates in a coherent value-schema the most productive features of the noetic, sympathetic and aesthetic styles of life, *in accordance with the most elemental needs of the proactive individual.* Although this style of life may contain some feature of the mystic, utilitarian, and authoritarian value-system; when it does, these features are either attenuated or at war with the basic character of the individual. When their clash with the essentially proactive nature of the individual is pronounced, he is in the grip of a neurotic ailment. The experience of existential and other self-oriented therapies, such as Rogers', for instance, shows that neurosis is the inhibition or denial of the authentic self, or the individual's unique life-style, as we would describe it.

The goal of life in the proactive style is a dynamic fusion of contemplation, compassion, and sensuous enjoyment. Although these values are integrated into a unified scheme, they may express themselves differentially in accordance with the combined needs of the inner individual and the external situation. Orthodox psychology would describe this condition as a form of adjustment; but it is in fact a mode of self-expression and becoming. The proactive individual, guided by his coherent life-style, does not merely react passively to his environment, but makes productive changes in accordance with previsioned ends. He has an *active need* for reflection, loving encounter, and enjoyment of beauty. He combines in himself the "male-female" principle of life, by which every individual strives to achieve an 'inner form" — the inner form in which masculine striving and feminine creativity are harmonized as a developing whole. Goethe was aware of this and expressed it in his well-known line: *Das Ewig-Weibliche zieht uns immer hinan* — "The eternal feminine lures us ever upward."

The proactive life is thus an endless seeking of a perfection that can never be attained. Like the artist, poet, and creative scientist, the proactive individual is never certain of the outcome of his search. He feels unfinished and never wholly fulfilled. Every creative life, like every creative art and science, is even at best highly problematic. Even while he exults in the joy of his life, every proactive individual is haunted by the feeling that every achievement is but the start of another beginning. Proactive life, which is to say the truly human life, is indeed an endless becoming. Plato knew this, as did also Goethe and Beethoven; as did Shakespeare and da Vinci before them; as does every individual for whom life is more than a crude material transaction — an Einstein, a Schweitzer, a Laurence Olivier. The man who reflects, loves, and enjoys, is the man who knows that the meaning of his life is a titanic struggle to create that perfection which is immanent in his human nature: *Ecce homo* — "Behold the man."

CONCLUSION

Humanistic research and self-oriented psychotherapy have disclosed what wise men have always known, that man is not only a store-house of habits, memories, and attitudes, but a person who is constantly engaged in actualizing himself by means of his individual life-style. This life-style is an individual's interpretation of reality, which may or may not correspond with reality "as it is." This interpretation cannot be described causally, but only through immediate experience. Strict causal explanations, as we saw in Chapter 1, hold with certainty only in the fictitious world image, but not necessarily in the human self-picture.

In the broadest sense, then, style of life is one's philosophy of living. When we know an individual's life-style, i.e., when we know what life means to him, we know *him*. Every individual guides his life by this meaning, either by design or unwittingly. We believe that this is also what Adler meant, when he described the individual in terms of the latter's goals and meanings. While he did not, except in casual sporadic remarks, call it a philosophy of life, this is what Adler in fact meant by it.

Finally, style of life as a psychological datum is always a convergence of a preformed individual structure and the molding force of the environment. But the manner in which this convergence is achieved is dependent on the unique character of every individual.

10

Wer immer strebend sich bemüht,
Den können wir erlösen.

("He who strives ever forward,
Him can we save.")

J. W. VON GOETHE

The Proactive Personality

The controlling purpose in this book, which we have sedulously
and singlemindedly pursued, is to lay bare the individuality of the
human being; to show that his being is constantly changing in the
direction implicit in his style of life. Man is a multiform being,
seeking to actualize his potentialities. He cannot be meaningfully
described by means of such separate elements as drives, motives,
memories, and cognitive structures. Rather, he must be viewed as a
life-totality.

It is false to say that this way of conceiving the individual aban-
dons empirical evidence and constructs a purely fictitious view of
man. On the contrary, this way of conceiving man is familiar to
many biologists, especially modern geneticists and evolutionists,
and is substantiated by all holistic psychologies and psychotherapies. It is based on empirical evidence, but its method consists
in the investigation of totalities. It gladly uses data discovered in
the clinic or the hospital, but it also relies on personal experience
and the dispassionate study of men long dead, as they reveal themselves in their lives and their productions. In studying Leonardo or
Goethe we can learn about man uncontaminated by the blinding
force of our own contemporary culture. In this *Ganzheitsforschung*,
in this investigation of the total individual, we may not fully expose
the separate features, but we highlight the holistic nature of man.

It is our conviction, based on many years of study, experience,
and intimate acquaintance with living individuals, that human beings are inherently both reactive and proactive. Which of these

modes of being is selected as the dominant style of a person's life is dependent on the unique convergence in each individual of his elemental needs and the chosen values of his society. In short, proaction varies, like intelligence or artistic ability, on a continuum from most to least. That person whom we are describing as the proactive individual is characterized by a high degree of forward directedness, independence, and becoming.

It is fair to say that the history of psychology is in no small way the dissemination of fashionable ideas about the nature of man. This history should have taught us something about the folly of trying to account for human behavior by means of a single paradigm. It should also have taught us that the worship of scientific respectability impairs one's scientific creativity. When the spirit of adventure is stifled by the narrow demands of a rigid model, psychology must suffer — as indeed it has suffered — the penalty of closed-mindedness.

A proactive psychology, although recognizing the importance and legitimacy of the reactive pattern, chooses to investigate the propulsive orientation. Although something is lost in this decision, much more is gained.

PROACTIVE PSYCHOLOGY

All that we have written in the foregoing chapters points to a single, ineluctable conclusion: every individual has the capacity to resist the molding force of his social environment and become what he potentially is. The paradox of human growth is that the being that we are is ever changing. Each individual transforms the materials of his experience into novel forms. All experience is self-experience, all growth is becoming. Proactive psychology permits us to see the individual standing before a world of possibilities from which he may choose according to his own character and his own style of life. This is no mysterious process. It is but the persistent quest for one's selfhood, one's identity.

Again, proactive psychology rejects, as should now be clear, the view of man which makes him over-dependent on his past and his defenses. Proactive psychology rejects the all-importance of security, and the principle of homeostasis on which it stands. It sees man as a being who is lured by adventure and risk, by improvisation and conceptual experimentation.[1] It finds that man is stimu-

---

[1] See Chapter 1.

lated by dissatisfaction as well as the reduction of tension, by the
need to transform what is into what ought to be, as well as adjustment to things as they are. The more proactive an individual is,
the more he displays in his conduct that independence of conventional thought and action which we all acknowledge by lip-service,
but refute in practice. In his most healthy psychological condition,
man is a daring and challenging individual. We have been too impressed in conventional psychology by the negative and self-impairing traits of man, and closed our eyes to his Promethean, defiant,
self-propulsive characteristics. Every psychotherapist knows that
his patients resist the demand to face the truth about themselves,
which he brings to light in the healing process. Psychological illness is in large measure this fear by the individual of facing the
truth about himself. Psychological growth — which is to say psychological health — is the courage to face the truth about ourselves
and the daring spirit of actualizing our authentic lives in the face
of criticism, rejection, and the threat of isolation. Lack of personal
courage is so pervasive in the conventions in which our lives are im-
prisoned that many of us deny our human greatness.

At his very best, however, man is capable of that "holy insecurity" which Buber ascribes to man in his relation to God — or as
we would say, in his relation to his authentic self-hood. All proactive psychotherapies plainly demonstrate that authentic human
relationships are embedded in honest self-acceptance. The more a
person accepts himself the more open he is to the selves of other
persons. In his psychotherapeutic work and research, Rogers has
witnessed a recurring confirmation of this basic human fact. The
lonely individual — which means every individual — can establish
a genuine bond between himself and other individuals only if he
has the courage to be himself, and is not denied his selfhood by
repressive and denying influences. Rogers adds, what our own experience and knowledge validates, that in being ourselves and encouraging others to affirm themselves, we are actually helping each
to become an authentic person.[2]

The Self-Process

By its popularity and prestige, psychology has unwittingly — and
sometimes deliberately — dictated the kind of conduct it defines
as acceptable. Much of the conforming behavior which is now re-

[2] See, for example, C. R. Rogers, *On Becoming a Person* (Boston:
Houghton Mifflin Company, 1961), pp. 15–27.

ceiving so much belated attention, is a product of the overwhelming stress on social adjustment. Social adjustment is necessary, but an excess of it leads to the weakening of individual responsibility. It is much easier to do what our conventions demand than to expose ourselves to censure and ridicule. It is much easier to follow the crowd than to practice the difficult art of self-discipline. The fear of individualism is so intense and widespread, that self-affirmation is often equated with egocentrism and selfishness. The increasing rebellion against social engulfment, when it is genuine and sincere, is proof that self-affirmation is our most despairing need. It challenges psychology's belief that man is scarcely more than a drive-reductive being. It argues, instead, for man's desire for and capacity to determine his destiny within the limits of his capacities and his finitude. It questions in a most radical way the concepts of adaptation and survival as motivating forces in human life, and recognizes them as the half-truths that they are.

It questions also that other half-truth which is deeply entrenched in the romantic attitude in American life, that happiness is the goal of life. Alongside of adjustment, self-preservation, and happiness, proactive psychology would place at a higher level man's need to discover and enhance himself. If this search for identity, this seeking to find one's selfhood, is fraught with risk and suffering, as it always is, it but demonstrates that for many people happiness cannot be the ultimate good. A psychology that defines health and "normality" in terms of the degree of happiness and social adjustment which we display in our daily lives, not only encourages self-deception but destroys or weakens the basis of our moral strength. Wise men have always known what many adjustment psychologists cannot understand, that a life built by the individual's own efforts is attained only by means of individual strife and torment. The search for tranquility characterizes those individuals who have stopped living and are waiting to die. The proactive individual works to confirm his life, to actualize his selfhood.

This way of conceiving the healthy personality has important therapeutic implications. Proactive psychotherapy would not aim for personal happiness, but for a continuing self-fulfillment. It would not value social adjustment above other psychological goods, but value the enhancement and deepening of our emotions and feelings, and the heightening of our human sensibilities. It would glorify for the sick individual the life-giving qualities of physical enjoyment and reverence for beauty in man and nature. Psychotherapists have yet to explore to the full the healing and renewing power of beauty in art and music. Healthy men are always recognized by their *surrender* to "peak experiences," whereas neurotic individuals are *overcome* by crippling anxieties. Reverence and wonder are emotions not listed in the psychologist's taxonomies. Not only are awe and sensibility qualities of mental health, but they are positively related to personal insight and clinical perceptivity. It is well known that many creative people, despite their occasional eccentricities, rightly intuit another's selfhood. This capacity is not basically cognitive, but is a function of a simple wonder and openness to experience. Unlike some psychologists, whose perceptiveness is impaired by a strong tendency to partition and abstract, the aesthetically-oriented individual more readily perceives persons in their totalities. The psychologist, like other narrow specialists, is the victim of a "trained incapacity," to use Thorstein Veblen's well-known phraseology. He depends too much on fixed categories and misses the essential fluidity of the healthy individual.

We now have evidence from varied sources, that clinical insight is enhanced when the psychotherapist approaches his patient not alone as a trained expert but as an artist entering into the life of the sick individual. Existential and "client-centered" therapists conceive of their relation to their patients as creative — as a loving encounter between two people both of whom are changed by the vital relationship. In this sense, psychotherapy is an art as well as a science, a creative engagement of two people, as well as the skillful use of a technique. This is so true that Maslow rightly argues for the training of the psychotherapist in "aesthetic perceiving and creating."[3]

We have said that the heightened perceptivity of the proactive individual, be he a trained psychotherapist or a highly perceptive layman, is partly a function of his tendency to perceive totalities. The rigid scientist views things not only as abstractions but as relatively fixed categories. Even his "variables" have a way of becoming constants. The aesthetically-oriented person, on the other hand, approaches life and people with spontaneity, individuality, and freedom. He has fewer defenses to cope with, and he is never handicapped by the need to defend a system or theory. He sees the self of another in the light of his own spontaneous selfhood. Not being on the defensive, he need not defend and justify himself in the eyes of others. Not having a need to reduce human singu-

[3] A. H. Maslow, *Toward a Psychology of Being* (Princeton: D. Van Nostrand Company, Inc., 1962), p. 86.

larity and uniqueness to constants, he need not engage in that de-personalization of the other individual which is characteristic of the empirical psychologist. Unlike the latter, who paradoxically removes the self from his observations, the more humanistic observer makes it the focus of his interest. Instead of banishing the human element from his perceptions, the proactive, aesthetically-centered individual, uses it as the ultimate standard.

The "successful" therapist is thus a person who differs from the ordinary or the mediocre one, not in his possession of greater intellectual powers, or of a greater mechanical dexterity, but in his greater capacity for self-experience and self-realization. He is more complete in his selfhood, and this enables him to grasp more easily another in his totality.

This capacity of grasping another self in his wholeness is not a mystical power possessed by some and denied to others, but a wider and more intense development of the perceptive power present in all healthy individuals. It is wider and more intense because it is not dissipated in wasteful defenses of either oneself or one's view of man. The spontaneous, proactive individual is less self-deceptive, less inclined to lie to his inner self. The inauthentic self has little sense of direction, and to render himself confident, he makes himself absolute, and so whatever he perceives and does is veridical in accordance with his self-affirming fiction. Thus the therapist who sees almost every patient as suffering from insecurity (as if this were not true of everyone) is notably deficient in security himself.

The Internal Act

We take it as self-evident that selfhood is influenced in very important ways by the social environment. An individual perceives himself as a person in the framework of the social expectations of the world in which he lives.

By no means evident is the more important fact that every individual's view of himself is shaped by the unique way in which he internalizes the social world. Each person interprets the values of society in accordance with his own experience and style of life. The view which other persons have of him and his image of himself are transformed in the light of his individual intentions. His image of himself — that precious thing which radiates the meaning of his life — is his unique perception of himself as a person. This self-image is precious because it is the self which the individual recognizes to be truly and intimately his own. It is the unique, subjective organization of organic, interpersonal, and cultural aspects of the integrated personality.

The self-image, though related to the roles which a person enacts in his social groups, differs from them. The role-personality is what each individual is when he fulfills society's expectations, according to such categories as age, sex, marriage, and occupation. The healthy individual enacts these roles easily and comfortably because they make his functioning as a social being possible. There is a great deal of clinical evidence which shows that deficiency or failure in enacting one's social roles is the source of maladjustive behavior. Although the self-image changes with every increment of personal growth, compared to the role-personality, or the image of ourselves conferred upon us by the customs of our group, it is the more enduring aspect of the total personality. The self-image identifies a person over time and differentiates him from other individuals. Paradoxical as it may seem, we can predict a person's behavior more confidently from his unique, personal self-image, than from the roles he enacts. There is more consistency and integrity in the "core" of his personality, than in the social self imposed upon him by society.

In this analysis of the self-image, we attribute great importance to the subjective life of man. The internal act by which each individual "classifies" his life into a consistent but growing image of himself, cannot be observed "externally." By means of our self-image we can talk to ourselves, and in a way objectify and evaluate ourselves, and "size up" the objective situation. This is introspection in the best and most effective sense, a process of seeing ourselves objectified.

The internal act by means of which every individual recognizes himself as a person by objectifying his inner life, challenges the dominant objectivism of mechanistic psychology. The latter does not recognize the internal act, and rejects the introspective approach to the study of man. It denies the reality of subjective consciousness, and in so doing rejects the personality which the self-image brings into existence. Positivistic psychology would deprive man of that self-confrontation by which each of us intensifies his being and validates the being of another. It closes its "mind" to the nature of the self as *inwardness* — as the reworking of objective facts and subjective trends to form an image of the total person-in-a-situation. It is blind to the most important fact about creative psychotherapy, namely, that the therapist, through a vigorous and courageous effort of self-objectification, enters *into* and *lives with* the self of the other, instead of merely observing him. It means, furthermore, that the therapist operates not merely with clinical knowledge and skill, but by means of his own subjective meanings. He sees the image of the other as he freely meets it within his own self-image. Psychotherapy is always the acceptant confrontation of self-images — the self-image of the client and the self-image of the therapist — in which both are mutually modified. All psychotherapy, by whatever label we identify it, is subjective.

The self-image originates and grows in the framework of the internal act. Many individuals, when they search for the first glimmerings of their own selfhood, will find its sudden acute emergence in the form of self-awareness. We are not referring to the dim awareness by the very young child of his own "bodily" self. This is but the child's experience of sensory stimuli, visceral activities, and muscular movements. Although these processes may indeed serve as vague antecedents of the more developed self, the discovery of the self in the form of a consciousness of myself as an "I," as a subjectivity, is something both sudden and intense. Although its occurrence varies with individuals, it appears most often after the fifth or sixth year in a child's life, but often in preadolescence.

In a significant recent article, Spiegelberg describes this self-discovery as the "I-am-me" experience.[4]

Using testimony supplied by autobiographies of literary figures, Spiegelberg shows the sudden and acute oncome of self-awareness, of the exultant "I-am-me" experience. Later he elicited the origin of self-awareness empirically by means of questionnaires designed to disclose its occurrence. He found that the age of its discovery varies, and that some find the experience of discovery unusually enjoyable, whereas others find it upsetting. Some, especially those who lead a solitary and ruminating life, find relief in being given the opportunity to express their experience of it, and especially in discovering that the experience of acute self-discovery is shared by many individuals. Some individuals did not report the experience of self-discovery. Although Spiegelberg does not account for its absence in some individuals, it is certainly not improbable that it has been lost to memory, rather than having never occurred.

Another explanation of its seeming absence in some individuals is the possibility that in many instances the experience is the result

[4] H. Spiegelberg, "On the 'I-Am-Me' Experience," *Rev. Exist. Psychol. & Psychiat.*, 1964, *4*, 3–21.

of a traumatic event. Accordingly, in those people in whom it occurred in less dramatic circumstances, the experience might well have been forgotten.

The role of trauma is acutely evident in a few cases which the present writer has studied in some detail. In two cases which are well-documented, the experience of self-discovery was unpleasant and occurred in connection with traumatic experience. In one instance a boy, slightly over five years of age, discovered himself as being "different" or "bad." It came about when his mother spanked him lightly with a hairbrush, having never experienced physical punishment before. The other instance was that of an immigrant boy, slightly over eleven years of age, who was harassed and persecuted, physically and emotionally, for being a "dirty wop." Our own feeling about the matter, based on the study of both literary figures and living individuals, is that the "I-am-me" experience is universal, but most acute in highly sensitive and emotionally intense individuals.

Although one is always grateful for additions to one's understanding of the human person, it in no way minimizes the value of Spiegelberg's study to observe that the I-am-me experience has been a subject of profound interest in the psychology of the self for a long time. Much of the value of Spiegelberg's investigation lies in its timeliness and in its confirmation of a generally proactive view of man.

Transcendence

Conventional psychology has bogged down and denied its own potentiality for growth by stressing, in excess of supporting evidence, that psychological health consists of individual and social adjustment. Yet, because of the damaging consequences of this extremely one-sided emphasis on the externals of behavior, our strictures cannot be repeated too often. There is mounting evidence deriving from existential, humanistic, and proactive psychology, and from all forms of creative psychotherapy, that the principles of adjustment are not universally valid. Worse yet, they reflect the premises of a mechanistic psychology and the bias of individual psychologists. If one defines mental health as the capacity to adjust oneself to the dominant mores, then quite clearly every individual for whom integrity and autonomy are more important than a comfortable social acceptance is *ipso facto* maladjusted.

Furthermore, many of us feel that even those psychologists who have advanced the dynamics of the human personality by expanding the adjustment model and defining health in terms of competence, are still conceptualizing human behavior within the adjustment framework. This is true of White's stimulating concept of competence.[5]

Characteristic of every healthy individual is a strong resistance to engulfment and influence by the immobilizing power of convention and custom. This resistance appears early in the socializing process of some individuals, and is probably present in all of us. It is not necessary to be a psychologist to discover this simple fact, for everyone who has guided the growth of children and young people knows this from personal experience. There are astonishing differences in the resistance and docility of the human organism.

Despite the obviousness of this condition, most psychologists persist in the established routine, describing all behavior as modes of social adjustment. Some of them, baffled if not chagrined by the resistant autonomy of some individuals, label this independence as persistent non-adjustive reaction. What saves this concept from absurdity is that it is recognized to be a class of responses, not a description of total beings. Yet, the concept is largely irrelevant, for man is a whole, not a part-reaction.

Countering this one-sided and exaggerated emphasis on adjustment, but not contradicting its place in the total psychological economy, is the view that the individual, quite early in his psychological growth, shows signs of maintaining his autonomy. Resistance and transcendence are intimately related. The person who resists enculturation is more free to transcend his former being. Resistance refers to the degree of freedom from external social pressures; transcendence means the capacity to transform oneself in the light of personal goals and values. Contrary to a view expressed by some, transcendence has nothing to do with a state of existence beyond the known world; it is not a "spirit" world, or an immortal condition. Every individual who has succeeded in transcending his past experience knows full well that there is nothing beyond it but *more* experience. There is no need to posit a supra-individual being, or supra-social existence, in this view.

Thus, transcendence means the continuous change of one's life in the Rilkean sense, of beginning again after every attainment. It means that man is that species of animal who strives to attain a

---

[5] See R. W. White, "Motivation Reconsidered: The Concept of Competence," *Psychol. Rev.*, 1959, *66*, 297–333. For the same criticism, quite independently reached, see A. H. Maslow, *op. cit.*, pp. 168–169.

higher state for himself and his fellow human beings through his own efforts. Man is truer to himself as a proactive being when he transcends the individual and social frames which inhibit his full growth. As a distinguished geneticist put it, the future for man is "one of his own making, if only he will have it so."[6] This view clearly implies that, since even the manifestations of genotypes are changeable — as Dobzhansky, for instance, has pointed out — man can in principle direct his own evolution. If this is true of human evolution, what is there to contradict the belief that man can transcend the narrow and imposed limitations of his existence to become a more perfect being.

Transcendence is not ordinarily stimulated by an overpowering need for social adjustment, but by the search for adventure and tension. It is evoked by what Jaspers so aptly names "frontier situations," the conditions in which the human self feels its integrity and identity at stake. Healthy life is not a homeostatic condition, but a disquietude. Accordingly, a psychology that will rescue man from disintegration in his activities, must offer us a counterpoising process: the transcendence of the social situation and the transformation of the individual in the direction of meanings and values that will achieve and sustain a creative selfhood. Creative selfhood is not some ineffable state of being, but the heightened sense of awareness of oneself and our relation to other human beings.

Consciousness

The most incredible and far-reaching event in the history of psychology was the banishment of the process of consciousness from its domain. This rejection of consciousness is the more astonishing because it was not based on sound and necessary reasons, but on the biased and willful demand that psychology become a completely objective science. Once this premise was accepted and given the most honored place in psychology, few psychologists dared to question it without the risk of losing that most questionable and perishable of commodities: the virtue of scientific respectability.

The "proof" of the non-existence of consciousness is invulnerable, for it has a built-in necessity. In order to experience consciousness one must be capable of self-consciousness, a condition which is

[6] H. J. Muller, "The Human Future," in J. Huxley (ed.), *The Humanist Frame* (New York: Harper and Brothers, 1961), p. 414.

obviously impossible if consciousness is non-existent. The consciousness which the behaviorists discarded was the inert consciousness in general. But consciousness does not exist *überhaupt:* it is always the property of an individual. Consciousness is but another term for *experience.* Experience is characterized by the fact that it is *my* experience. As experience, consciousness includes the capacity of being aware of our own consciousness — of self-consciousness. The denial of consciousness is the denial of human experience and self-awareness. Yet, it is a commonplace fact that the psychologist who has disowned consciousness is nevertheless engaged in the observation and recording of the experiences of subjects — their learning, memory, motives, and other psychological activities. These scientific procedures require an exceptional degree of awareness, even of self-awareness on the scientist's part, for his relations to the subjects can and do influence both his observations and the behavior of his subjects. Indeed his consciousness is the end-term of the relation between himself and the object of his investigation.

Consciousness, then, is not the entity or receptacle which its biased critics have made it, but a function, or individual process. In this process the self is the focalizing center, the relationship in which experiences are ordered into a spatio-temporal continuum. The conscious self is thus not an epiphenomenon, not the fringe of experience, not a set of habits, but the core of organized and meaningful experience, the organizing and self-regulating capacities of the total personality.

The human subject in the laboratory experiment is more than an organic instrument which is sensitive to stimuli. Unlike a thermometer which simply registers the temperature, or a lower animal responding to heat sensations, the human self is both conscious and self-conscious about the external condition. He can comment upon the temperature and communicate his response to others. The animal can only withdraw from the warm register, but the conscious self can turn the heat off at will.

Psychotherapy would be impossible if there were no states of consciousness in both the therapist and the patient. Roughly speaking, the mentally ill person is notably deficient in self-awareness. In this connection, self-awareness should not be confused with morbid self-consciousness, or the fear that one's subjective behavior, which has been projected, does not belong to oneself. Psychotherapy is the exploration of the patient's states of consciousness, including unconscious — or as we would say, potential —

states, as yet unborn. Successful therapy consists in a reconstruction of the patient's inner world, a heightening of the awareness of himself as an experiencing person. The psychotherapies of Jaspers, Minkowski, Binswanger, Boss, Frankl, and Rogers, as representatives of the creative explorations of the patient's inner life, all bear witness to the presence in patient and therapist of states of consciousness. The patient's delusions themselves presuppose an active conscious process. The presence of delusions indicate a temporary disruption in the stream of consciousness, in the unity and continuity of the patient's mental life. The fundamental purpose of every therapeutic interview is to understand and appreciate the patient's subjectivity, his awareness of himself as a person. This concern for the patient's subjective life is rapidly replacing the outmoded preoccupation with his symptoms and past history, with syndromes and taxonomy. Behaviorism, in other words, is giving way in psychotherapy, as in the whole of psychology, to a phenomenological study of states of consciousness.

Wholeness

The stress on the wholeness of the human being is a marked characteristic of the newer trend in personality theory. Whether we call it organismic, holistic, personalistic, or proactive, the stress is always the same: personality is a relatively consistent and unique whole. This is in strong contrast with the mechanistic-statistical view which, when it gives any serious attention to the nature of personality, deals with the generalized or statistically average individual, or the whole as a *compound* of discrete variables. From the holistic point of view, the individual holds transactions with his environment, not by means of part-reactions, but as a whole person. The "parts" sustain their relations to the external world integrally, not separately and atomically. The order of reality in holistic psychology conceives personality as the ultimate standard, an order which also obtains in the natural sciences, as we are continually discovering.[7]

One of the greatest advantages of the view of personality as an

---

[7] In this mode of conceptualizing personality in its relation to science lies the hope of once more uniting the sciences and the humanities. It is perhaps not so remarkable, in view of his own uncompromising stress on the wholeness of life, that Goethe saw life and art and science as a "whole united in flaming fusion" (*das zusammenbrennende Zusammentreffende Ganze*). The idea is particularly stressed in his *Wilhelm Meisters Lehrjahre.*

integral whole is that it unites in a single conception the view that personality, whether we refer to the scientist, the poet, or the "ordinary" healthy individual, is always a more or less integrated whole of reason and intuition, feeling and imagination, drive and allurement, understanding and appreciation.

We have said that personality is always "a more or less integrated whole." This way of phrasing the matter is not an expression of doubt or uncertainty, but the reiteration of a former observation, namely, that man is a highly selective individual. He selects from the many possibilities in his life organization those which best satisfy his needs, interests, aspirations, sentiments, and passions. In this view the authentic person and the authentic science of the person are both irreducible totalities.

From the holistic point of view, then, personalities differ from one another, not merely in their intelligence and motivation, but even more so in the degree of their capacity for integral personal experience. For the integrally structured person every experience has a greater completeness in itself and a greater openness to experience at the same time. This is our understanding of Rogers' discovery that every person is "an island to himself" and that each of us can build bridges to other islands, if each is willing to be himself.[8]

We dare to hypothesize that the more integral a person is, the more veridical and authentic are his experiences and the more he can trust himself. For this reason, the individual who trusts his experience, which is to say his immediate, or intuitive, grasp of a situation, usually has a more reliable understanding of life and people, than one who is bound too closely to technical knowledge and conventional belief. In short, understanding other people is a function of the integral unity of the total personality.

Admittedly, the concept of integral unity is difficult to establish empirically. It is an experiential, not an experimentally verifiable, state of being. It is not something above, or in addition to, the integrated functions, but the integration itself. It unites all those separate activities which have historically divided human nature into subject and object, inner and outer, implicit and overt, mind and body, behavior and consciousness. In our view, all these have a place in the individual, but none of them by itself or in mere combination, explains the holistic character of the personality. But

---

[8] C. R. Rogers, *op. cit.*, p. 21.

it is precisely the latter, the holistic element in reality, that accounts for personality as a whole.

Again, the integral whole is not a fixed condition. It is not something fully identifiable and achieved, but a process, a being-in-becoming. Since we cannot use empirical procedures or experimental-statistical formulations without destroying its essential unity, the integral personality cannot be formulated in the strict cause-effect, stimulus-response paradigms. Being unique, it lies in the realm of the unpredictable. It is not a derived particular, but a complex arising anew in every individual. Biological inheritance does not account for it, but only for its organic capacities. Although each of us inherits from his parents and other ancestors the various endowments, the personality as an integral whole is always a new creation. In our personalities we are thus not bound to our heridatary past, but lured by the possibilities of freedom that are inherent in the creative evolutionary process. The "parts" we inherit genetically, but the integral whole is a blend which is different from the organic particulars. The appearance of the integral personality on the biological scene marks a new and momentous event in the process of evolution. For this reason psychology, in so far as it pretends to investigate part-functions empirically, is unable to deal with the integral personality. The science of personality, therefore, needs yet to be born. When it is finally fully developed, psychology, especially in its study of the human personality, will be a harmonious blend of the naturalistic and the humanistic modes of investigation. We believe that the present volume is a foreshadowing of, if not a complete introduction to, the psychology of man. We believe too, that the science of personality serves at least as a footbridge, if not as a firmer structure, between the so-called "third school" of Vienna (logotherapy and existentialism) and the poorly named "third force" in the United States (humanistic and proactive psychology).

The Social Encounter

It should now be evident that proactive psychology is the study of the social nature of man, as well as his unique individuality. Much space has been given in this book to the study of the social situation, the estrangement of man from his fellow human beings, with its concomitance of anxiety and guilt, and of sensibility and the loving encounter. To the extent and degree that man inescapably participates in the nature of being, he is a part of the subjectivity of other human beings. The concept of freedom which we discussed in Chapter 5, is meaningless except as man actualizes himself in a determinate sociocultural environment. The self is always discovered in association with others — in love and strife and reconciliation. It finds its fullest expression in care and sacrificial surrender to the person of the other one. Although man values above all else his personal integrity, he suffers deeply when he has only himself as the object of relatedness. Engagement in the life of other individuals is necessary for one's own growth and renewal. No individual is a mere spectator; no one a complete outsider. Man is the being in whom sacrifice and reception comingle; for whom giving is already a form of receiving, as Marcel expressed it.[9] Personality can come into being and actualize its potentialities only when we enter into meaningful relations with other persons. We learn of the nature of man not only in the manner in which he actualizes himself, but also by the way he relates himself to other human beings. Human life is individual expression and social encounter. In the absence of encounter, a life ceases to be a dialogue and becomes "monological."[10]

The social encounter is not a bare relation or interaction. In these forms of relationship we can learn about an individual, but not necessarily understand him. Social encounter is, rather, that sensibility which we described in Chapter 8. It is found in every form of creative human relationship and in every form of good psychotherapy. May notes the well-known fact that in psychotherapy, as distinguished from a knowledge obtained from case records and clinical interviews, we often have the experience of "here-is-a-new-person."[11] In the social encounter we can know an individual not only in the external modes in which he adjusts himself to others, but also in the unique quality of his being as he spontaneously reveals himself in his participation in the being or subjectivity of another human being.

The unique character of an individual is discovered also in the pluralistic nature of the social encounter. In the encounter of one

[9] G. Marcel, *Homo Viator: Introduction to a Metaphysics of Hope.* Trans. by E. Craufurd. (London: Victor Gollancz, Ltd., 1951).

[10] See M. Buber, *Between Man and Man.* Trans. by R. G. Smith. (London: Kegan Paul, Trench and Trubner, 1947), p. 22. The term "social encounter" is Allport's. See G. W. Allport, *Personality and Social Encounter* (Boston: Beacon Press, 1960).

[11] R. May, "Contribution of Existential Psychotherapy," in R. May *et al.* (eds.), *Existence: A New Dimension in Psychiatry and Psychology* (New York: Basic Books, Inc., 1958), p. 37.

self with the self of another we see man as he reveals himself in his several modes of being: diadic, plural, and anonymous. The diadic mode refers to the intimate encounter of two beings, such as those of a parent and child, and lover and beloved. The plural mode is the encounter among several individuals, and is most common in the daily interactions of competition, conflict, accommodation, and assimilation. The anonymous mode we described in detail in Chapter 3. It is the type of relationship found in the impersonal, socially distant relations of people in our mass society. Some forms of this social encounter are essentially negative and destructive, and Ellenberger, who has described the several modes of encounter, cites as examples the dancer at a masked ball, the soldier who kills others or is killed by them. He cites also the interesting case of the author of anonymous letters who is, in effect, conducting anonymous battles with his audience.[12]

The social encounter does not refer merely to the social interactions so well described by the sociologist, but also to the diadic engagement, as we have shown, of patient and therapist in the healing situation. Gebsattel refers to "the experience of an encounter with an unexplainable other being," in the form of wonder or astonishment. Like Ellenberger and May, Gebsattel has shown that our encounter with the troubled individual is not exhausted in the objective knowledge of his symptoms, defenses, and life history. What we experience in psychotherapy is the "being-different" of a fellow being in his human totality. A knowledge of his symptomatology and his life history, which is to say his past, is an intellectual encounter which appeals to our intellect and curiosity and leads to "scientific understanding." The truly creative social encounter, however, consists of an attitude of "wonder," in which the "unexplainable other being" is more deeply penetrated. Scientific knowledge of therapy may actually serve as a block or barrier to such a penetration. In the realm of wonder and contemplation new insights are created. This wonder, this sudden astonishment by the appearance of a new person not revealed in his symptoms and life history, leads us "beyond the bounds of purely scientifically-oriented intellect and its inclination to functional-theoretical and functional-mechanistic trains of thought."[13]

The wonder and astonishment are there because the social en-

[12] H. P. Ellenberger, "A Clinical Introduction to Psychiatric Phenomenology and Existential Analysis," in R. May *et al.* (eds.), *op. cit.*, p. 122.
[13] V. E. von Gebsattel, "The World of the Compulsive," in R. May *et al.*, *op. cit.*, p. 172.

counter is not a static state in which one person reacts to another person, but a process: the process of being-in-becoming, the process in which the being of the other appears to us as a new being — the "being-different" of each person to the other. In this "being-different" we see the other person not as he was, but as he is coming to be. The social encounter is thus a process in which every individual experiences mutual self-confirmation and magnifies his self-actualization.

CONCLUSION

Psychology in the twentieth century made three important decisions which turned it away from the study of the conduct of man to a preoccupation with part-relations. The decisions were, first, to investigate the behavior of separate processes, such as learning and homeostatic drives; second, the denial of conscious experience; and third, the casting of all behavior, from the simplest sensory reaction to the most complex personality structure, in the paradigm of stimulus-response equivalence. The first decision partitioned man into separate and tenuously related part-functions; the second decision denied the inner life of man — the life of freedom, self-direction, and moral choice; the third decision put man in total bondage to his past, or at the mercy of mere mechanical reconditioning.

These decisions, which are themselves clear arguments for the freedom of man, have forced psychology to adopt a thin and trivial program of scientific investigation, from which proactive man, the true subject-matter of psychology, has been banished. Above all, total personality, or man in his fullest, has become the stepchild of a technologically burgeoning psychology.

This technologically growing science — science in its most impoverished meaning — is inherently unfit to deal with the most important fact of human life: the fact that man is a being who, while resting on his past, builds himself a future. Psychology is unintelligible if we do not assume that in personality we have a central organizing power which controls and directs the separate functions which empirical psychology has done so much to identify and measure. The personality is the center of reference which makes human experience intelligible. It is the "organ" of self-direction and self-actualization. It confers unity and wholeness on human experience. Personality is no mere collection of sensations, motives, and memories, but an inwardness which cannot be quantitatively defined. It is no mere outward structure: no adventitious process, no epiphenomenon, but is in its maturest form an inward grace which, lured by the adventure of growth and novelty, propels man into the future.

This proactive character of man is, on traditional grounds, a mystery and a delusion. Its reality can be established only by a psychology willing and capable of transcending the crippling limitations imposed upon it by an anachronistic conception of the nature and method of science. These limitations were explored and evaluated in our first chapter, to which the reader is asked to return for a fresh evaluation. The day has long passed when the positivist in psychology can continue to bolster a tottering psychology by means of an outmoded philosophy. The facts of genetics and evolutionary theory leave no doubt that the whole — of which the personality is the supreme example — is not a compound of individual parts, but a creative synthesis of the parts into a new being different from and transcending them. Conventional psychology is incapable of dealing adequately with personality, for it derives wholes from their parts. Modern holistic theory in genetics, evolution, and proactive psychology denies that the character of the whole can be inferred, or "extrapolated," from the characters of its separate parts. It demonstrates, on the contrary, that the essence of all wholes is found in their transcendence of the individual parts. The whole is not dominated by its parts, as mechanistic psychology would have us believe, but is self-determined. In this self-determination of the whole, as it applies to the total, proactive personality, lies the freedom and self-determination of the human individual. In short, personality is the most complete embodiment of that wholeness which is immanent in both nature and man.

PART
FOUR

Revival of Wisdom

11

Man's dignity stems not from his having been given a favored place in the universe but from the fact that while his existence is contingent, his life is his own creation.

HAZEL E. BARNES

Toward the Perfectibility of Man

When psychology declared its independence of philosophy — an independence which has been only partially achieved — it also renounced all pretension to wisdom. Although philosophy has by no means lived up to its name, its lovers and advocates have occasionally achieved a measure of understanding and wisdom, as well as scholarly erudition.

Psychologists, on the other hand, have resisted, as Boring once remarked, "the humanizing deviations that would bring their science over toward scholarship and wisdom and understanding." They have resisted, Boring goes on to say, "because they are dedicated to a narrow empiricism."[1]

It is therefore in vain that we look to psychology for wisdom about man. The search is the more disappointing in view of the fact that psychology, even more than philosophy, has the potential for making man more wise and insightful regarding himself.

When it is actualized, wisdom is the art of intelligent living. The meaning of one's life is fulfilled in the actualization of the values that constitute the human personality. But in this connection academic psychology has very little relevance to man's effort to make himself into a better being. Moreover, if the psychoanalytic view of man is to be taken as a guide to perfectibility, it will more

[1] E. G. Boring, in *Contemp. Psychol.*, 1958, 3, p. 62.

likely than not discourage every man of sensibility. This reaction would be salutary if psychoanalytic descriptions of man were congruent with man's forward-directedness. Unfortunately, this is not the case. Freudian man is the prisoner of his encapsulating past, and holds out little hope for growth and perfection. It promises only a recapitulation of man's past in a contemporary setting.

Although man is amazing, he is no masterpiece, as a character in Conrad's *Lord Jim*, ruefully complains. Rather than serving as a complaint about man's shortcoming, this observation is not an argument against his perfectibility. It implies that man can evaluate, praise, or condemn his life in the light of the perfect deed, rather than wholly in the shadow of a determined fate. It challenges Martin Luther's famous cry: *ich kann nicht anders* ("I cannot do otherwise"), as he nailed his *Theses* to the church door. It is the cry of every helpless individual, for in the face of possibilities he *can* but *does not* choose otherwise. His was not so much an act of courage, as a demonic show of defiance. The implication of Luther's defiance, as with all radical forms of revolt, is that inner turmoil is often a forerunner of vital improvement. Wisdom and perfectibility seldom result from a comfortable serenity. The enlargement of experience and the wisdom and perfectibility to which it may lead, is born in inner strife. For this reason the lessons of Goethe's life and art are better guides to creative living than many specialized bits of information furnished by orthodox psychologies. Faust is the symbol of man's eternal search for the meaning of life; of his capacity, through striving, to change himself into a better human being. The transformation of Faust, as he moves from the First to the Second Part of Goethe's tragedy of that name, is an eloquent argument for wisdom about life and the perfectibility of man.

Wisdom lies not in the fragments of life, but in its totality. Faust found the meaning of life when he exercised responsibility and renunciation, when in the midst of partial and fragmentary experience, he was able to envision life as a whole.

We believe that the psychologies which hold out hope for man are those which, although based on sound Freudian principles, have outgrown their negative and inhibitory features. Those psychologies present us with a picture of man full of possibilities for change and improvement, of which the psychoanalytic view of man gives us no hint. This is true of all essentially proactive psychologies, such as existentialism, logotherapy, humanistic psychology, the psychology of Carl Rogers, and the recent advances in the psychiatric work of Karl Menninger.[2] Although steeped in the Freudian framework, Menninger's view of man is oddly at variance with the metapsychological pessimism of Sigmund Freud. Menninger's proactive man is capable of self-abnegation that the pleasure principle cannot explain or justify.

The psychological investigation of perfectibility is the most difficult task in the study of man. Before we can take even the first faltering step, however, we must divest ourselves of the false belief that perfectibility lies outside the realm of scientific investigation, and overcome the timidity which inhibits us when we face an unexplored area. We believe that a first approximation to its understanding is possible, and we shall make the attempt.

INHIBITION AND RESTRAINT

Perfectibility can be understood better when we know the barriers which block or prevent the realization of one's potentialities. These barriers have been widely examined in connection with the problems of development and growth, but their relevance to human perfectibility has been largely neglected.

Early Socialization

Every reader who is familiar with the extensive research on socialization, child-rearing, or enculturation, both local and cross-cultural, knows that the manner of social patterning may enhance or inhibit the actualization of human potentialities. It is fair to say that many efforts to humanize the growing child are negative and inhibitory. Their chief objective is to fit the child into the conventional mode of thought and action. Although this patterning of the child's personality is both necessary and desirable — without it societal life would be impossible — there is inherent in it the ever-present danger of inhibiting the child's individuality.

Descriptions of the socialization process in the United States are often based on the unstated assumption that American life is more uniform than it actually is. Although our social life and our modes of child training differ by class and geographic location, nevertheless, there are discernible uniformities.

Socialization and control of the child rest largely with the mother. Without going into the details of toilet and genital train-

[2] For the last-named, see K. Menninger, *The Vital Balance* (New York: The Viking Press, Inc., 1963).

ing, the effects of which are often exaggerated by psychoanalytic investigators, it can be said that these forms of socialization are, on the whole, not too severe. Education in the home and on the playground encourages competitive and aggressive attitudes and behavior. This approach is embedded in our strong emphasis on success and getting ahead, or being on top in most of our activities. The child soon learns that success in most things guarantees parental love and acceptance. This success may have little relation to excellence. It involves the mother's fear of being found deficient as a parent if the child does not compare favorably with other children in the parent's social world. Nothing is a greater reproach to her as a mother than her child's failure to measure up to her conception of the child as she compares him with other children in the neighborhood.

The mother's anxiety over her child follows him in practically all his activities. If Gorer is right, the mother is particularly afraid that her child might turn out to be a "sissy." In this he is supported by Margaret Mead's study of the American "character."[3]

The mother's class-consciousness, which is typical of most Americans, is characterized by a strong need for conformity, a need which has been raised to the level of a moral principle. "The good man," as we have written elsewhere, "is not only the man who has made good but who does what all good men do: he follows the Joneses."[4] Nonconformity is proof of differentness, and this in turn is often a sign of idiosyncrasy, even of inferiority. We fear and dislike the black sheep among us. Thus, proponents of civil rights for everyone, friends of labor, and advocates of school desegregation are still often suspect.

The conforming behavior which begins in childhood is reflected in later life by an almost compulsive need to join and belong. The average middle-class American finds his friends and gains a needed acceptance in his clubs and lodges. The associations in these groups are based less on congeniality of character than on common interests and similar needs. It is friendship of a sort, but a companionship based on the need to be liked and accepted and rewarded for one's agreeable behavior. If many Americans suffer

[3] G. Gorer, *The American People* (New York: W. W. Norton and Company, Inc., 1948); M. Mead, *And Keep Your Powder Dry* (New York: William Morrow and Company, 1942).

[4] H. Bonner, *Social Psychology: An Interdisciplinary Approach* (New York: American Book Company, 1953), p. 287.

the emptiness of inauthenticity, as we believe they do, the vacuity
is one consequence of the fear of individuality and the dread of
estrangement and loneliness which nonconformity begets.

Educational Leveling

The uniformalization begun in the home and extended to the
playground and the peer group is continued and augmented in the
educational organization, from kindergarten to university. Despite
the increasing mania for hurrying up the educative process by
advanced placement, intellectual grouping, and similar devices
spawned by our professional educationists, we nevertheless do not
hold individual excellence in high esteem. Instead, what we are
doing throughout our entire educational establishment is to sort
out young persons who are able to survive the rigorous, but on the
whole mechanical, demand for learning and reproducing what they
have learned, on standardized examinations. The entire procedure
is based on the fallacious notion that the individuals who have survived the patterning process are a homogeneous group of people.
However, everything that we have said in this book points in a
different direction. If the youths who emerge from the terrible
process of patterning and deformation are very much alike, it is
because a bad education has dampened or killed their extraordinary
differences. Much of the degeneration in taste and the tendency
to slogan-thinking can be laid at the door of the leveling process
in our education. What we are creating is not the superiority and
love of excellence that a sound education can produce, but the
inhibition of talent and a spurious culture. In his sober moments,
when he can lay aside his inherited ideas about socialization and
education, every college teacher must be astonished by the results
which he has helped to produce. Our students, in and out of
college, have little understanding, let alone a keen appreciation, of
ideas outside their immediate application. Even in those areas
where the love of ideas and the appreciation of beauty can be most
readily expected, namely, the realm of arts and letters and the
humanities, we find a preoccupation, on the part of students and
teacher alike, with literary and aesthetic constants. Criticism and
the arts, it seems, are also straining to be exact and scientific, and
at a time when the great makers of science themselves are trying
to bridge scientific constants and humanistic variables. Our students of philosophy and literature are misguided by a narrow conception of reason and intelligence as abstract understanding. From
a proactive, humanistic point of view, however, understanding

means abstract intelligence, imagination, intuition, feeling and taste, integrated in the total personality. Every creative person, be he scientist, philosopher, artist, poet, or teacher, is marked by a profound capacity for individual experience, for love and sensibility, quite apart from technical intelligence and academic learning. Erudition is precious, but the life of the creative intellect and aesthetic feeling is more precious still.

It is precisely here that our educational concerns are largely irrelevant and our educational establishment breaks down. The dominant method of selection and the ruling philosophy of education are both based on a questionable factualism. This factualism has little or nothing to do with understanding and appreciation. It has imposed a pseudo-objectivism upon education which few have the courage to challenge. Since a fact can be challenged only by a contradictory fact, the factual disclosures of tests and examinations are invulnerable. Little thought is given by the factualists to another fact, which is less demonstrable, that our techniques of testing and measuring assure the survival of the unfit, which is to say, those individuals who have the capacity of factual memory. At the same time it rejects those whose intellects are characterized by independence and spontaneity. Every observant and thoughtful teacher, whose thinking is not impaired by the dominant tradition and emphasis in education, knows that too often those who survive the dispiriting drudgery that forces the student's mind to submit to the attainment of snippets and facts and technical skills, are mediocre in feeling, understanding, and loving appreciation. The exasperation and despair of the gifted intellect in the face of the tyrannical factualism, is a terror to behold. It destroys, in a very short time, the spontaneity and wonder and integrity of the student's mind.

We can save these precious qualities in our students only if we show vision and courage in revising our view of the nature of man and directing education away from factualism and conformity toward creative values and proactive personality.

The Consolations of Mediocrity

No one in his right mind deliberately seeks or approves mediocrity. Nevertheless, mediocrity is a refuge for all those for whom superiority and excellence serve as a threat to their comfortable stability. This attitude is not entirely an individual one, but is embedded in a false view of the nature of democratic equality in education and in daily life. This view holds excellence and democratic equality as incompatible attainments. Although it is a false dichotomy, it is nevertheless responsible for a wide-spread suspicion of the excellent and the superior. It is not true, as some apologists tell us, that our fear of excellence is a remnant of the American Frontier, when men had neither time nor inclination to cultivate intellectual and aesthetic virtues. Many generations have been born and died, since our uncouth pioneer days, and the explanation is anachronistic.

The fear of quality is based on invidiousness — the notion, as we have said, that quality and equality are incompatible. However, it is precisely in a democratic society, with its tolerance of diversity, that abilities of all kinds can be actualized. When it is free of the fear of individuality and differentness, as democracy is at its best, equality and excellence are among its highest values. It is not democratic equality that is at fault, therefore, but the false notion that democracy must aim for the average, lest it grow into an aristocracy of merit and superiority. That for many people a comfortable mediocrity is safer is not to be doubted, but this fact does not invalidate the belief that merit and equality are not mutually exclusive.

There is no significant evidence in our society that talent and superiority lead to hierarchical discrimination and snobbery. On the contrary, it is quite clear that men and women of talent are also persons of loyalty and responsibility. Talent, especially when it is also informed, as it tends to be, by sensibility and understanding, breeds democracy and other-mindedness. The spirit of aristocracy, which many fear will arise if merit is widely encouraged and rewarded, is not a spirit of separateness but of sympathetic understanding. Democratic pluralism does not tolerate, let alone promote, hierarchical power or authority. Excellence can have no official spokesman, and no machinery of indoctrination, by means of which to establish itself as a power that would successfully challenge our democratic institutions. The real danger in America comes, not from the able and the gifted, but from the mediocre individuals who would stifle creativeness and individuality, because these challenge the safety of their mediocrity and conformity.

Bureaucratization of the Intellect

One of the gravest dangers to our democratic institutions and to the actualization of creative potentialities, is the bureaucratization of the intellect. Astute men should have foreseen that sooner or later science and scholarship would capitulate to the collective spirit of the age. It seems that the last ramparts of freedom and independence are beginning to crumble before the onslaughts of a comfortable togetherness. The irony of this development lies, not in the social pressures of science to apply its findings to the betterment of our social order, but to the ill-supported belief that the group is superior to the individual in the solution of important problems. Accordingly, in science, as in industry and government, the virtues of consensus and harmony are challenging the disturbing qualities of dissension and individuality.

The search for consensual validation is a worthy aim, for no group can survive in the long run without its stabilizing influence. What is dangerous in this tendency is the stultification of originality and diversity. Bold and imaginative thinking is by its nature divisive, as Whyte has shown, and the bigger the decision-making committee, the more people are going to be offended.[5]

This condition is spreading and being rationalized and justified by many individuals. The anti-individualism which informs it is justified to the point where it is openly affirmed that the individual, as we remarked in Chapter 5, must be bent to the requirements of group thinking.

The illusion of harmony. The anti-individualistic character of much recent research is shown not only in the unpopularity and distrust of the lone investigator, but even more in the deferential overdependence on the team. This distorted notion of the democratic process easily results in sacrificing individual thinking for the sake of appearing harmonious and dedicated to the collective effort. Individual convictions, especially when they appear to be "erratic" and "wrong-headed" to the majority, are beaten down for the sake of organized research. A tragic outcome of this collectivization of human thinking is that it tends to stunt original ideas. The gifted mind, while pursuing its own thinking with a determination that baffles the ordinary and mediocre individual, is exasperatedly impatient with the inhibiting character of collective thinking. From the standpoint of creative science, one original idea, no matter how contrary to the demands of short-run investigation, may often be

[5] W. H. Whyte, *The Organization Man* (New York: Simon and Schuster, Inc., 1946), p. 223.

Some of the materials in the section on Bureaucratization of the Intellect were supplied by Karl Weick, in a seminar at Ohio State University, Autumn 1960, to whom indebtedness is gratefully acknowledged.

worth much more than all the technical minutiae of scientific "projectism."

Organized research is so often afraid of making mistakes that it impairs the individual's capacity for fresh insights. The coercive nature of much organized research — coercive because of the need to erect a facade of collective harmony — is often a paralyzing interference with that dedicated inquiry, which is the essence of scientific investigation. The creative mind, whether in science or the arts, has its own criteria of importance, rigor, and dependability within the framework of an inter-subjective system of logic.

Some research groups are less committed to the discovery of truth than to the appearance of collective harmony. In this they resemble the business establishment whose main concern is to make its products seem to be what they are not; or the automobile designers who, as Norman Cousins once pointed out in *Saturday Review,* compete with one another in depriving the passenger of essential space by allocating it to the rear trunk. "Baggage rides in splendor, but people are cramped," writes Cousins, ruefully.

The art of staging. Putting on a harmonious facade is an important factor in sustaining technological research. Members of the research team cooperate to maintain the impression that they are achieving their ends. This maintenance of a stance in the eyes of the public and their colleagues is designed to maintain the unity of the team. Like advertising in business, it results in a bureaucratization of reasearch which hinders research itself.

This art of staging is glaringly revealed in Noltingk's description of the work of the Tube Investment Research Laboratory, in Cambridge, England. It seems that the director of research must present two fronts. He must represent the outside world to his staff, but at the same time be ready to advertise and defend himself to his establishment. "His own people must know him to be honest and open," writes Noltingk, "though the higher circles of technical and industrial politics in which he moves will almost certainly turn him, while there, into a political schemer."[6]

In order to maintain, or seem to maintain, a high level of performance, a research team will communicate selected facts to its consumer. Accordingly, it must withhold any discrepant information from those who might judge its work adversely. This information is known as "inside secrets." These inside secrets in turn

[6] B. E. Noltingk, *The Human Element in Research Management* (Amsterdam: Elsevier, 1959), p. 49.

pose a difficult problem for the researcher — the problem of mutual suspiciousness and the danger of group disruption. Those who are not permitted to share the secrets feel excluded, and their feeling of group solidarity is undermined. On the other hand, the more persons share the secrets, the greater the possibility of their unintended disclosure.

This dual situation in collective research sows the seeds of its own destruction; for when the team project has been completed, the group is dissolved unless it is ingenious enough to expand or prolong its project. However, research teams have been known to maintain themselves even in the absence of any problem, merely by appearing to be busy in the eyes of their sponsors. This process is aided by keeping research "within the family." An almost inevitable consequence of this behavior is the formation of a tightly knit bureaucracy, in which loyalty to the team guarantees its survival. Clearly, this condition is not conducive to genuine experimentation, novelty, and the expression of independent ideas.

The role of ambiguity. The project researcher must have skill in making his investigation satisfy the sponsor's demand for utility. The written report serves as an ideal technique for accomplishing this purpose. In the report, the project director, by the use of such bromides as "empirical," "quantitative evidence," "applied," and "conceptualized observation," gives his sponsor plenty of opportunity to interpret them in accordance with his own knowledge and understanding of scientific techniques. Most of all, the investigator is able, behind the verbal facade, to convince the sponsor that his wishes are being satisfied while the former is in fact performing a different task. This is a new twist — a form of reseach "payola."

This practice of calculated ambiguity is probably most glaring in the application for funds for sponsored research. A research proposal, it has been found, is most likely to receive governmental or business subsidies when it is a blend of sufficient practical ideas to assure a prospective sponsor of what he wants, and ideas ambiguous enough to permit the investigator sufficient latitude for his own definition of research. Futhermore, the calculated ambiguity requires several experts to pass judgment on a proposed project before it is approved and granted funds. Robert Weiss, conducting a study of the Bureau of Government Research, found that, for the approval of one project alone, six groups of additional consultants had to approve it before funds were allocated for its investigation.

A deadly evil of this procedure is that the researcher is often less concerned with an accurate description of his proposal than with satisfying the several committees and judges who will evaluate it. The practiced researcher is skilled in verbalizing his feedback to the sponsoring agency in such a manner as to assure the agency that it is getting what it wants.[7]

The specialist in verbal fronts has been effectively described by Wilensky. The specialist, he points out, is expected to assemble and present his project in such a manner as to lend maximum support to the claims of the team as a whole. In this presentation the facts more often than not are only incidental; what is more important is to be able to anticipate and meet the arguments of the prospective opponents, to sense the attitudes of the public to which the team may want to appeal for support, and to know the principles to which everyone concerned with the project is most likely to give lip-service.

But the whole procedure is faced by a dilemma. The more the applicant is able to forget or rationalize his professional standards and think only of the interests of the team which employs him, the more effective may his arguments for them be; yet, at the same time, the greater his reputation for being an independent professional who is interested only in the facts bearing upon the case, the more effective is he likely to be when he presents his findings to his intended audience.[8]

This mediocritization of scientific scholarship is making inroads on "basic" science as well. Intrinsically, there is no need to make a sharp distinction between "pure," or basic, and applied, or "operational," research; but in practice the difference has been widened by the practitioners of applied, or "horizontal," research. Its large-scale character is rapidly relegating basic research to a position of secondary importance. This is aided by the fact that large-scale research is largely subsidized by government and industry, and because its achievements are usually more spectacular than the long-term — and for the time being apparently "useless" — ideas of the pure scientist. Furthermore, the sponsors are usually much more impressed by, and find it easier to evaluate the results of, quantitative research. Also, the number of persons working on the project is more dramatic than its implications for further research.

[7] See R. S. Weiss, *Process of Organization* (Ann Arbor, Mich.: Survey Research Center, University of Michigan, 1956).

[8] H. L. Wilensky, *The Staff Expert: A Study of the Intelligence Function in American Trade Unions.* Unpublished Ph.D. dissertation, University of Chicago, 1953.

Vast expenditures of public or private funds on a research project add to the glamour of applied investigations. Consequently, there are projects subsidized by the government, for example, which exceed the bounds of good sense. This absurd situation is compounded when the project has the additional quality of propaganda value. When, for example, the Soviet Union announced its wish to join the International Geophysical Year, the project suddenly assumed an importance far out of proportion to its accomplishments. Consequently, the members of the Executive Committee of IGY had to evaluate and approve expenditures which seemed to the Committee disproportionate in relation to the scientific merit of some of the projects involved. Various polar expeditions and rocket flights were financed by our government in amounts which would have "subsidized the physical sciences at all our universities in great luxury for many decades." Merle Tuve, head of the Department of Terrestrial Magnetism, at the Carnegie Institution in Washington, D. C., and Chairman of the aforementioned Executive Committee, pointed out that all the money was spent by our military establishment. "We encountered or produced in the IGA," he wrote, "many examples of drastic loss of a sense of proportion between the costs of a project and its substantive content."[9] This lack of a sense of proportion is magnified by the incredible fact that many governmental or industrial project directors can give no more satisfactory explanation of the importance of their projects than that they cost large sums of money, employ a large number of individuals, and involve great expenditure of effort.

In fine, there is no paucity of evidence to support the conclusion that the economic waste associated with governmental support of research is causing wasted talent and scientific stultification. Excellence and perfectibility are neither encouraged nor rewarded, and moral considerations take a decided beating.[10] The irony of this situation is that many scholars and scientists are themselves engaged in the anti-intellectualism from which men of sensibility have defended science and the arts for more than a century. It weakens, if it does not destroy, the moral and intellectual integrity and responsibility which have always served as civilizing forces in

[9] M. A. Tuve, "Is Science Too Big for the Scientists?" *Saturday Review*, June 6, 1959, pp. 49–52.

[10] For a brief consideration of "the moral obligation of the scientists as trustees of public funds," with special reference to the National Institutes of Health, see the editorial, "Whose Responsibility?" *Science*, 1962, *138*, p. 160.

both the individual and society. It inhibits the creative intellect, enslaves the individual thinker, and thrusts the dedicated scientist into the market-place. When this happens, we all lose.

SPONTANEITY AND CREATIVITY

Implicit in all democratic institutional arrangements is the belief that every individual has the right to actualize his own powers and gifts. Although in practice this ideal is often rejected, as we have seen, in favor of a comfortable mediocrity, it nevertheless has the greatest promise of realization in a free society. Basic to this belief is another one, seldom recognized and infrequently examined. It is, simply, faith in man. This faith in man gets little support from conventional psychology, as should now be very clear. Psychoanalysis and behaviorism hold out little or no promise for perfectibility and individual self-transformation. In both psychologies, despite psychotherapy in one case and reconditioning in the other, man has no choice regarding his psychological future. Both believe that the idea that man can profoundly change himself through his own volition and in accordance with his own value-system, is false and sentimental; and the notion that man is often moved by moral and philosophical beliefs even more than by physiological and defensive needs, is usually either dismissed or rationalized by means of a brand of learning theory.

This way of conceiving man's limitation is all the more remarkable — and disturbing — in light of the historical fact that all great civilizations, including our own, have held a conception of man as a being who is motivated by his own ideal of what he aspires for and desires to be. Only contemporary positivistic psychology denies the obvious fact that man aspires to be someone other than he is, and that he aspires to grow morally and spiritually. Only modern mechanistic psychology refuses to look upon man as an "evolutionary novelty," as a being who has not really fallen, as we have said before, but who has risen and can rise to even greater heights. If neither psychology nor education has perceived the proactive vitality of man, this failure is the consequence of a one-sided rationalistic emphasis. Growth and perfectibility are not matters of reason alone, but of reason informed by character and feeling. The automaton, which our narrowly rationalistic tradition in psychology has made the prototype of human nature, exists only as an abstraction, and is pitifully at variance with the self-discovering and self-transforming living being. Our social institutions, notably our schools and colleges, being dominated by the mechanistic-rationalistic tradition, hold out little hope, except in periodic commencement addresses, for the perfectibility of man; and these, it may be assumed, are wholly without lasting consequences. Like other aspects of human life in which wholeness is an alien idea, both our psychology and our education are artificially removed from the main stream of life. Neither psychology nor education can be of benefit to man unless each is informed by a vital moral purpose. But in their legitimate yet exaggerated faith in the scientific enterprise, each has conceived its function to lie wholly outside the sphere of human values. Each describes man as a reaction system instead of a being moved by what Allport calls "propriate striving."[11]

Most readers of these pages can cite cases of individuals who changed themselves in accordance with an ideal image, even though conditions of heredity and environment would have indicated otherwise. Instead of describing cases from our own files, or from our own observation, we shall refer to the exceptionally well-documented instance of Jean Genet, as it is expounded in Sartre's biography of him.[12]

Genet was a thief and a homosexual who lived a sordid and criminal life. After spending some years in prison he was, at the urging of Sartre, Cocteau, and other French intellectuals, pardoned. Sartre analyzes and diagnoses the case in the manner of a clinical psychoanalyst. Despite his life of crime and perversion from early days, Genet "cured" himself in the sense that he transcended his past and directed his life toward a future of superior artistic creation. He is the author of poetic and fictional works, including *Notre-Dame des Fleurs* (*Our Lady of the Flowers*), now translated into English. Perhaps the most crucial psychological fact in Genet's self-transformation was his awareness of having freed himself from his past, from his hereditary and environmental patterning.

One may criticize the use of this case on the same ground that

[11] G. W. Allport, *Becoming: Basic Considerations for a Psychology of Personality* (New Haven: Yale University Press, 1953), *passim*.

[12] J.-P. Sartre, *Saint Genet: Actor and Martyr*. Trans. B. Frechtman (New York: George Braziller, Inc., 1963). The original French edition, *Saint Genet, Comédien et Martyr*, was published in Paris, in 1952.

See further, E. Clark, "The World of Jean Genet," *Partisan Review*, 1949, *16*, 442–448.

The reader who might wish to acquaint himself with most of Genet's writings, should consult his *Ouvres Complètes* (Paris: Gallimard, 1951).

Freud was criticized, for the use of the dramatic instance. In view of the fact that there are numerous cases of this form of self-transformation on record, the objection is not a serious one.

Belief in Man

The most urgent need in contemporary psychology is to instill hope regarding the sanctity of man. A careful look at human history reveals that its greatest and most inspiring moments were periods of hope for and belief in the perfectibility of life. Whether the object of belief was God or man, the period was characterized by dedication to ideals that transcended man's immediate concerns.[13]

When psychology traded the human for the animal paradigm, it took a fatal step backward. It turned away from conscious and moral conduct to mindless and automatic behavior, from the deliberate human act to the determined animal response. No amount of logical sophistication designed to save the positivistic theory from disproof — for example, the specious argument that *if* we knew all the innumerable factors determining a man's choice, *then* we would be able to show that every choice is indeed not free but determined — is convincing. This is without even noting that the argument is illogical since it initially assumes what it professes to prove.

A psychology that believes in man, fully aware that he is a remarkable phenomenon but not a masterpiece, is open to the vision of man as a perfectible personality and of an ideal society made up of perfectible human beings. It believes in man as a being capable of error and evil and cowardice, yet as a person who can transcend these human defects and create of himself a better person and of his society a better commonwealth. Each person can be, within the limits of the human condition, his own philosopher, the creator of his own personality. When properly nurtured and lovingly guided, many individuals *could*, in the idiom of their own knowledge, experience, and value-orientation, become a cross between the poet and the philosopher. If so many fail in this fusion, the fault lies in part in our cynical disregard of man's native idealism. Beyond that, his failure is his own responsibility, for he does not, even though he can, set himself the task of transforming his own personality.

But even here, the fault does not lie altogether in the individual

---

[13] For extensive confirmation of the above statement, see P. A. Sorokin, *Social and Cultural Dynamics*, 4 vols. (New York: American Book Company, 1937–41).

himself. Our socialization, formal as well as informal, shares the responsibility. Our psychology breeds fatalism in many men. Instead of helping man to emancipate himself from a deformed regard for his own nature, it convinces him that he can do little more than to adjust himself to an unalterable human situation. Psychology fails in the vital center of human life; *instead of cultivating the human hunger for perfection and self-transcendence, it saddles man with the paralyzing fear of his human limitations.*

Man needs for his perfection the attributes which positivistic psychology refuses to acknowledge as a subject for legitimate scientific investigation. We have in mind again the love and sensibility which we have discussed all too briefly. A psychology that takes man seriously is impressed by the fact that every individual can actualize himself most fully when he takes responsibility for building his personality and promoting the well-being of other human beings. Consecration to life is based on faith in the perfectibility of man, and the giving of oneself to another or to a worthy cause. This is not a religious doctrine, but a fact borne out by the experience of the human race. A psychology that ignores this very simple truth abdicates its responsibility as the science of man. It has lost faith in the power of man to transcend the barbarism of his past to create in his maturity a better human society.

Differentness

The fear of the odd, the different, the "deviant," seems to be widespread among many lower animal forms, and is an important cause of alienation in human society. We have already taken note of this fact in our discussion of the fear of individuality and the need for conformity. One of the surest ways to inhibit novel behavior and the growth of creative personality, is through the discouragement and suppression of divergence from the average or the ordinary.

The psychologist, who strongly aspires to be a scientist, should be among the loudest to acclaim the differentness of scientists and other productive individuals. Differentness challenges the psychologist's belief in the uniformity of human nature. The psychologist would rather close his eyes to the independence of the human spirit than admit to the violation of an established principle. Independence of spirit, of differentness, may follow the law of uniformity, but we seriously doubt it. Every individual who frees himself from the sovereignty of determined habits, is different from the ordinary. Every person who does more in life than adjust himself to the demands of convention, is different. It is destructive for psychology and education to judge every individual by the norm of social adaptability. Amrine has put the matter with discernment and wit when he imagined this improbable situation: Albert Einstein being both a good scientist and a fine citizen, *and* a Rotarian. "I find it ridiculous," he writes, "to imagine [Einstein] at Rotary meetings wearing a button, 'Call me Al.' "[14]

The scientist, like the artist and every individual of quality, cannot be circumscribed by the stabilities of a nomothetic science. These stabilities can be calculated for the average, but they break down when they are applied to those who differ not only from the average but from each other. In its determination to describe the extraordinary by means of the ordinary, psychology adds to the inhibiting and restraining effect of modern life upon the individual's striving for self-actualization and independence.

Differentness must be permitted its way even though it lead to wrong-headedness and mistakes. Many a blunder has led to a new insight. It is characteristic of the independent thinker to be impatient, and to resent anything that impedes his eager aspirations. Even the harmless conceit of the superior person, especially when he is still immature, is infinitely preferable to the arrogance of those who would inhibit his superior mind.

Creativity

Many years of devoted attention to the personality of the creative person have taught the writer one solid and dependable truth: although a number of similar traits are found in artists, scientists, and other creative individuals, the fact that stands out most sharply is that creative people reveal their creativeness in divergent ways. There is no single pattern to describe them, even though all of them possess good, but not necessarily superior, intelligence, are intensely interested in ideas, and are all profoundly motivated by aesthetic considerations. The creative individual, like every individual, differs from other creative individuals, but to a greater degree than the average individual differs from other average individuals.

The desire for perfectibility is strongest in the creative individual, whether he be a person with a special gift, such as scientific or artistic ability, or only with a strong need to transform himself as a

[14] M. Amrine, "Scientists and Jesuits, Gypsies and Jews," *Science*, 1963, *142*, 913–914.

person. He is the truly proactive individual, propelled by the need to grow, change, and actualize himself. The conventional categories of introversion and extraversion, remnants of Jung and traditional adjustment psychology, do not describe him adequately. The introvert tends to recoil from the external world because too often he perceives it as a threat. He is deficient in the eagerness to meet life, thereby limiting his growth.

The extravert, on the other hand, although relating himself comfortably to the external world, is a person whose inner life is deficient. Not being normally reflective, and his sensibilities being blunted, he develops little aesthetic sensitivity and does not learn to cultivate and refine his robust feelings.[15]

No doubt some creative individuals show strong introverted, or occasionally extraverted tendencies, but our own observation has taught us that neither of these terms adequately describes the forward thrust that is found in most creative personalities. These individuals are strongly proactive, in whom reflection, the need to know, and aesthetic sensibility comingle in a more or less integrated form. The psychological traits that have most often appeared in the creative personalities of the individuals in our study, are independence, perseverance, intuitiveness, enjoyment of the "strains" of work, a marked degree of self-confidence, and an intense need for self-actualization.[16]

Fortunately for psychology, the creative personality is now being intensively investigated by MacKinnon and his associates, at the Institute of Personality Assessment and Research, of the University of California. Their findings confirm our own, but more specifically and in greater detail. It will profit us to state them briefly.

The nature of creativity. Creativity is by no means the mystical condition that superstition and tradition have made of it. Basically, it is a biopsychological process characterized by originality, flexibility, and actualization. These traits can be used, as MacKinnon used them, as "measurable" variables, i.e., traits which are used as empirical indicators after they have been expressed overtly.

These indicators are externalized differently in the fields of creative writing, architecture, mathematics, and physical science, MacKinnon believes. Our findings are somewhat different, in that they indicate a remarkable similarity in all creative people, irre-

---

[15] See H. Bonner, "The Proactivert: A Contribution to the Theory of Psychological Types," *J. Exist. Psychiat.*, 1963, *3*, 323–328.

[16] Unpublished memorandum, August 1939.

spective of the area of creative interest. We do not find the pronounced personality differential in the artist and the scientist. On the contrary, the scientist, like the artist, perceives the world in personal and aesthetic terms. This finding is more in accord with the claims of such scientists as Polanyi and Bronowski, both of whom find basic similarities between scientists and artists. The scientist and the artist each externalizes something of himself into the domain of his creative activity, but in different degrees, the scientist less than the artist.

Creativity and intelligence. In agreement with MacKinnon's findings, we would say that the relation between creativity and intelligence is not especially significant. Although few, if any, artists and scientists are below "average" intelligence, many of them are not exceptionally intelligent as defined by standard intelligence tests. As MacKinnon has found, "above a certain required minimum level of intelligence which varies from field to field and in some instances may be surprisingly low, being more intelligent does not guarantee a corresponding increase in creativeness."[17]

Intuitive apperception. The creative person, whether as an artist or scientist, or a generally healthy person, can readily transcend his past experience and trust his intuitive understanding. He does not need to depend on "objective" evidence and logical proof. The "openness to experience," as Rogers has called it, makes it possible for the creative person to detach himself from stimuli and antecedent motives, and rely upon an almost instantaneous "closure," which constitutes his insight. In this he is the examplar of strong proactive tendencies and autonomy of motives. In MacKinnon's sample, 90 per cent of the creative writers, 92 per cent of the mathematicians, 93 per cent of the research scientists, and 100 per cent of the architects are intuitive, or "alert to the as-yet-not-realized."[18]

The noetic-aesthetic component. In describing the proactive style of life in Chapter 9, we described it as an integration of the most productive features of the noetic, sympathetic, and aesthetic styles. MacKinnon, commenting on the same subject, says unequivocally: "all our creative groups have as their highest values the theoretical and the aesthetic."[19] Not only is the creative individual motivated

[17] D. W. MacKinnon, "The Nature and Nurture of Creative Talent," *Amer. Psychologist,* 1962, *17,* 484–495.
[18] *Ibid.,* p. 489.
[19] *Ibid.,* p. 490.

by the desire to know, but his knowledge, or his creative act, must be expressed with elegance or beauty. This is sharply at variance with the belief, held by many American psychologists, that the scientist concerns himself only with truth; and with the absurd contention that the scientific psychologist should avoid elegance and "style" in his research. "For the truly creative person," writes MacKinnon, "it is not sufficient that problems be solved, there is the further demand that solutions be elegant. He seeks both truth and beauty."[20]

This image of the creative individual differs sharply from the stereotype. He is neither sickly, nor pathological, nor unusually self-centered. Rather, he is physically and psychologically healthy, independent, original in thought and action, and hungers for truth and beauty. He rebels not only against restraining custom, but also against his own achievements. This is so because all things on the way to perfectibility disturb him, for deep in his heart he knows that he shall never be equal to them. We have found that the creative person, and the proactive individual generally, is particularly dissatisfied with his creative achievements and his rather restricted social relationships. He often fails in making his life a work of art, and he is seldom satisfied with himself as he is. Although he is self-confident, intellectually competent, and generally mature, he nevertheless strives to surpass these qualities in himself. He is an examplar of the need for self-transcendence and self-transformation, for a continuing self-perfectibility. These qualities he perceives less as traits of character or moral virtues, than as mileposts on the road to excellence and perfectibility.

Finally, creative personalities combine in themselves traits that our culture evaluates negatively — namely, feelings, passions, intellect, self-appreciation, and a generous share of femininity. These traits when combined in the same individual do not normally lead to peace and equanimity, either in the person or in his relations to his fellow men. Like da Vinci, or Goethe, or Einstein, creative persons are men of great intellectual and emotional turbulence, and a receptiveness to novelty and change which baffles the "average" individual. Beware when a thinker is let loose in the world, someone has written; and this is the warning we should heed when we try to

---

[20] *Ibid.*, p. 490. For a brief consideration of the psychologist's attitude toward style in writing, see the following: M. B. Smith, "Editorial," *J. abn. soc. psychol.*, 1961, *63*, 461–465; S. Rosenzweig, M. Bunch, and J. A. Stern, "Operation Babel," *Amer. Psychologist*, 1962, *17*, 237–243.

understand the creative individual. As MacKinnon reminds us, such persons may not be to our liking, but we believe it is our responsibility not merely to tolerate them, but to encourage them to actualize their potentialities.

WISDOM

The human relevance of psychology lies not in whether it is a science or a philosophy, but in its power to promote wisdom about ourselves and productive human relationships. Wisdom may be promoted by technical knowledge, but it is not identical with it. Indeed, technical information can actually serve as a barrier to the rise and growth of wisdom. The folly of many persons, filled to the brim with poorly digested empirical knowledge, is that they mistake possession of facts for understanding, and scientific fervor for the love of truth and wisdom. Wisdom is not achieved by pursuing it. It cannot be attained by observing and measuring human behavior or by comprehending man only in his intellectual and social embeddedness. Psychology must study man in the context of all that makes for his betterment; in the framework of what he has been and in the aspirations that he seeks to actualize. If wisdom makes men sadder, as we have been told, it is because we expect of wisdom what wisdom cannot in its very nature give us: peace of mind. The wish for surcease from the dread and anxiety of daily living is a sign of immaturity, of a belief in that which cannot be completed, namely, the being of one's own life. Contrary to a widespread belief, fostered by our educational system and implied by our dominant reaction psychology, wisdom, like the creativity we have described, is not primarily a product of intelligence, but a matter of moral values and character. We understand the world and the individuals who inhabit it, not through abstract knowledge alone, but by means of that rare courage in which each of us lives his life and fosters the freedom to encourage others to lead their own lives freely. Wisdom, then, is that capacity, partly acquired, partly a matter of gift and grace, by means of which every individual is continually discovering and rediscovering himself, creating and transforming himself, fulfilling and actualizing himself.

To the extent that these traits are rejected as legitimate concerns of scientific psychology, that psychology cannot help us to attain wisdom concerning the nature of man. Psychology should concern itself with man's moral and spiritual growth, but since it denies their place in our science, it is doomed to a narrow and specialized preoccupation with technical concerns. Engineering, whether human or technological, can make our lives more comfortable and pleasant — and this is no small gain — but it cannot by itself humanize our spirit.

The human personality, we have said, is not a mere structure of psychological modalities. It is not even primarily, to repeat, an intellectual experience, but a profoundly emotional form of existence. When we forget this fact, we make the error of defining wisdom as a form of abstract understanding, instead of a powerful feeling about the human condition.

> It is not wisdom to be only wise,
> And on the inward vision close the eyes,
> But it is wisdom to believe the heart.[21]

As long as psychology continues to offer us nothing but facts and abstract principles, and to deal only with public and measurable phenomena, it cannot attain for us that self-knowledge which is the beginning of all wisdom. Mankind has meanwhile embarked on a new mission, a new adventure: the determination to be mindful of the meaning of man's existence. It is no longer satisfied, as it peers into the uncertain future, with mechanical descriptions. It longs for the power and understanding by which each man can make of himself a better human being, a more beautiful work of art. Only by reaching for his perfectibility, especially his moral perfectibility, can man in the long run avert the destructive power which he has himself invented. It is therefore not the discoveries of science, but the *spiritual community of scientists,* that is of greatest importance in the preservation and enrichment of human life.

The wise man does not demand rational proof for the values which he holds dear, and he is skeptical of every dogma. His wisdom is an unconfirmed answer to perennial questions. He knows from experience that wisdom lies not in textbooks nor in technical demonstrations, but in staying close to human life and his own experience. The crisis and desperation of modern life are in part generated by the psychologist's addiction to the external and the superficial. Like the times themselves, our psychologies are

---

[21] G. Santayana, "O world, thou choosest not the better part!" in *Poems* (New York: Charles Scribner's Sons, 1923), p. 5.

sick with an "emotional deficiency disease," as Murray described the present social situation. Although we are all aware that psychology is not designed to create hope, its findings are so abstract and generalized that they appeal only to man's intellect and to his "shallow sentiment."[22]

In this matter psychology promotes the narrow rationalism and the inhibiting behaviorism which permeate our cultural life. In so doing it is profoundly guilty of maximizing the ills of contemporary civilization, namely, the trivialization of man and the totalization of society. It helps to bring the aseptic world of *Walden Two* nearer to becoming a reality. In the mistaken belief that rational and behavioristic analyses of the human person give us the only scientifically defensible view of man, psychologists have created the illusion that their discoveries give us a total image of the human personality. They are guilty, furthermore, of divesting man's full stature of all aesthetic imagination and of all striking and powerful metaphors, by means of which thinkers from the days of the Bible to contemporary humanistic psychology, have expressed the exultant temper of man. They are guilty, finally, of closing their minds to the creative power of ideals in the formation and growth of personality — the ideals which, though variable with time and individuals, have made man, as Kant described him, a legislative being, a self-directing and self-transforming person. The external aspects of personality can be easily and accurately described and measured by our behavioristic methodology, but its vital and creative nature can be apprehended only by experiencing its inwardness, its fructifying ideals. The mutilated individual who emerges from the standard psychological measurements scarcely resembles the proactive being who unceasingly strives, against all barriers and impediments, to actualize his own ideal of the kind of person he has chosen to become.

Wisdom concerning the nature of psychological man is thus to be found in the words uttered almost four decades ago: ". . . Personality realizes itself by producing unity and wholeness in the personal character; and when through its weakness the character is degraded and a course of conduct embarked on which constitutes a denial of that fundamental tendency and aspiration toward wholeness, the force of the Personality in the individual is often strong

---

[22] For a brief diagnosis of our time and a prescription for its ills, see H. A. Murray, "A Mythology for Grownups," *Saturday Review*, Jan. 23, 1960, pp. 10–12.

enough to rescue the individual and sometimes even through a more or less violent crisis to convert him to sanity, self-respect and moral wholeness."[23]

In these days of pessimism and cynicism, a state of mind confirmed if not fostered by our self-limiting psychology, this hopefulness of the human spirit sounds sentimental to the psychologist who has learned his trade by studying the behavior of animals. However, wisdom is always based on hope and belief, as well as upon skepticism and denial. Man needs both inspiration and refusal in order to make life meaningful, and to remind him that life is both difficult and changeable. Poets and dramatists, humanists and existentialists, have shown that life is tragic, paradoxical, and absurd — but also full of untried possibilities. Optimism is no easy exhortation to a stiff upper lip, but an awareness of the positive chances when most of the cards are stacked against you. Optimism is an essential ingredient of the human adventure. It is that sense of buoyancy which nerves and sustains man in his darkest adversity. It has nothing of consequence to do with mere resolution, but is the expression of man's inward character. It is free of those vain expectations which make men's lives drab and meaningless, for few things can be more disappointing to the wordling without wisdom than to be virtuous without reaping its rewards. The wise man, nurtured on confidence in his own selfhood, has access to the whole universe of goodness and beauty and truth, and it is without limit.

CONCLUSION

The recurrent theme of this book is that man is a creative and proactive being. He can choose the attitude which he takes toward his past and transform it in order to create his own future. By means of this self-determination man can create his own good, his own system of values, and through both make of his life a work of art.

The attainment of a creative selfhood exceeds in difficulty, in success and failure, anything with which a mechanistic psychology can confront a human being. Contrary to the belief that a proactive and humanistic psychology is too easy and optimistic, all the evidence that we can muster shows that self-transformation is the most difficult of all human tasks. Unlike the easy optimism inherent in

[23] J. C. Smuts, *Holism and Evolution* (New York: The Viking Press, Inc., 1961), p. 300. The original edition was published in 1926.

mechanistic psychology — which would explain the formation of character and personality as a process of learning and reinforcement — proactive, humanistic psychology throws the greatest weight of responsibility on the self-determining individual. We believe that it is no achievement when one's personality is molded by the laws of association and conditioning, of tension-reduction and reward. In this molding process, man is basically a passive being, a reflector of the mechanical patterning by others. His own intentions play a minor, or perhaps a non-existent, role. He is the helpless victim of those who manipulate and control the socializing conditions. He is bound to the stimulus-situation to which he responds, not freely, but in accordance with the laws of reinforcement and conditioning. This, we submit, is a pitifully easy and unfulfilling brand of psychology. It breeds a false optimism which, if it were proposed by a non-positivist, would be dismissed as the expression of a tender-minded sentimentality. Indeed, positivists take strange positions when their mechanistic constants are seriously questioned. Their defending ideas tend to become dogmatic and absolute.

In proactive psychology the view of man's growing nature stems neither from the theological belief in man's favored place in nature, nor from the positivist's dogma that it is but a structure of learned habits. Both explanations are distorted: the first by wishful thinking, the second by the rejection of man's capacity for intentional growth and self-transformation.

Perfectibility is neither a response nor a product, but a process of growth. Whatever the degree of this attainment, which varies from individual to individual, its motivation arises within and with free responsibility. Although it differs with individuals, it is the same in everyone in that it is a striving for the realization of the maximum of values of one's life. It beckons a man to strive with all his energy to be what he can be, and to be it *wholly*. It is the determination by each individual to refine or transform the crude being that he is into the cultivated person that he can become. It is, in fine, the adventure of spiritual growth.

This idea of perfectibility is no easy doctrine. It is that virtue which the ancient Greeks practiced: ἀρετή (*arete*), which is the perfectibility of physical, intellectual, aesthetic, and moral virtues. It means the development of the potentialities of the individual. It is a form of excellence that cries out against all forms of negation of the vivacious self; "the music of our conscience," as Nietzsche described it, "of the dance in our spirit." (*Es ist die Musik in unserm Gewissen, der Tanz in unserm Geiste. . . .*)[24] The proactive individual bestows his own finality upon himself. He creates his own values and transforms those which he learns from his social world. In this sense every individual creates his own reality in accordance with his ideals. His very act of striving for it maximizes its reality. Although he strives mightily to create his own world, he is not deluded by the belief that he will in fact perfect it. His optimism and self-confidence are always informed by a profound awareness of life's gratuity. It is ironic that Freud, who was most pessimistic about man, believed with Goethe and Nietzsche, both of whom influenced him, in the former's idea of ennoblement and the latter's concept of sublimation, as means toward increasing perfectibility. Perfectibility is thus not an ineffable state, but a condition in which, as Nietzsche put it, a person, having "attained" an ideal, thereby surpasses it. (*Wer sein Ideal erreicht, kommt eben damit über dasselbe hinaus.*)

The psychology expounded in this book is neither new nor unshakably held. It is a cognitive experiment, in the sense in which we used this term in our first chapter, performed to observe its outcome. It is characterized by a strong belief in man and a reverence for his potential human qualities. It is, we like to believe, an antidote to the partitioning of the human personality, and an attempt to rescue man from the inauthenticity to which both psychology and life have subjected him. In this we heed the plaint of Heidegger, that each of us is the other one and nobody is himself.

It should be clear that this stress upon self-affirmation and self-validation does not exclude sympathy and the loving encounter; on the contrary, it confirms them. The fusion of self-confirmation and compassion constitutes that self-ennoblement which man alone among animals hungers to achieve. This need of self-ennoblement, rather than grace and revelation, lures man on to the moral life, which at his best he must achieve again and again. The bankruptcy of so much contemporary psychology lies in its neglect and renunciation of this important fact. If this observation regarding psychology is for many unacceptable, it is in part because the defenders are also the persons who have created it. If we are to save the science of psychology from the human irrelevancy toward which it

---

[24] F. Nietzsche, *Jenseits von Gut und Böse*, in *Friedrich Nietzsches Werke* (Leipzig: C. G. Naumann Verlag, 1906), vol. 8, p. 171.

is rapidly pointing, we must have the wisdom and courage to perceive that, despite psychology's remarkable achievements, psychological man cannot be the object of rigorous positivistic investigation. To affirm the contrary is to surrender the scientific temperament to arrogance and illusion, which for the scientific understanding of man is an unpardonable offense.

There is nothing in the pages of this book that even remotely suggests that we declare a moratorium on science and rigorous experimental research, for that act would be a sure return to the errors of the prescientific era. It is, rather, a plea for once more joining forces with the broad humanistic idea of the artist and the philosopher. Science narrowly defined cannot lead us to a better understanding of the whole man, for science without the wisdom that comes from experience and reflection is blind. Without wisdom we are in danger of losing our moral values and through this our sense of proportion. The "disastrous oversights of the scientist," as Whitehead phrased it in his *Science and the Modern World*, have been the forgetfulness of values and the rejection of the great humanistic tradition. It is these values and this tradition that we must revitalize for both the beginning and the end of our search for a fuller understanding of man.

Epilogue

> *Science . . . shows remarkable and highly surprising things about man, but as it attains greater clarity, the more evident it becomes that man as a whole can never become the object of scientific investigation. Man is always more than he knows about himself.*
>
> KARL JASPERS

The impetus behind the writing of this monograph has been the need to begin the study of man where conventional psychology leaves off. Basing our conviction on an intimate knowledge of the empirical facts of human behavior and the significant contributions of the philosophy of science, we have set out to present a psychology of man that views him as a unique individual. We believe that science consists not alone of experimental procedures and theoretical formulations, but even more of openness to criticism and a fresh approach to perennial problems. We believe that psychology as a scientific discipline should place no limits to the field of its investigation. We believe that every psychologist should take as his motto Terence's famous utterance: *Nihil humanum a me alienum puto* ("Nothing human is alien to me"). The exploration of every possibility should be the psychologist's overall goal.

A fully scientific psychology is the constant interrogation of established conclusions. It is a radical questioning of every conviction. This is the more true in view of the fact that science is always, in the final analysis, provisional and incomplete. Psychology must admit what is true of every science, that science cannot be fully established and widely apprehended within the domain of science itself, but must be reflective, which is to say philosophical, as well. When it fails in this, science is blind. When it ignores this fact, it becomes scientism — a dogmatic attitude toward science. Even when the scientific view of man is objectively veridical, it is one-sided when it ignores the scientist's attitude toward his description of man; for in the end, it is always man's *interpretation* of scientific findings which makes a difference regarding them. The danger of mistaking the partial or incomplete scientific discoveries about man for the total explanation is always present, and must be combatted with vigilance. Psychology alone cannot interpret the meanings and implications of its own discoveries. This task belongs to human reflection, or philosophy. Conventional psychology has placed an excessive and unsupported faith in sheer methodology. But psychology is much more than technical proficiency; and when it goes beyond technique and tries to understand human conduct, it becomes philosophical.

Psychology must rid itself of dogmatic "nothing but" assertions. These are never scientific, but "scientistic." "Nothing but" pronouncements belong in the category of causal-functional relations; and these break down, as this monograph has tried to show, in the most vital areas of human behavior. Truth about man is always wider than the truth which we already possess. This is why method alone, however sound and rigorous it may be, is inadequate. We take second place to no one in stressing the great importance of a rigorous methodology, for without it no science of psychology is possible; but we believe that when method becomes the whole of psychology, the science of human behavior degenerates into a technological exercise. Having developed a rigorous methodology, psychology is now in need of a vision — a vision of the greatness of man, a greatness that has failed to show up on the finished psychological photograph.

The fundamental question for psychology has been, and continues to be, the perennial query: "What is man?" It must ask this question, neither in the spirit nor for the sake of religion or morality, but in the interests of psychology as a behavioral science in the broadest sense.

Today psychology answers the enduring question — if it asks it at all — by the results it obtains when it manipulates a replaceable organism. However, there is yet another way: we can use the phenomenological study of the unique and irreplaceable individual. The first always courts an authoritarianism which denies man's freedom; the second leads to a view of man who is free to actualize his potentialities and to realize himself as the human person that he is. We do not deny the value of the first, despite its implied danger, but we prefer the second, even though in principle it cannot be empirically demonstrated. We agree with Jaspers' profound observation, that man's freedom cannot be an object of empirical investigation. Debate over the problem of freedom, therefore, should not be over whether it is possible, but whether one is ready to assume the moral responsibility and the consequences of denying it.[1]

The mechanistic psychology of our time has nullified, through neglect or denial, that which makes man the human being that he is: his freedom. The denial of freedom, so contrary to man's capacity for creative living and to democracy's *raison d'être,* holds the seeds for the authoritarian individual and the tyrannical society. We must not forget that the first acts of every political tyrant were the abrogation of individual freedom, the control of science, and the terrorization of society. Any idea that denies the freedom and dignity of the human being, be it political, ideological, or scientific, destroys the basis and meaning of self-directing persons and free institutions. Determinism has taken many forms in human history, but the most insidious of them has been the psychologist's denial of individual choice.

The behavioral sciences have been adept at enumerating and describing man's limitations and defects. Sociologists have detailed them in statistics on crime, delinquency, and marital discord. Psychoanalysts have recounted them in biographical analyses of hatred, aggression, and mental disorders. Behaviorists have accounted for all of them by means of the learning process. That these limitations and defects abound in profuse numbers only a very uninformed and experientially naive person would deny. If this were all there is to human nature, our cynical scholars would be the greatest bearers of wisdom. But to believe that it is, is as naive as to be foolishly optimistic and sentimental about man's superiority and goodness. Nevertheless, psychologists are greatly remiss when they close their minds to man's powers and the great dreams in his heart.

Is there, then, no dependable discipline that would devote itself to the study of the greatness of man? We believe there is. It is a new psychology that has the courage to envision a bolder view of man and construct a more imaginative science of human behavior. It is a psychology fully open to man's complexity and the breadth and depth of psychological understanding. It is not content with mere descriptions of part-functions, but is open to what man, in-

---

[1] See K. Jaspers, *Allgemeine Psychopathologie,* 6th ed. (Berlin: Julius Springer, 1953), pp. 630–631.

cluding the psychologist who investigates him, really experiences. It affords neither cynicism nor uncritical optimism, for each in its own way leads to a caricature of man. It does not shrink from the risk of leaping into uncharted territory, from proposing bold ideas, from facing calumny and ridicule. Psychologists have been notably timid about losing their scientific respectability. Too often they have been followers of its fashions instead of creators of new ideas. Their timidity is particularly odd in view of the changed nature of contemporary science, the changed science which we discussed in detail in our initial chapter. In the broadened view of science, it is possible to envision man as the maker of his own life, not merely as the reactor to external stimuli.

It is not necessary in this broadened view of man to overrate the average individual, but only to recognize that self-transformation is a human possibility. The world is full of dullards and philistines, of sadists and destroyers, and it always will be; but clearly, these facts cannot destroy the truth that men are also moved by love and justice and a sure sense for constructive living.

We think it is false to believe that the study of the whole of psychological man precludes the attainment of concrete and particular insights. Particularistic knowledge can be as deadly and dogmatic as the sweeping pronouncements of a holistic psychology, and we have many examples of it in our positivistic tradition. Psychology must always be sensitively aware of the limits of its knowledge; and yet, in order to advance the study of man, it must always go beyond the limits themselves. It can be vague and wrong in some details and yet give us a believable vision of man as a whole. It can be scientific without recourse to laboratory or clinic, by founding itself upon observations and one's own and other people's experience. Empiricism is necessary but not indispensable. When empiricism claims absolute validity, it generates into dogmatic scientism. There is much dogmatism in psychoanalysis and behaviorism disguised as science. Psychoanalysis shows a dogmatic faith in a mode of medical thinking about man which was in vogue at the end of the nineteenth century, and which modern medicine has outgrown. Behaviorism has shown a naive faith in a methodology whose basis is an anachronistic philosophy of science. The consequence of both ways of thinking about man is that man no longer needs to be man, but only an automaton or machine. The degradation of man by each of them is offensive, not because it violates moral or religious sensibilities, but because it is contradicted by evidence from genetics, evolution, and a broadly humanistic and proactive psychology. Positivistic psychologies are narrow and disabling: psychoanalysis, because it rests on the model of the medical-psychiatric case study; behaviorism, because it is based on the animal-statistical paradigm.

Having said all this, we are nevertheless driven to the necessary conclusion that a holistic knowledge of man is an ideal, not a reality. A total knowledge of the whole man is impossible, and we must rest satisfied with partial insights into the whole. In this fact lies both the agony and hope of every sincere investigation of human behavior. An understanding of man as a proactive being can be attained only by a disciplined use of knowledge from experience, logic, experiment, and spontaneous intuition, but without attaching an absolute value to any one of these. Authentic scientific knowledge of psychological man cannot be achieved by any specific mode of investigation, but only by their wise and judicious integration. There are no recipes for the study of man, and every method and formula will be ineffective if it is uninformed by a wide range of humanistic and scientific knowledge, and of that most precious and difficult of all human capacities, wisdom.

A psychology that will fulfill this requirement must be fully mindful of man as the being who, unlike any other being, has reverence for himself.

Name Index

Subject Index

238